FROM OLD CHAPEL FIELD

Selected letters of
Robin Tanner

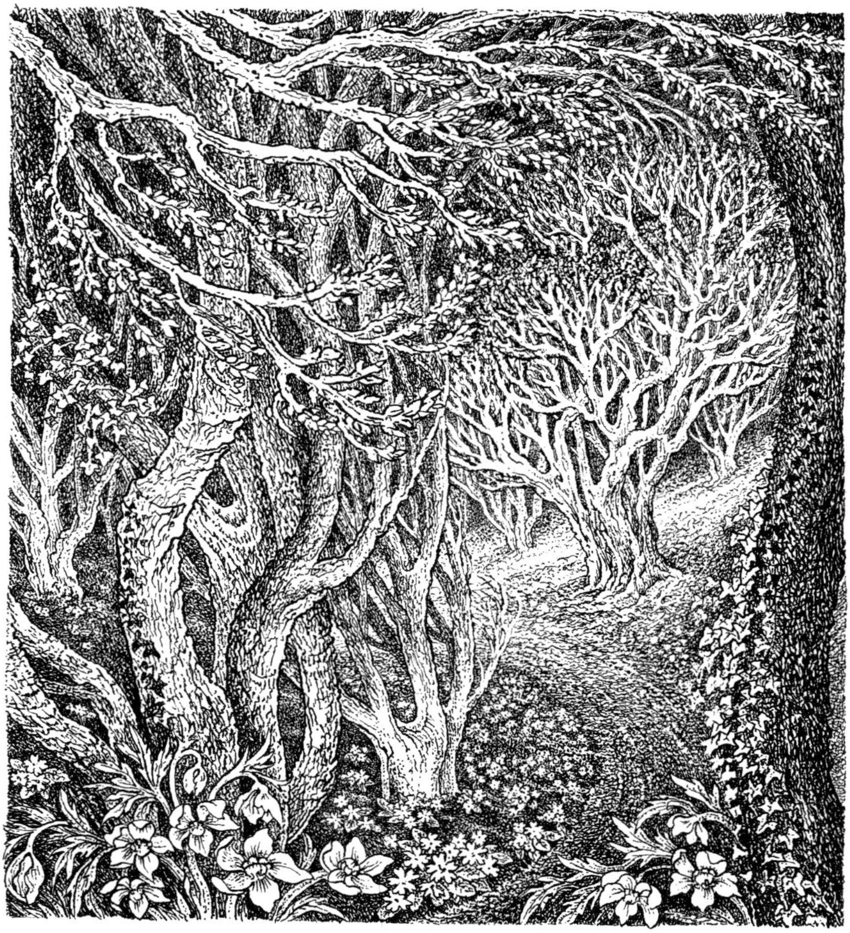

Twelve years ago the hazel copse
  Was builders' rubble, docks and nettles,
Where now the sloe-tree snows its petals
  On scattered nuts the squirrel drops.

Robin Tanner, 1943

From Old Chapel Field

Selected letters of

ROBIN TANNER

1920–1988

edited by

TIM FENN

i

Impact Books

First published in Great Britain 1991
by Impact Books, 112 Bolingbroke Grove, London SW11 1DA

ISBN 0-245-60406-5

Typeset in 11pt Baskerville by
Photoprint, 9–11 Alexandra Lane, Torquay

Printed and bound in Great Britain by
The Bath Press, Avon

The Editor and Publishers are grateful to Robin Garton for kind permission to reproduce, slightly amended, the biographical note on pages xiv–xvi.

Frontispiece: *The Hazel Copse*, Robin Tanner, 1986

To
Friends,
Teachers and Etchers
everywhere

I'm writing at the studio window facing the
snowdrop-filled copse and the mass of hellebores.
Every day some fresh flower opens and the mist
of green on shrubs and trees thickens.
There has surely never been such a Spring.

Robin Tanner, 5th March 1988

Contents

I never cease to marvel that
a few black marks on paper can be
made to communicate deep feelings. . . .
My only means of protest
against distance.

Robin Tanner

Foreword

One morning in January 1990 Dietrich and I were pleased to spot two white envelopes in familiar handwriting among the usual waste of postal advertisement in unsalvageable polythene. The first we opened was from our headmaster friend C., who was helping to plan a Tanner day. Did we think it a good idea to replace the traditional poetry programme with a well chosen selection of Robin's letters, to be read where possible by their recipients? A new and bright suggestion, we agreed. The other letter was from Robin's former HMI colleague, Tim Fenn. He had been recollecting the many celebrations of Robin, both as etcher and as teacher, in London, Bristol, Bath, etc., but nowhere as yet as letter-writer. And surely he was equally well known and loved for that? Had anyone suggested collecting his correspondence?

No one. It was true. What an extraordinary coincidence that two people who had never met should raise the matter on the same day! Tim's letter continued: 'If you approve I would be willing to do the editing.' What a generous offer! It put a different complexion on the whole enterprise, for my heart, responding at once to it, had at the same time sunk as I envisaged the house, with reviews, letters of condolence, and fan mail still not re-read and sorted, being submerged yet again. Thankfully we accepted, and introduced the two writers to each other.

Neither we nor they, however, could have foreseen the sheer volume of paper that began to arrive. For Robin loved writing letters. Calligraphy for him was one of the fine arts, and moreover a craft that every single person could and should take up. Legibility was the first essential of good manners in common social intercourse. And letters were so much more. He was forever pursuing better tools – well designed, more responsive pens; richer, more manageable ink; smoother, more alluring paper; alphabets of basic heritage forever combining into fresh significant form. 'The watermark on this heavenly paper is Ƨtowford Mill 1841', he writes excitedly, 'with the S the wrong way round, but it is too blue to print on: I shall use it for letters. It has a most seductive surface, and the texture is divine.' And as though 300 correspondents were insufficient practice, he would keep up the entries in his own handmade books in his best script – etching records, lecture notes, garden diary, commonplace books, transcriptions of the Wiltshire parts of *Kilvert's Diary* and of William Morris's letters from Kelmscott – 'a nice job to pick up at odd moments, like knitting'. 'How amusing it will be to write 77!' he exclaims early in 1976, and doodles a line of five sevens.

Letters received were another joy. The daily post was opened ritually, with a wooden paper knife of his own fashioning, the careful slit made only after full investigation of the mode of address, stamps, postmark and any other clues. At last the text itself would be read, preferably aloud, for us all three to enjoy and comment on.

To answer by return is a natural reaction, and time permitting would have been Robin's. It permitted best before breakfast. All his life he liked to rise with the birds, and having laid the table 'as if the Lord or whatever were coming' would settle down to write, head slightly aside and eyes a trifle too near the paper, till I appeared, my time clock incorrigibly later than his. Addressing the envelopes was an additional ceremony, calling for some embellishment.

Their sheer beauty alone could have accounted for so many letters having been preserved, and ideally they should have been reproduced exactly as written, but this would have prevented necessary editing. Moreover the 'marvel' of the 'few black marks on paper' was that they 'can be made to communicate deep feeling', and 'deep' is reiterated. 'What is friendship for if not sharing one's deepest thoughts?' – this in an unfinished letter begun ten days before his death. 'Life is getting very short' says Robin (eighteen years earlier!) – 'too short I think for mere politeness.' 'People do not want to think or to be made uncomfortable,' he complains. 'I go about dislodging everybody who is sitting at all comfortably!'

For his job telephoning might have been more suitable, and would certainly have been for confidences and for trying to fix dates simultaneously with several different people. But he fought it until May 1969. He hated 'poles and wires', especially in his own garden, and waited till we could afford to banish them underground; he reminded us that his colleagues kept late hours, whereas we all liked to be in bed by ten; and that the telephone would expose him, making him available to all and sundry. This proved all too true, and he maintained: 'On the whole I feel I am able to communicate more readily on paper.'

Would he have minded his letters being published? 'My naturally extravagant and excessive nature gets in the way when I try to write,' he says; 'I am too much in love with words.' He was in love with people too. Recognising Michelangelo's words as speaking for him also, he copied them into his commonplace book: 'Wherever I behold man or woman lovely of mind, . . . or one who can do or say something more appropriate than the rest of the world, or wounds me with his goodness, I am compelled to fall in love with him . . .' But he asserted that the friends he was so personally and warmly addressing might well be less embarrassed to read the words than to hear them.

When his work eventually became purchasable through agents a thought struck him: 'Suddenly it comes over me that – rather stupidly perhaps – I have allowed all these private, personal things to become public, which was never my intention.' On the other hand: 'I must tell you of one unexpected and comforting feeling that has come to me since writing *Double Harness* – I feel singularly *safe*! Everybody knows everything about me! Nothing has been hidden! And I have nothing to lose! "He that is down need fear no fall!" ' The words occur so often that it must be the prevailing attitude. We personally believe that Robin would enjoy re-reading the letters.

Happily, owing to the reassuring prospect of safe-keeping by the Bristol University Library, not one letter of those as yet unfound and those most regretfully excluded for lack of space need be lost to posterity. The Library's warm hospitality is most comforting, as is the patience, tact and loving involvement of both editor and publisher. For those letters presented here we are most grateful to the donors, and do hope that any who are disappointed at not finding their own included can say with one of them: 'If none of my examples reaches the final draft I'm still delighted to have been involved, and look forward to reading the collection.'

Heather Tanner
Dietrich Hanff
1991

Introduction

Most editors of selected letters mention the problem of deciding which to include since usually only about a tenth of those available can be accommodated. In this book the proportion is even smaller since a number of correspondents are unaware of this publication (a letter sent to two daily newspapers and one weekly announcing the proposal was not published). There are in fact very few examples of letters to friends abroad.

When the writer of the letters is a literary figure an obvious main theme is the discussion of his or her writings. This cannot be applied here since writing was not Robin Tanner's main interest ('I write straight from the heart and make no claim to being a writer.'): he referred to himself as teacher and etcher; but his teaching included many other crafts. Teaching and etching are of course often discussed and form two of the main themes. Others include natural history, his beloved countryside, gardening, music, poetry and books, not to mention nuclear disarmament and peace. His concern for the environment, his continuous involvement with the quality of what surrounds children in primary schools and the relationship between pupils and teachers run through a great many of the letters.

This continual reference to certain themes could lead to too much repetition; many of the letters reproduced here have therefore had parts deleted. Selection has also been determined by the wishes of correspondents: private matters may affect others and personal relationships might be endangered. The principle of the editing has been to include only what has been agreed by those concerned. In consequence a few topics on which Robin Tanner had interesting and constructive views have been omitted. These include homosexuality and marriage and divorce. But, as mentioned in the Foreword, it is hoped that all letters, whether originals or copies, will be available in due course at the University Library in Bristol.

Since this is a companion volume to Robin Tanner's autobiography, *Double Harness* (Impact Books, 1987), the arrangement is broadly chronological. Despite the large number of letters to choose from, there are significant gaps, even besides those years for which Robin Tanner's oldest friend, Cecil Crouch, who kept all his letters, was the only source. All the love letters, for example, were destroyed by mutual consent long ago! But fortunately the illustrated envelopes of Robin's daily comfort to Heather during her long stay in hospital were kept and some of these have been reproduced.

In selecting and compiling the material, I have been greatly helped by a number of correspondents who sent a selection of their letters, giving reasons for their choice. And, most importantly, Heather Tanner and Dietrich Hanff have helped and guided me throughout: but for that, the editor's job would have taken far longer or would never have been completed. I should also like to add my very warm thanks to Villy Craddock and Benita Plows who not only typed the manuscripts, work made more difficult by having to cope with so many extracts, but also made a number of very useful suggestions.

A postscript about the editor's background: I first heard of Robin Tanner in 1946 when I visited Ivy Lane School, Chippenham, and saw the murals there. Then I heard him talk about primary education at HMI conferences before he retired. But it was only after visiting the exhibition at the Ashmolean Museum, Oxford, in 1981 that I wrote to him. Our correspondence was mainly about handwriting and etching. I obviously regret very much that I did not know him better. But the fact that I have not been closely and emotionally involved has perhaps made it easier to select the letters to show the many-sided nature of this extraordinarily versatile man.

Tim Fenn, 1991

Biographical note

1904 Born in Bristol, the third of six children. His father worked in Bristol for a short while as a carpenter and joiner before returning to Chippenham.

1915 Pupil at Chippenham Grammar School where he met Heather Spackman.

1921 Student teacher at Ivy Lane School, Chippenham.

1922–4 Student at University of London, Goldsmiths' College, learning to teach.

1924 Teacher at Blackheath Road Boys' School, Greenwich by day; in the evenings student at Goldsmiths' College where he studied life-drawing and etching under Clive Gardiner and Stanley Anderson. Fellow students included Paul Drury, Edward Bouverie Hoyton and Graham Sutherland.

1926 Saw Victoria and Albert Museum exhibition, 'Drawings, Etchings and Woodcuts by Samuel Palmer and other Disciples of William Blake'. Visited an exhibition of paintings by pupils of Professor Franz Cizek in London.

1928 Became a full-time art student at Goldsmiths' during the summer. Bought paddock in Kington Langley known as Old Chapel Field with Heather Spackman, and returned to Wiltshire.

1928/9 Began to etch full time, working at his parents' home in Chippenham.

1929 Met F.L. Griggs on varnishing day at the Royal Academy, having successfully submitted *Christmas*.

1930 Started teaching full-time at Ivy Lane School, Chippenham. Vivian Goold, uncle of his future wife, designed the house to be built at Old Chapel Field.

1931 Married Heather Spackman on 4th April, at Corsham Church.

1931/2 Taught Workers' Educational Association evening class on English ecclesiastical architecture in Swindon. Became involved in teaching teachers the crafts associated with book production.

1932 His pupils painted murals of Summer, Autumn and Spring.

1934 Commissioned by Harry Peach, founder of Dryad Handicrafts, to produce books on block printing and lettering for children.

1935 Appointment as HM Inspector of Schools necessitated two-year sojourn in Leeds.

1936 Met Christian Schiller at a course for teachers of young children.
Made Associate of the Royal Society of Painter-Etchers and Engravers; later he became a Fellow.

1937 His move as HMI to Gloucestershire enabled his return to Old Chapel Field. Met Phyllis Barron and Dorothy Larcher whose printed textiles he had long collected.

1939 The Tanners welcomed Dietrich Hanff, an eighteen-year-old Jew from Germany. They registered as conscientious objectors. Publication of *Wiltshire Village* commissioned by Collins. Work begun on the sequel, *Woodland Plants.*

1941 Work as HMI concentrated on Bristol.

1950 *Flowers of the Meadow* by Geoffrey Grigson with illustrations by Robin Tanner, published as a King Penguin book.

1952 Addressed International Conference of Craftsmen in Pottery and Textiles at Dartington Hall on 'Children'. Formed lasting friendships with Hans Coper and Lucie Rie. Elected member of the Royal West of England Academy.

1956 Appointed HMI for Oxfordshire.

1964 Retired as HMI. Death of Phyllis Barron who left all her work to Robin Tanner. This formed a founding gift to the Crafts Study Centre, housed in the Holburne of Menstrie Museum and administered by the University of Bath.

1966 Some etchings included in the exhibition, 'A Gothic Vision; Etchings and Drawings by F.L. Griggs' at the Ashmolean Museum, Oxford.

1970 Resumed etching after an interval of 24 years.

1974 A set of twelve plates in portfolio, 50 impressions of each, published by Joe Graffy of Penn Print Room, included in an exhibition which toured Kendal, Bath, Bristol and London.

1977 Awarded Hon. MA by the University of Bath.
Retrospective exhibition of etchings at the Robin Garton Gallery, London.
Publication of *British Etchers: 1850–1940* by Kenneth Guichard (Robin Garton) including impressions of *Wren and Primroses, Full Moon* and *The Old Road.*

1978 Second and third editions of *Wiltshire Village* published by Robin Garton.

1980 Exhibition of etchings, water-colours, egg tempera, drawings, books and his Ivy Lane pupils' work at City of Bristol Museum and Art Gallery.
Publication of *The Etcher's Craft* by the Friends of Bristol Art Gallery.

1981 Exhibition moved to the Ashmolean Museum, Oxford.
Publication by Robin Garton of *Woodland Plants*, and Gray's *Elegy written in a Country Churchyard*; the latter printed by The Old Stile Press.
BBC Nationwide short film on the Tanners followed later in the year by *A Vision of Wiltshire* documentary.

1984/5 Exhibition of etchings, drawings and books toured the libraries of Wiltshire.
Publication of *A Country Alphabet* by The Old Stile Press.

1986 Publication of *A Country Book of Days* by The Old Stile Press.

1987 Publication of *Double Harness, An Autobiography* by Impact Books. Paperback editions of *A Country Alphabet, Woodland Plants* and *Wiltshire Village* published by Impact Books.

1988 Died on 19th May.

Family tree

Emily Collins Baker (eldest of family of 13, Aunt Win the youngest) 1876–1938 = Sidney **Tanner** 1876–1960

Percy	Bert	**Robin**	Leslie	Olive	Grace
m. no children 1899–1980	m. 2 girls 1901–61	1904–88	unmarried 1907–48	unmarried 1910–90	m. Cyril Rice (1904–89) 6 children 1912–81

Daisy Goold 1865–1945 = Herbert **Spackman** 1864–1949

Sylvia	**Heather**	Faith (Olive)
unmarried 1898–1965	m. Robin Tanner 1931 no children b. 1903	m. Hugo Sharp no children b. 1905

List of correspondents

BILL ASBRIDGE: a Liverpool headmaster who went to Oxfordshire in 1963 to work with Edith Moorhouse in her advisory team; in 1967 he went to West Africa to help set up the Oxfordshire–Gambia Education Link.

AUNT WIN ALLEN: see WIN.

ROY BATEMAN: engineer, lived in Kington Langley, near the Tanners.

LES BENNETT: primary school headmaster in Dorset; lecturer at Froebel college, Roehampton; primary school adviser in England and abroad.

SAM BLACK: HMI Art Specialist in England (1947–9); Principal Lecturer in Art at Jordan Hill Training College, Glasgow; Professor of Fine Arts in University of British Columbia. Thereafter, Director of the Shieling Gallery in Bowen Island, B.C.

MICHAEL BLAKER: painter and etcher; editor of the Journal of the Royal Society of Painter-Etchers and Engravers of which he is a Senior Fellow.

DENISE BROWN: member of the Royal Society of Painter-Etchers and Engravers and of the Royal West of England Academy.

HARRY COLES: pupil of Robin Tanner's at the Deptford boys' school and twin brother of Teddy who became an Anglican monk in Johannesburg. Harry Coles is a retired organist of Southwark Cathedral.

FAY CORI: lives in Pembrokeshire. The Tanners stayed in one of her holiday houses. Robin Tanner advised her about calligraphy.

CECIL CROUCH: fellow student at Goldsmiths' College. Taught in schools in Cambridgeshire. Letters to him cover the years 1922–88. All these were left to Heather Tanner in his will.

ROSEMARY DEVONALD: senior lecturer in Art Education.

DAVID EVANS: primary school headmaster in Oxfordshire and closely associated with courses run by Robin Tanner.

JIM FAIRBAIRN: Oxfordshire primary school headmaster; head of the Education Department at the College of Ripon and St John's, York.

MARY FOOKS: Deputy Principal, Bath College of Higher Education.

DAVID GOULD: art historian and restorer.

JOE GRAFFY: print collector and dealer.

FRANCIS GREENACRE: Curator, City of Bristol Museum and Art Gallery, who, with Kate Eustace, organised the 1980–1 exhibition of Robin Tanner's work in Bristol and Oxford.

ELIZABETH DE HAAS: a friend who inherited, lives in and cherishes the home of Dorothy

Walker, daughter of William Morris' friend, Sir Emery Walker.

ROBERT HAPGOOD: Professor of English at the University of New Hampshire; Marilyn, his wife, is a teacher and adviser.

TONY HEALD: headmaster of primary school, Yorkshire; artist.

RAYMOND LISTER: author of catalogue raisonné of Samuel Palmer and of other books concerning him and his circle. Emeritus Fellow of Wolfson College and Litt. D. of Cambridge University.

EDITH MOORHOUSE: Chief Primary Adviser in Oxfordshire. Robin Tanner worked closely with her from 1956 to 1964 and, after his retirement, on courses for Oxfordshire teachers. The extensive correspondence covers the years 1959–88.

CHARLIE NAYLOR: headmaster of primary schools in Yorkshire. Co-operated with Robin Tanner on courses, particularly at Woolley Hall, Yorkshire.

JOHN AND BETTY PARR: HMIs who worked with Robin Tanner. John was a skilled photographer.

MARGARET PEDLEY: HMI who worked with Robin Tanner.

JANET POYNTON: Co-ordinator of Primary Education, Norfolk.

KEN PRITCHARD: Primary Adviser, Wiltshire; then Senior Primary Adviser, West Sussex.

PETER SOWREY: headmaster of Wiltshire primary school; calligrapher.

KIM TAPLIN: writer and reviewer.

KEITH, GERALDINE AND PETER TAYLOR: voluntary wardens of Leigh Woods Nature Reserve and publishers of *Eye on Local Nature* in Bristol.

DENIS THOMAS: writer and critic.

JIM TURNER: retired headmaster of a Gloucestershire secondary school; poet.

TOBY WEAVER: as Assistant Education Officer in Wiltshire, first met Robin Tanner before the Second World War. Became Deputy Secretary in the Department of Education and Science and was knighted. Subsequently, Visiting Professor at Sussex University and Professor of Education at the Open University.

JANET WEBB: wrote an MA thesis on art teaching in primary schools with special reference to Robin Tanner's work.

DON WILLIAMS: Chief Primary Adviser, Wiltshire.

WIN (see also AUNT ALLEN): sometimes called 'Ginge', only five years older than Robin Tanner.

TONY WINTERTON: Robin Tanner's doctor.

I

Up to 1935

This section covers the years up to the time Robin Tanner joined HM Inspectorate of Schools in 1935. It is the period described in Chapters 1–6 of *Double Harness*. There are very few letters available and only three correspondents. Of the 20 letters or extracts, sixteen are written to Cecil Crouch to whom Robin Tanner wrote by far the most during his life.

The earliest letter (undated) was written to his Aunt Win who was barely five years older than Robin Tanner. He would have been in the sixth form of Chippenham Grammar School and the year was probably 1920. (His aunt is described on page 20 of *Double Harness*.)

LETTER 1

At present, I am in the Chemistry Laboratory, supposed to be swatting Chemistry, but I'm sitting by the open window in the sunshine and I really DON'T feel like work!!!!!!!

I've been amusing myself by making sketches of our very energetic science master who is giving a lecture on 'Carbon and the Nitrates and Phosphates in the soil, and their chemical relationship to plant life'! – which, I might add, does not greatly interest me!!!!!!! You *would* think him funny if you could see him now, raving about in his gown.

I'll sketch him for your special benefit and amusement in a minute or two.

Continued .... 3.15 p.m.

I will now continue this scrappy 'letter'. I was bound to leave it off for a few minutes and hide it with my blotting paper! – because the master marched up to me, (just as I was writing about him to you), with a none *too* pleasant look on his face – but he did nothing dreadful!

Bert's[1] gone and joined up!

– He was absolutely fed up. – Has tried everywhere for a job. He went to Melksham, Devizes, Trowbridge, and Bath and could get nothing (this was on Tuesday) so he did the trick and joined up.

We had a card on Wednesday saying he had passed as Electrician.

We hope it's only for the 90 days Defence Corps. – but have not yet heard.

Silly ass! But I s'pose we can't really blame him. He absolutely *can't* stop here doing nothing, but it seems jolly rotten to think a chap has to join the army though, cos of no work.

However, we must make the best of it, and hope he will not be in it for long.

– Oh! Here's our Bert just coming!

– Oh what a scream! I *wish* you could see him!

Just wait a minute till he comes in, and I'll describe him ——— If you could see him you'd raise the roof. Boots – 2 ft long. Like iron. Trousers – Baggy. Sloppy. Too big. Hands – Black! Coat – Indescribable! Hat – Oooh!!! – He *does* look a lad!!! He has come home for the weekend to bring his civvies etc. He's only joined for the 90 days. Is Electrician in Royal Engineers. – Stationed in Bath. – at Weston. And not having *too* bad a time.

---

1. Robin Tanner's brother.

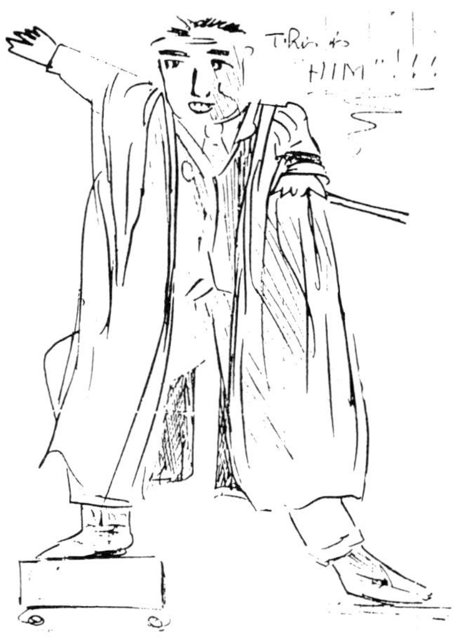

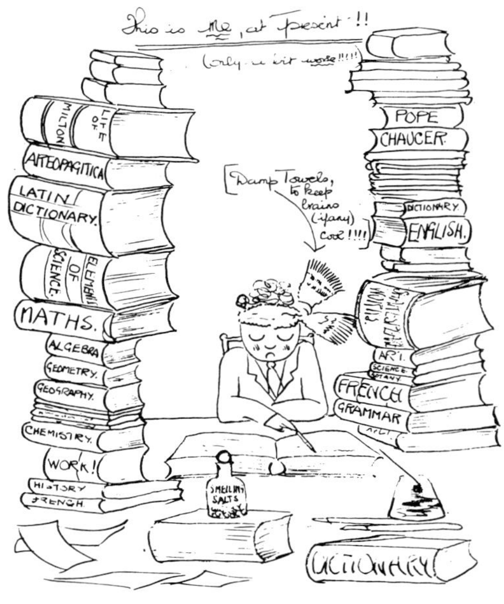

The next letter, also to Aunt Win, was written from Goldsmiths' College. The names of two friends and fellow students, Percy Friend (Ami) and Cecil Crouch, occur for the first time. Robin Tanner's arrival at Goldsmiths' is described in Chapter 4 of *Double Harness*.

LETTER 2

[probably 1922]

I like Coll and Hostel now awfully. Two fellows at the other hostel are splendid. One is Head of the Coll! Aren't I honoured? We have lovely times together, in the City on Saturdays etc. They'd do anything to help me and I don't know what I should do without them. They want me to go home with them at Christmas. Percy lives at Chatham and Cecil at Tonbridge Wells.

Our food is edible! and really I mustn't grumble. Of course I can't compare it with home, but it's quite decent. For example:

1. Supper last night was bread, marg., cheese. Plenty of it.
2. Tea yesterday was salmon, bread, marg., apricot jam. Breakfast today was a boiled egg each, bread, marg., marmalade.

Midlunch is always decent. Something after the style of Mother's Sunday dinners. You understand so I will not grumble.

The colossal organ in the Hall is a wonderful 4-manual instrument. Doctor White makes it thunder for miles! I have never experienced such thrilling music.

The large Common Room possesses one of the loveliest pianos I think I have ever heard. It is a Berlin rosewood. Its tone is sort of milky, low, silvery and mellow. Several of the Senior Hostellites are students of Advanced Music and they play wonderfully.

The next letter is the first to Cecil Crouch written from home during the Easter holiday.

LETTER 3

Monday. [16th April, 1923]

My dear Cecil,

I haven't kept you ages this time for a letter, . . . but somehow, with a house full of visitors who won't budge but want 'entertaining', and Adv. Art, and 259 other things I have put it off till now. . . . Besides, what *can* I write about, except the few things that happen here?

. . . I'll now proceed to tell you all the news, trusting you will be interested, and pleased to receive so much writing from me!

1. This morning I went to get measured for a suit, and on the way I met three old school chums. They were going to Bristol by bus for an examination in mechanics.
2. It rained on my way home. We have been having wretched weather all the week; I am told it is because the moon or sun or something is in the wrong quarter.
3. I lost my collar stud and a button last Wednesday.
4. We have 3¼ wallflowers in bloom in our garden.
5. *Ma petite soeur* got five sums right today at school.
6. On Saturday I went to Bath to see *Much Ado about Nothing* and *Richard III* by the Henry Bainton Company. These plays were written by a man named William Shakespeare who died on April 23rd 1616, and who wrote lots of plays.
7. We had tea in a café in Bath.
8. It rained on Sunday.
9. I put 3d. in the collection on Sunday morning. I went to our Parish Church, a fine old 15th Century edifice that stands in the old market square, near an antique shop where they sell volumes of Chopin for 6d. per volume.
10. I made two holes in my socks this afternoon.

11. We had pork for lunch today.
12. The text at church yesterday was 'God is a spirit; and they that worship him, must worship him in spirit and in truth.' I am awfully sorry, but I have quite forgotten the context, but as soon as I discover it I will send it on to you with full particulars.
13. My little sister is at present playing 'Wonderland', a marvellous harmony by the great composer Ezra Read. It is written in ¾ time and in the key of C. The page of music is torn at the bottom.
14. A cock crew five times just now.
15. I hear that butter is 2d. a pound cheaper today than it was at 7.43 p.m. on Saturday last, April 14th.
16. ——— The *Latest* News.

    ——— I am *19* tomorrow!

    Isn't it ghastly.

    I refuse to get any older!

LETTER 4

London. [20th December, 1925]

Dearest Win,

This is not a letter: I am too busy, restless, excited, bewildered, dazed, and tired to write a letter. I am in a terrible muddle, physically and mentally, for there is so much to be done. There are rehearsals for our school play, letters and shopping to do, registers and books to mark, and 274 other things to do.

At present I am just swimming on and longing for end of term. I am so London-smothered. Three solid months' work from 8 a.m. till 10.30 p.m., in foggy, filthy London makes me long for one beautiful thing – a breath of quiet, pure, leaf-scented Wiltshire air. I am feeling ever so Home-and-country sick. I would give anything for a lone white Wiltshire lane with giant elms above and squishy grey mud beneath. I am dying for some long Wessex dream-days, when I can wander down the fields again, and listen to great silences and feel a clean cold wind whistle through my hair.

Thank God I have nearly three weeks' holiday. Isn't it wonderful. I wonder if I shall see you. I go down next Wednesday, I hope, and – ugh! – return on

Jan. 11th. I am scribbling this note in case I get no opportunity to write before Christmas, to wish you and Horace a most Beautiful Christmastime, and a 1926 to follow, that is secreting much happiness and peace for you. I wish you *wealth*, – in the Ruskin sense of the word. Of course, Mother and all will write separately to you.

Having poured out my own jeremiad to you, let me hear how you are. . . . What holiday – if any – do you get, Win? Are you having a Fancy Dress Dance? Tell me all your news. It is ages since you wrote, and I don't feel I have *really* spoken to you for long, for years.

Is Horace doing well? I have finished Art School for the Term, and it is a relief. I have also been going to English Lectures at the University, with Cyril, my college chum, on Modern English Poetry. It has been thrilling. I have another Art Examination in Italian Painting of the Renaissance, and the History of Gothic Architecture, Stonework, Stained glass, costume, and design, to face next May.

You know we are in MARLOTT[1] now I expect? It is very pleasant and jolly. Everyone likes it exceedingly. I know you will too, – especially the colour-schemes, eh!!

I am going to stop now, when I have written down a lovely Christmas poem by my well-beloved Thomas Hardy, for you to read and cherish as I do.

I will write it on a separate sheet. Goodnight, Win.

Write to me.
Love
Fred.[2]

---

1. The Tanner family house in Chippenham.
2. Robin Tanner was known as Fred at home.

LETTER 5

Marlott. [31st December, 1925]

Your letter has just come, Cecil. I had just returned from a 10-mile walk! There! That shows you I am better, doesn't it?

This is really to thank you ever so for your Christmas letter and present. It was most lovely of you. I was delighted with the *Cherry Orchard.* It is more interesting to me even than I imagined it would be, because the translation is a different one from that which I heard at Hammersmith. I *shall* treasure it. Thank you, again. You have had a glorious Christmas, I hope. As for me, – *I have been thrilled every minute.* The crowd has gone now, and we are left to enjoy ourselves as wildly as we please.

. . . I was amazed to see fields of snow soon after passing Reading, and when I reached home-station, I was greeted by my young sisters all muffled up snow-style. Then we Trojaned[1] home across the snow, under the trees in the starlight.

Christmas Eve was aglow with silver. Every field and blessed lane was a wonderful white and glistening downland. At 9 p.m. we all went for a walk down the lanes, and trudged bravely over the frozen snow; and sang Lüther's Cradle Hymn and other lovely Carols, just because we felt we must. There was one huge star over a barn, and we called it Bethlehem. (The star was Venus really I believe!) On Christmas morning we awoke to more spotless snow. My brothers, and Grace and Olive and I walked up Derriads' Lane to the grey farm, through the grey gate past the grey crab-apple tree, to the big meadow. We Hudsoned, all of us. Chaffinches, Wagtails, Bullfinches, Robins, Wrens, Starlings, Blackbirds, and even two shaggy old Crows came to our feet and ate our crumbs and scraps. It was most wonderful. I shall never forget it.

Since Christmas we have done strange things! I am *so* happy, *so* desperately well, *so* excited, *so* flushed with the beat of the wind and flying leaves. Now all the snow has 'thawn', and the brooks are swollen, and the white roads are mud roads; and yesterday we had much rain from the West; but today is a 'mad March day' really.

. . . *Jude* [*the Obscure*] is making a big impression on me. I have read very little really, for there are so many out-of-doors things to do, and so little time to do them in. The wind is screaming and rushing all round and through the house. Thank your Mother and Daisy and All for their card. Give them my love. I hope you are as happy as I am. Goodbye.

---

1. Brother Leslie's car.

LETTER 6

To Cecil Crouch, written from the school in Deptford, London, where Robin Tanner was teaching.

Wednesday. [2nd February, 1928]

Thank you so much for last night's letter. I will write as soon as I can fix up a time to come to you. I am frantically busy. Let me tell you what has happened: I retire from teaching at Easter 1928. I go to Goldsmiths' Art School for three days a week next term (till June 29th). The remaining days I spend in museums and things. On June 29th I go home to start work in my studio (as yet unbuilt!) at etching. I have signed a three-year contract so far, to do a min. of four and max. of seven plates annually. I shall earn over £400 a year I hope. I shall just work alone there, wander, draw, paint, walk, sleep, design, and read. The work won't be hard. The '*hours*' will be of my choosing. I can earn as much or as little as I like. Seven plates would give me £565. But the cash doesn't interest me as much as the *work* and the *life*. I can draw just what I like and when I like! I shall have the studio in the garden of course. I'll tell you all the details when I *do* see you. Next term I shall 'get ready', you see.

The thought of leaving *schools* for art and home – almost kills me with excitement, and I am afraid I shall wake to find I've dreamt. I don't deserve it all. Cyril,[1] Heather, and Home are wildly excited of course.

I *can't* stop, really, to tell you all, though I feel so mean.

Love to all at home.
Love Robin.

---

1. Cyril Rice, fellow student at Goldsmiths', who married Grace Tanner, Robin's sister, and later became a headmaster of a Wiltshire primary school.

LETTER 7

A postcard to Cecil Crouch, headed 'Blackheath, Monday afternoon, 14.5.28'.

Helen[1] and I have just returned from Petersfield and Steep, down in Hampshire. We have walked in all the old places of Edward's poems, – sat in the fields and woods and lanes and combes about which he wrote; and felt the lovely yielding spirit of the earth again in the sunshine. Oh it has been so lovely, Cecil. I have been to Bedale's School, and met lots and lots of ever such interesting art people. At Whitsun I am going HOME (for a week) on Whit Tuesday. So I cannot come to Soham then. But please I want badly to come soon. Get *A pocket-book of songs and poems for the Open Air* (Collected by Ed. Thomas. Jonathan Cape 3/6). It is the beautiful anthology Edward made for Helen in the 'As it Was' times. I had £130 for *Martin's Hovel* etching. – I've written heaps more than you.

Love Robin.

---

1. Wife of Edward Thomas.

LETTER 8

To Cecil Crouch. Written from Marlott, Robin Tanner's parents' house, in the garden of which his father had built the studio.

[1st December, 1928]

I have just come back from Derriads-Mead where I've been wandering along the hedges, gathering berries and pretty leaves, listening to tits and wrens, playing with the water of full ditches, watching the slow daffodil clouds stretch thin across the west with a wavering light, thinking about my place on the map and about London and all the herded folk there and about you up in Soham somewhere. I've been thinking a long while about you Cecil. Are you well and happy? It was lovely having your letters. I was thrilled that you were playing again. The Bath Pumproom Concerts we hear. They are splendid often. Tell me about school and village 'drama'. Tell me about Cambridge.

I am doing my huge Christmas Eve plate now. *The Gamekeeper's Cottage* is published. Ami wants badly to paint Wiltshire, having once seen it. I think his weekend here did him a good deal of good. All Marlott loved Ami, making allowances for his ravings. He was surprisingly at home and eager and un-arty. I mean he fell in with things and didn't bore. He let up though. I think school is rather awful for him.

This is a most perfect December day. The good rich earth imprisons me. I never never want to go away from it. The brown soil, the white stones, the deep mud with leaves inlaid, the homesick sky, the indigo dark woods low down in the hollow where the brook roars, the plainting peewits, the old roads, the old hedges, the lost-away-forgotten feeling that broods over the fields, the old people going homealong – these things hold me. They are so real and so intense. The old allround English life that Chaucer and Shakespeare knew lives on in these lovely places.

Do read the works of Mary Webb, especially *Precious Bane* and *Gone to Earth*. They are marvellous things, and have helped me marvellously.

Goodnight Cecil dear,
Mother and all send their love
The owls are out
Love Robin.

LETTER 9

An undated letter to Cecil Crouch, probably late 1928.

Sunday morning.

I know I ought really to write you a lovely long letter, Cecil. The days fly by ridiculously. I am busy biting my Woodman plate. Heather and I have drawn all the materials for The Harvest Festival and The Cheese Room.

I can't afford those records for a long time. I must earn. I've done two etchings and am doing *Monday Evening*, a big 7″ × 9″ plate of a cottage interior, ironing, supper laid, folk in garden, grandfather's clock etc.

There is a piece of news for you, which maybe you'll be surprised to hear. Because of the 'local fame' because of the R.A.,[1] the Wiltshire Education Authority want me to start a handwork and art scheme in a school half a mile from here. It is the school where I student-taught. They are keen to begin this new stunt, and since I can do exactly what I want I'm going to take it in my stride. I don't see why I shouldn't earn as much cash as I can and the job will be just as I like to make it. Of course it means I shan't have so much time for being idle and so on, and for my etching, but I can manage it. It is a full-time post. I thought a lot about it before I took it. You see (but don't publish it at all, Cecil) Heather and I want to make our little home next year, and I simply must save as much as I can. Dreadful it sounds, but it isn't really, and I want to save what I earn by teaching. It will be queer, but I shall love it, because I have to do what I like with the kids – bookbinding, etching, woodcuts, etc.

Tell me what you think of me. Tell me how normal I am. Ami goes madder.

Goodbye now, and my love to you, and all at home.

Mother sends her love.

Robin.

---

1. Robin Tanner's work had been accepted at the Summer Exhibition of the Royal Academy.

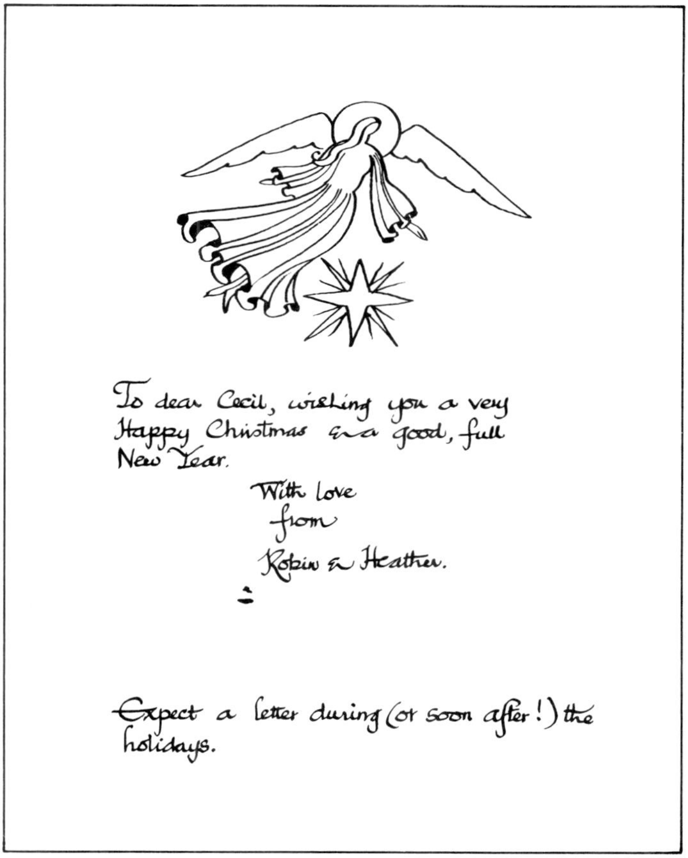

Studio. Monday Evening. [March 1929]

I would love to write a long letter Cecil, but . . . I haven't written because I have worked. Already this year I have done one enormous plate – a square foot of copper! It is the plate I told you of, called *Christmas*. There is the whole village under the moon, seen from the church tower, and all around are the bare hills and ploughed fields and tall trees. And carol singers are singing under lanterns by the pond. It was a terribly difficult piece of work, but I loved trying to do it, – but of course the result is pretty hopeless. But etching makes you go on etching. Now I am thinking of my next three plates – The Woodlanders, The Dairy, and Harvest Festival.

I was THRILLED, Cecil, about the playing you've been doing, and how I'd love to hear the 2nd *Scherzo* again. Though Chopin doesn't give me much. I am ignoramus supreme, but I know that of all the music I've heard I love these people most, and in this order

Beethoven

Brahms

Bach

Delius

Mozart.

Now laugh heartily at me!

I saw Ami in London when I went up to the Dutch Exhibition. He still raves over most things! But he's dreadfully miserable – but it's rather the kind of misery you sort of *enjoy* – and is determined to leave London in the Summer. I drilled some sense into him, and bossed him about and made him declare he won't leave teaching and 'do nothing'. He *does* need some looking after and 'pummeling'. He could do *such* good work: he has it in him, but he's too fond of theories and 'reality' and 'life' and 'spiritual impulse', and 'mysticism'. I try – when I see him, to make him *live*.

. . . Cyril was here for the weekend. A marvellous sunny time. We saw fieldfares, redwings, marsh tits, bullfinches, woodpeckers, nuthatches, tree creepers, coal tits, and a jay: and we watched them each for a long while.

The celandines and primroses are only just blooming. It is all very late because of the drought. I wish for a week of rain. Still, every day is marvellous. Heather comes home on Wednesday week for her month's holiday – and we shall walk and walk.

One day I shall make you come and stay here, and I'll take you everywhere like you took me. Mother sends her love and hopes you don't have any neuritis now. Your letter was so happy. . . . Even our piano – only a £60 Benson! – you won't really object to playing on, I think. . . .

Are you walking on the common or somewhere or are you eating those funny little breakfast biscuits made by Mr Huntley and Mrs Palmer – that your landlady orders by the ton for you?

All the evening has been golden, and now the blue of the sky is dark and open, with the 7-days' moon swung up high and clear, and Jupiter chasing Venus down to the west. The owls in Derriads are lovely. No day ends well without the owls' cries, I think.

Goodnight Cecil,
and my dear love to you. . . .
Robin.

LETTER 11

To Cecil Couch, written from London.

[28th April, 1929]

I'm staying here with Cyril until the morning, I'm staying with Paul Drury tomorrow night, and then on Tuesday I'm going home again. I'm homesick for Home and the swallows and the cowslips already.

I came up for Varnishing Day at the [Royal] Academy, which is tomorrow, and this is only a selfish little note to tell you the lovely news that Ami has a watercolour accepted by the R.A., and I have two etchings. They are the last big plate (the Christmas one) and the little Roadmaker.

At least I'm not sure yet if they have *hung* Ami's or not, but I do hope they have. It will be such an encouragement. He has done some fine work. I bought two very good satisfying watercolours from him this time. . . .

LETTER 12

To Cecil Crouch, written from Marlott.

[10th May, 1929]

Your absolutely BRILLIANT letter is the loveliest I've read for ages. You *are* a good creature to describe so vividly all your Ami-time. I roared with laughter at some, and nearly cried at other paragraphs. And I can't tell you how *real* it all sounded.

About your poor Mother I feel so sad. Cecil, do try to bear it somehow, for I know how dreadful it must be for you, and I cannot understand how life goes at all. Be ever so brave: as I know you are. Send my dear love when you write. I feel so much for you and those at home.

. . . Ami is a queer sort of genius, with a lovableness in him. He is ghastly in his selfishness, yet I don't believe he *knows* he's selfish. Well! How can you help him? If I write to him he writes back wails and jeremiads and 'poems'. *Thank your God you are normal!* Please Cecil, I am normal too, eh? I don't want to be anything else. I want to LIVE, vulgarly and broadly. I want to love and hate and eat and drink and sleep and work and walk and talk and be quiet and think and have kids of my own and let them do likewise.

The worst of me is that I am so 'lustful'. I like butter and bread – not bread and butter. I always want *too* much of everything. I could smell a flower to death. I want to drink *lots* of beer. I want to learn *lots* of things. I want everything to be so ample. I want to give heaps and take heaps. It's a good job my Heather is 'lustful' too. We are both rather 'black notes only' I suppose. Well, that's how we were made and there's no altering it, Mister Crouch.

Why won't you ever come to Marlott? Why will you pass-in-the-night sort of. All here would be lovely, you'd find. They are so intensely homely and true. I'm glad you love all Mothers. They are marvellous. . . .

I simply *can't* come though, because of work. I've finished my edition today. Filthy foul work: printing. One day you *must* come and see my press. . . . I'd let you print an etching: marvellous privilege! . . .

This letter is to Harry Coles, twin brother of Teddy Coles, both pupils at the Deptford school. The latter became an Anglican monk who worked in Soweto, Johannesburg. Mr Nunn was headmaster of the school.

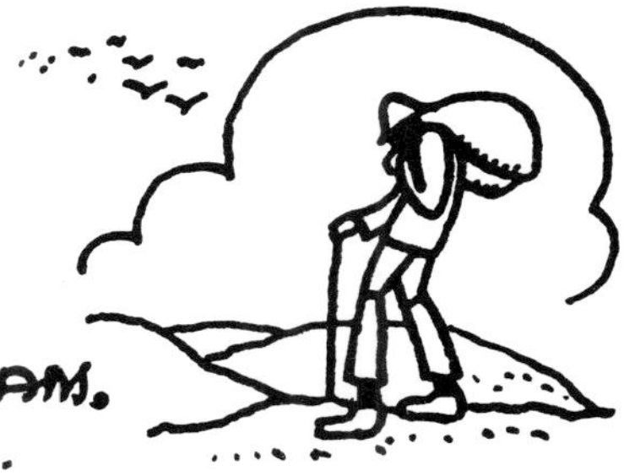

Marlott,
Frogwell,
CHIPPENHAM.
WILTSHIRE.

August 21. 1930.

Dear Harry,
It was a great surprise to find your letter awaiting me one afternoon when I returned from a lovely walk. While my sister peeled the mushrooms we had gathered I read your letter to her, and it was all a jolly surprise. But what a pity I missed seeing your aunt. It would have been so nice to have a chat with her about 'the dreadful twins'!

I have been staying in Hampstead, and I had hoped to jump on a '48 Bus' one day, and come and see you all. But I loathe London so much that I was very glad to be home again. One day I shall certainly come to see you. Mr Nunn writes to me often. Of course, you do not often see him now. I think you will get to like your new school as much as your old one. You *have* improved a great deal in your English, Harry. I am glad you and Teddy still like to draw. I often wish I could have you boys here, to see the lovely things I see. This is a wild wet morning, and the wind smells of hay and straw, because the men have been thatching the ricks at the crossroads.

Already you can tell that Autumn is near. There are ripe blackberries, nuts, and horse chestnuts, and the stubble fields are golden. I like to see the farmyards grouped with tall corn ricks and a good store of hay for the winter. I can never say which season I like best. The winter is a glorious time for some things, and I do not feel the cold.

Give my best wishes to all at home. I expect Cynthia is a big girl now! Does Betty still draw sometimes? Don't worry mother *too* much these holidays! Goodbye now, and tell me all your news again some day.

R. Tanner.

LETTER 14

Marlott. [21st December, 1930]

My dear Cecil,

May you have a simply lovely Christmastime, with peace and pleasant thoughts, and some music and reading and jolly talk and food(!) and walks. And may you be very well, all through next year; may you get a job near home, and more time for music and drawing and reading. I half – or three quarters – promised to write you a long Christmassy letter, didn't I? Well, I am deluged with packing and writing and house-business, so even now I fear my letter must wait. But here are the best wishes of all Marlott to you, and everybody sends their love.

It is a glorious, crisp, sunny morning. Cyril has just set out on his motor bike for London. Dad and Grace have cycled out to Kington Langley, where the house progresses ever so well. I think you will love the fireplace in the Living Room. It is just finished. Leslie started making a hedge yesterday. The poor child has sprained his ankle so has to 'lay up'. Olive is very busy making new curtains. Heather is cleaning the room, and Mother is all of a bustle with cooking.

We have a lovely holly from Langley. The sky is blue and Christmassy. A fox barks at night. Thirty-seven pullets were killed by him at Derriads last week. The lanes and fields are beautiful. I want to walk for miles and miles. I feel that primroses will soon be out and catkins will be blooming.

And so goodbye, and my dear love to you.

Your Robin.

We were a bit worried about our roof. The tiles look so dreadfully raw and pink and new at present, but are hand made, and therefore weather quickly.

LETTER 15

Heather and Robin were married on 4th April, 1931, so this was written during their first week at Old Chapel Field.

[9th April, 1931]

You poor dear Cecil,

Grace and Cyril have just been, and told me how you are ill: and here am I, not having written to you for so long. But I know you'll not mind when you know that I have been working day and night on a set of four etchings and four drawings for the photogravure supplement of *Nash's Magazine* (an article on the Thames). All has to be done by the 17th. And I've *heaps* to do yet.

April 10th.

The post goes at 7 p.m. here, so I couldn't post before. I've been so busy all day and am dead tired, but as happy as a robin should be in spring.

It is very good of you and Daisy to want to give me something for our cottage. Of course we want *everything* really: but our greatest need immediately is a chest for the hall. It is a very big place, as big as a small bedroom, so it is crying for a chest, and we have wanted this one for ages. Could you give us a contribution towards it? Perhaps you'd rather on the other hand give an independent object. If so, let me know, and I can furnish you with a list as long as a poker. (By the way, since I'm sending you this page, look at the fire irons. We have some like these! The log roller is a mephistopholean delight in store for you, at our big fireplace.) You'd not recognise this place now. Come down definitely when we're a trifle settled. At present we have the kitchen and living room half done: the rest, untouched! I want you to have a lovely quiet holiday here, and I'll make a fuss of you.

Please don't mind saying if you and Daisy would rather not give us something towards the chest. Some of our friends haven't minded their gift being a part of some big thing, but some have wanted rather to give us separate things. Anyhow, we shall all understand, and it is perfectly lovely of you to think so lovingly of Heather and me. I only hope you'll come and share the place with us. Already we have a thrush's nest with four eggs and a blackbird's with five in our hedge. There are primroses and wild parsley leaves and celandines everywhere. I do so hope you are better now, and having a good holiday. I *will* write, one day.

My dear love to you, and Heather sends hers.

We feel like Hansel and Gretel or The Babes in the Wood: very happy Babes in a very lovely Wood.

Goodnight Cecil.
Love, Robin.

People from Home come out daily. Les is helping and everybody marvellous. Dad and Mother are spending Sunday here. Heather is putting plates away in the gay kitchen.

LETTER 16

Robin Tanner was now teaching full time at Ivy Lane School, and had less time for etching. However, he continued to make drawings whenever he could: this letter indicates that he sent work to the Royal Academy during this period.

[17th May, 1931]

You dear Cecil,
To write to me thus when I neglect you so! There's a 'congratulatory epistle' from Ami that came weeks ago, it seems, and remains unanswered. The truth is that days come (each with beauty and joy and hours that are crammed full), and weeks go, and I feel nothing gets done. Yet really heaps and heaps of things must be being done! And our life here is so without knowledge of the-world-outside-our-field that to write a letter and send it out into the wide world is a wonderful event: truthfully that's how it feels.

We read your letter on our way down through the village to school. You are a lovely faithful creature and a perfect friend to me. I love to feel you are so happy about the R.A. I simply *must* get on with something in the Summer Holidays for *next* year. So far there's nothing done. I like to hear your news. I haven't been to London for ages, but we *may* go up for a couple of days during Whitsuntide. Then I have to be busy with a set of illustrations for 'The London Docks' by Virginia Woolf (*Good Housekeeping*) – perhaps a *Series* of articles. The Thames etchings have reproduced quite reasonably in *Nash's* (June No.).

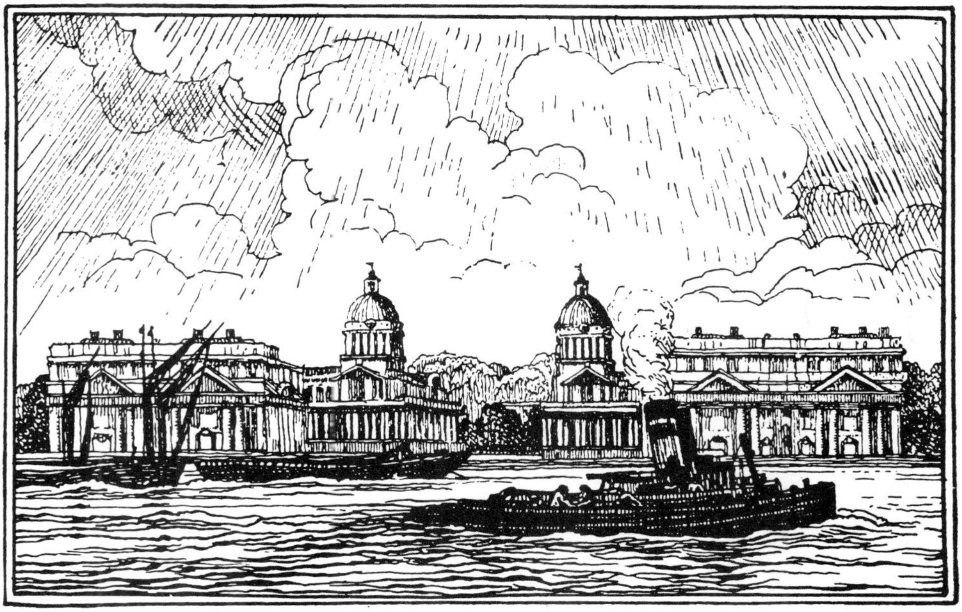

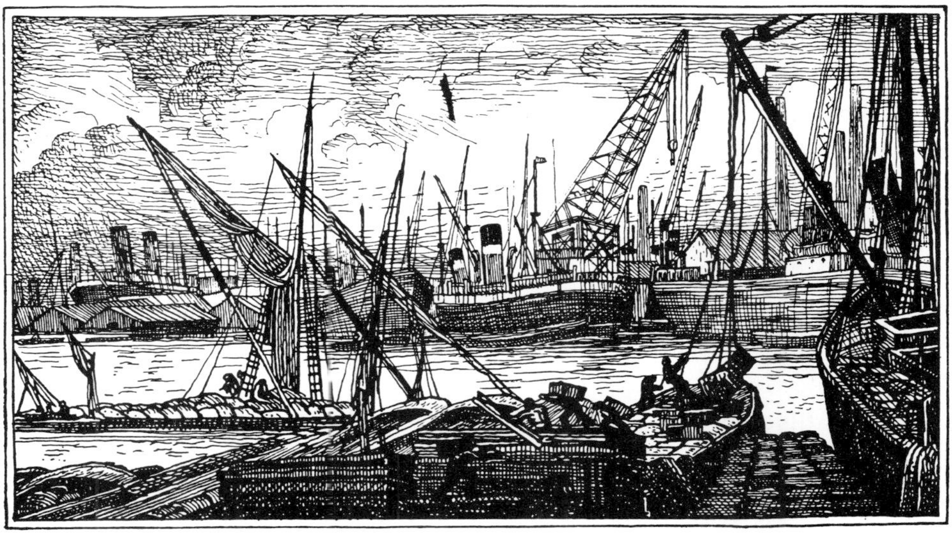

Drawings for Virginia Woolf's 'The Docks of London', *Good Housekeeping*, December 1931.

And then I may have told you I have to give three lectures to the Wiltshire Teachers' Summer School and they must be prepared pretty soon. And we are *very* gradually doing the house. Heather conquers some new patch every day: it is lovely to watch things develop. By the way, Gordon Russell is making your chest[1] for the hall after all – a *much* nicer one than Heal's, in *chestnut*, very modern and plain, for not much more. So I readily let him do it.

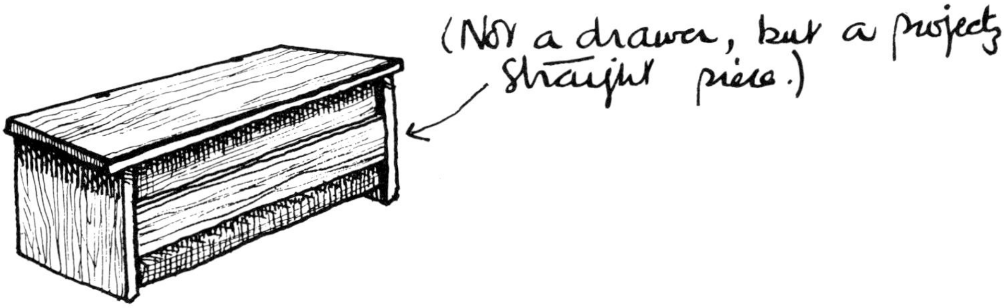

. . . I'd like Ami to come down here for a while. I wish you could come. The field is deep in green: we feel like a long old-fashioned story. Our thrush, having bred one lovely brood has built another nest and already has five eggs. We *see* and hear the nightingale down Morrell Lane. 'The cuckoo sends afloat his note on the air all day.'

Never was rain so light nor leaves so green nor buttercups so yellow nor hedge parsley so white as now. Heather is busy cooking a rib of beef and sundry puddings. She's loving all the housewifery and has gained much repute as a cook, Mr Crouch! In fact, we are both proving what marvellous gardeners, whitewashers, washerwomen, winemakers, window-cleaners, and workers at all things we are. Heather sends her dear love with mine. Have I ever answered your lovely Shakespeare Birthday letter? That gave us great joy, you precious creature.

Write us another letter. Have a lovely Whitsuntide, too.

Goodbye now, and God bless you.

Robin and Heather.

---

1. Wedding present from Cecil Crouch; see letter 15.

LETTER 17

[9th October, probably 1931]

My dear, thoughtful, and kind Cecil,
Here we are, by the Studio fire, after a busy day. Heather has been pulling up old plants, setting the garden to rights, and solignuming a new extending ladder we've just bought, and I've had a good day at school, with kids fabric printing, lino-cutting, and drawing alarming portraits in charcoal on big sheets of paper.

The walk home through Birds' Marsh was very lovely. – Dropping chestnuts, rich smells from rotting leaves, screeching owls and blackbirds, and a lovely sunset. And now all is cosy, and it is dark and wintry outside. Your pot of guelder rose berries (you wanted to photograph) still flourishes in the corner of the window! I wish you were here, so that I could tell you how happy your parcel made us. It was a lovely letter . . . and as for the photographs! . . . They are marvellous. We have loved them, and Olive (Spackman) loved them, and begs me to ask for one for her please. Today I dared to let Grace and Cyril share the whole packet (Cyril is much better, and hopes to start school within a fortnight or so) and they'll add an order I expect when I see them again on Thursday. Then I'll write again. Heather and I have enjoyed *all* the photographs, – the Easton Piercy *lovely* farm ones, even the dragonfly failure, the new Circus ones . . . Anyhow, I'll write later and ask for lots of things which you must refuse if difficult. . . . Do let us see the others, and tell us more about everything. . . .

Don't forget that we have no O.C.F.[1] photographs yet as those you sent were for Cyril. . . . Cyril is now reading *Cry Havoc*. Heather is just reading to me from *Headway* that England exports more armaments than any other country! We *are* a rotten lot! I'm so glad you are having an Art inspection soon. It will give you the praise you jolly well deserve. We'll send back the Music book and *Cry Havoc* as soon as possible. I *should* like to see your Peter Mitchell drawings – I expect you're *very* rushed. All my lectures are beginning. Tomorrow it is Swindon, which place I loathe. Picture me quoting Bannister Fletcher like mad! . . .

I *must* have an enlargement of the 'distant' view of Easton Piercy farm. That was a lovely day, wasn't it? And it now seems long ago, because of the darkness and the turning of the leaves and the weeks of school work.

Heather is feeling very well, and looks well, too. She sends her dear love with mine. We talk about you very often, and look forward tremendously to your letters and exciting enclosures. . . .

And now Goodnight. I feel ashamed of this dreadful scribble. It is all idleness and this comfortable seat low down by the fire. Do let us see *all* your photographs, as convenient. There is a very lucid account of fabric printing called *Fabric Printing* (Hours of Leisure series), published by The Studio Ltd, worth having. The method of printing can be modified. The block can be painted instead of covered with a roller.

Much love, you dear faithful creature.
Robin Redbreast and Jenny Wren.

P.S. Heather, on reading this says, 'Well, what a letter! It's just a long clamour for more photographs from beginning to end!'

---

1. Old Chapel Field.

LETTER 18

[3rd April, 1932]

You dear, long-suffering Cecil,

I cannot remember when I last wrote to you. It was in Winter, and now here is Spring. We have watched a thrush build her nest in our hedge near the top of Morrell Lane (and she has one egg in it), 'our' blackbird has built in the holly tree, our banks are full of celandines and primroses, and Birds' Marsh is full of daffodils. But alas, they are not the little frail wild kind I love. What primroses there are in every field! And now the marsh marigolds, violets, willows, and ground ivy are in bloom.

This weekend is the anniversary of our wedding. The hedges were greener at this time last year than they are now. I planted two lilac trees, two laburnums, and a red may tree and a hedge of quick along Leslie's front bank, and they all look healthy. The trees stand in the field, on this side of the bank. All this birdsong and greening grass after the long drought make us both so full of joy. I hope you are spending a nice homely holiday with your Mother and

Father. Give them my love. And I hope Daisy and her baby are flourishing.

It is a still and misty evening, with blackbirds still screaming along our hedges. I have just lit the lamp and have a big fire. I remember that last year we needed big fires for two months after we were married. I have started to needle my big Autumny plate, my eyes being much better. I don't know quite when my show will be. I shall be glad to have this plate ready to send up for the R.A. next year. The XXI Gallery, I think, have submitted a drawing of mine this year – a large brown one of the thatched cottage round the lane.

At the end of this sentence Mother and Leslie arrived by surprise; so I am finishing writing to you on Monday morning, just after 7 o'clock, before Breakfast, Mister Crouch. It is a soft wet morning. Heather is having her fortnightly washday too. We were awakened at midnight by pouring rain. The field is drenched, and the grass is extremely vivid. Our thrush is singing with great force. It will be a wet muddy walk through Birds' Marsh, and we shall love it. The field opposite us, to the South, has been full of lambs. . . . We had such a lovely time here last night, Mother holding the floor most of the time, to our delight; and Leslie in marvellous new Harris tweed plusfours, looking far more grownup, I fear, than his elder brother. Mother still has no teeth, but has been very brave and courageous having none. Dad has been very unwell. He couldn't even pay us his usual Sunday morning visit, but Mother says he is getting better.

Our holiday was short but beautiful. There is a new arrangement, whereby we have six weeks (instead of four) in the Summer. Then we both hope to do some egg tempera painting, just in the way our beloved Botticelli used to do. We have a great bath of plaster of paris slaking in 'bedroom 3'. It has to slake for a month. We shall mix it with parchment size (which we shall make) to make the gesso ground for the picture. The gesso is applied to a wooden panel. Heather is going to paint some cowslips, and I am 'using' her for a sort of portrait with masses of Spring flowers. Needless to say the so-called portrait bears no resemblance at all to Heather. But it will be lovely to do. The powder colours we are using are only those which are absolutely permanent, – mostly natural earths. It is a thrilling study.

Then, in preparation for Heather's Matric marking in June, we have been re-reading Browning. What a wonderful, *most* wonderful creature he was! Somebody after your own heart I should think. He puts the Moderns to shame.

It really is time to go to school. I should have liked to write a long letter. Tell me all about Stanley, Charlie, the Johnsons, Ching, what music you are studying, home, Ami, and all sorts of things.

Much love, – far more than I can tell on paper.
Your neglectful Robin and his beloved Jenny Wren.

Heather says I am to send her love, in a special sentence!

LETTER 19

[undated, probably 1934]

Sunday afternoon, May 8th; very quiet, except for the cuckoo and innumerable small birds, including a fluting cock blackbird who sits in the young elm near the studio calling with pride to his mate (who sits tight on five eggs in our bank).

We have decked the house with young beech leaves, and we have said old Tom Hardy's lines,

'When the May month flaps its glad green leaves like wings,
Delicate-filmed as new-spun silk . . .'

Our pots are filled with primroses, cowslips, bluebells, marsh marigolds, cuckoo flowers, anemones, stitchwort, gorse, and hedge parsley. . . .

It is a beautiful day. I have just finished the cartoon for my first egg tempera painting (a head of a woman with a very detailed background of woodland Spring flowers). Heather is embroidering daisies on a new hat. It is a day like 'The first cuckoo in Spring'. (By the way, do you know the very thin and poor piano arrangement of it? If not, *don't* know it!)

But this is to thank you for the heavenly record for my birthday, and to tell you how happy your loving thought made me (who treats you so shamefully with regard to letters – and I haven't even finished your Christmas drawing yet!) You are more faithful than any other friend. It is nearly ten years ago that you first took pity on a bewildered country child who didn't know a tram from a 'bus, and whose thoughts were all on Wiltshire and none on Goldsmiths' College. I often remember those early days, mixed up with Lyons' Teashops,

Dear Brutus, St Margaret's, Lee, *The Immortal Hour*, *Candida*, the 2nd *Scherzo*, Greenwich Park, and the Lecture Hall piano!

Well, thank you very much. . . . I will try to write more often, but (a) I have to draw, (b) my eyes aren't always good, (c) letters are so feeble.

There is little news. We are very happy, and hope you (and all at home) are. Ami's dovecote watercolour is in the R.A. I sent a big brown drawing of our darling thatched cottages, and that is in. I am needling my *Autumn* plate.

Tell me what you are drawing, playing, and reading. . . .

Our dear love to you.
Robin and Heather.

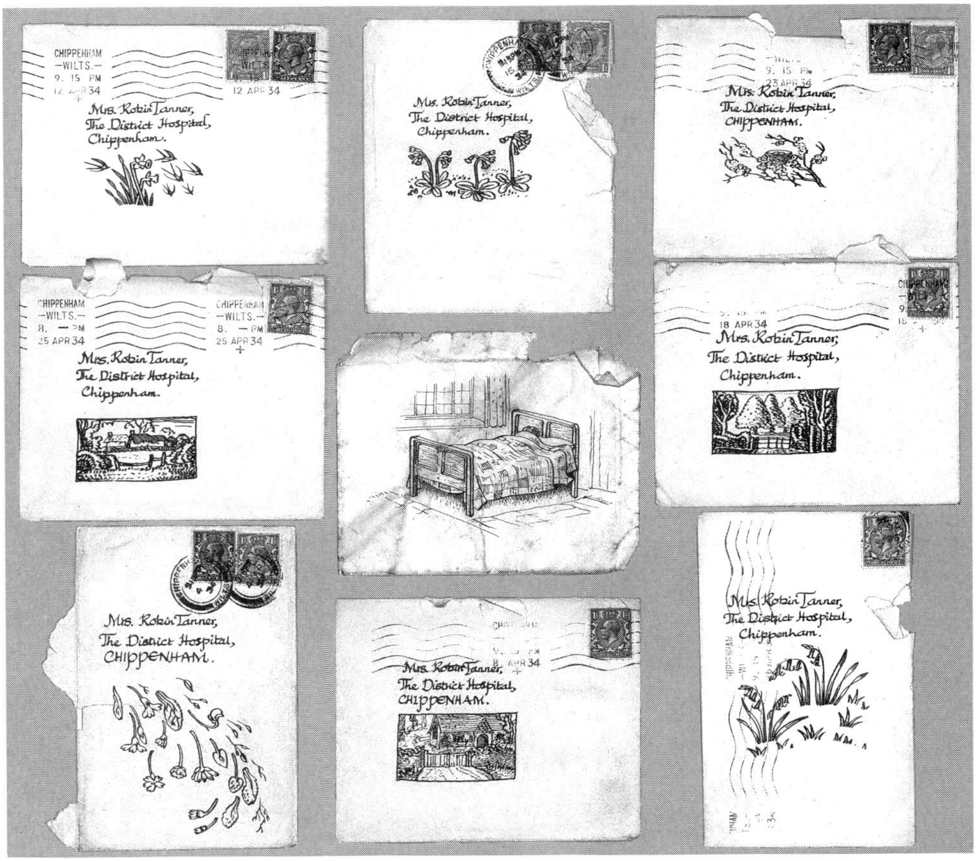

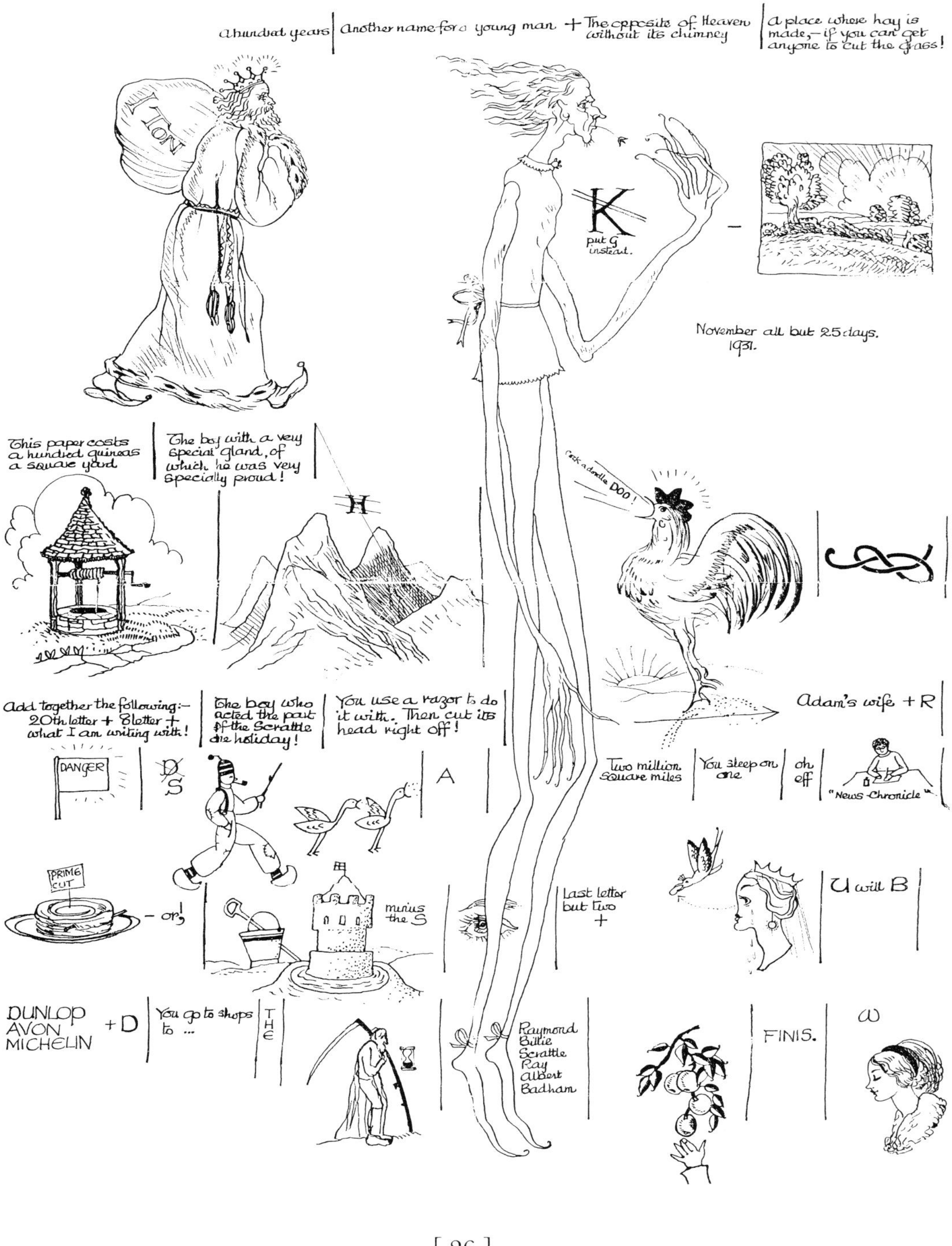

a hundred years
Another name for a young man
+ The opposite of Heaven without its chimney
a place where hay is made,— if you can get anyone to cut the grass!
TON
K
put G instead.
November all but 25 days. 1931.
This paper costs a hundred guineas a square yard
The boy with a very special gland, of which he was very specially proud!
H
Cock a doodle DOO!
Add together the following:— 20th letter + 8 letter + what I am writing with!
The boy who acted the part of the Scrattle one holiday!
You use a razor to do it with. Then cut its head right off!
Adam's wife + R
DANGER
D
S
A
Two million square miles
You sleep on one
oh off
"News-Chronicle"
PRIME CUT
— or,
minus the S
Last letter but two +
U will B
DUNLOP AVON MICHELIN
+ D
You go to shops to ...
THE
Raymond Billie Scrattle Ray Albert Badham
FINIS.
ω

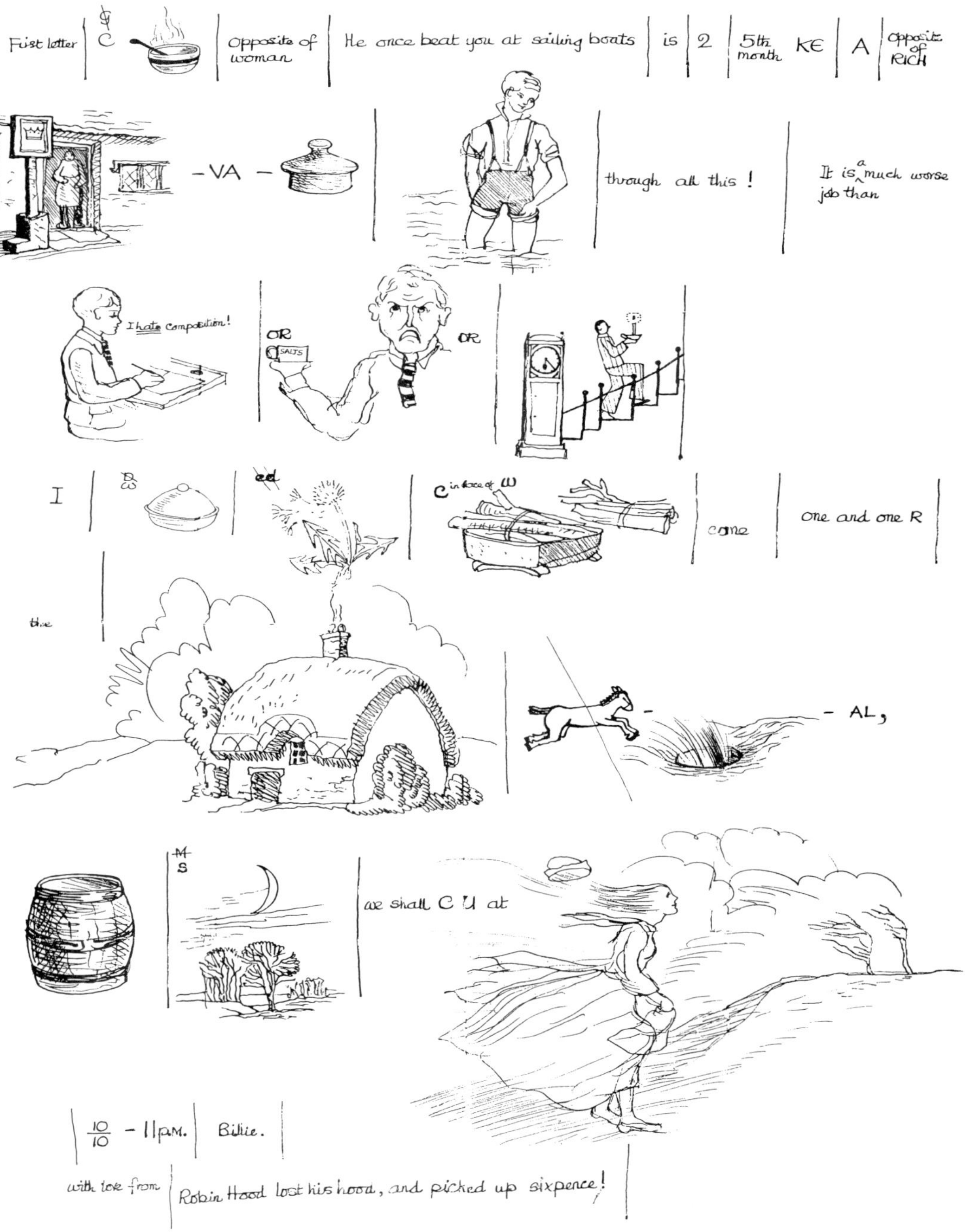
First letter
C
Opposite of woman
He once beat you at sailing boats
is
2
5th month
KE
A
Opposite of RICH
-VA-
through all this !
It is a much worse job than
I hate composition!
OR
SALTS
OR
I
ed
C in place of W
come
One and one R
the
- AL,
S
we shall C U at
10/10 - 11 p.m.
Billie.
with love from
Robin Hood lost his hood, and picked up sixpence!

LETTER 20

Undated letter written in 1935, before Robin Tanner took up residence in Leeds as HMI.

Thursday afternoon.

My dear Cecil,
We are sorry not to have answered your letter before, but were ever so glad you arrived home safely, and to find all well.

We are in the midst of a very dark time. Mother is much worse. She has been in Bath Eye Hospital – but the doctors are sure hers is not an eye case, and we have just returned from Bath now, having taken Mother to the Forbes Frazer hospital. It is feared that she is developing a tumour on the brain, and we are feeling most desolate and worried. She is already beginning to find it difficult to concentrate: she couldn't feel any interest in anything at all when we saw her this morning. She is now in a most lovely private hospital – and there she has to lie – and oh, it breaks my heart to think of her so. And I can hardly dare think far into the future.

We managed very well in Leeds. It was not so bad as we had expected. Our address next September 14th is likely to be The Gables, Moor Drive, Headingly, Leeds, 6.

Our goods go on Wed. The hall is full of them. Les. made us a beautiful little table (which we hope to use here one day as a dressing table) and we have a nice divan bed, and Heather is making some lovely curtains as I write. We shall soon make the Gables an extension of this heavenly little home. Next Sat. at 4 p.m. we are due to arrive. . . .

Our dearest love to you.
Robin and Heather.

(previous page) A pictogram drawn for Raymond Badham [Billie], a seven-year-old boy from Ivy Lane School who was in hospital. It reads: 'Old Chapel Field, Kington Langley. Dear Billie [Ray]. Well I do not think you have ever read such a large sheet of paper before and I expect you will be tired by the time you reach the end. What a cruel man he is to make a poor invalid wade through all this. It is much worse than writing composition, or taking medicine, or going to bed. I wish we could come to the Cottage Hospital but soon we shall see you at Windyridge [home]. Good night Billie. With love from Robin Tanner.'

2

1935–1945

This section covers the period between 1935 and the end of the Second World War. The Tanners lived in Leeds for two years, and then returned to Old Chapel Field when Robin Tanner was working as HMI in Gloucestershire and Bristol; during this time he travelled to many parts of England on courses and conferences. Chapter 7 of *Double Harness* describes the same period.

All the letters in this section are to Cecil Crouch.

LETTER 21

Maundy Thursday. [1935]

Dear faithful creature to write for my birthday, when I never remember yours. It was very lovely of you; and don't think you're going to persuade me that you're a nasty, cynical old man under a veneer of niceness, because I know far better, Sir. But I seem to embarrass you if I write with affection, so let me be modern and businesslike, and hasten to say:

1. I think the fabric printing is *extremely good*, whoever did it. Personally I'd prefer it without the yellow – or, at any rate, *under* the brown; I mean, printed before the brown. Thank you very much.
2. Pinion is a good person, isn't he? We thought that a fine letter for an inarticulate fenlander to write. – And what an excellent life drawing, too! You must be a good teacher to get a kid to be so keen. I'm so glad he appreciates you.
3. Greedily, we *should* love the record, one day, if you find us good enough to deserve such a gift.
4. Very much thanks for the photographs, each of which is very interesting in its way. I marvel that you can get such results, amateurly, and – believe us or believe us not, you contrary little devil – we are very proud to have them.
5. And thank you for all the congratulations and good wishes from you all. How nice, if I were stationed in Kent, and I could visit your mother and father . . . Tell me how everything is. In fact, sit down and write us a really

long letter! Holman wrote a note, and said wild things (for him) about the excellence of your piano. I am greatly looking forward to hearing it, one day.

6. Good, about painting the house. What colour? I remember most your ornate lavatory pan, – with willow pattern or some other discreet pattern. There's a little tap near the door, and one Sunday morning it decided to flood the whole house, I remember. The view from your bedroom windows must be lovely now, with all this mazy green. There are many nests in our hedges, and the garden and fruit trees are lovely.

Next week I hope to paint away at my tempera panel. . . . Mother is very well, but dad is very poorly, with indigestion and neuritis. It is a shame. He hasn't had a decent day this year, really, and looks *so* thin.

I'm trying to get Cyril to do some of my W.E.A.[1] lecturing next winter. He is busy with his garden and with bird watching.

Leslie has done *lovely* bowls in bands of different woods – not inlaid, but in solid bands – in good colour combinations.

. . . Heather, who is very well, and radiant in a bright cherry-coloured jumper, sends her dear love with mine.

May you have a really good, homely time this holiday. *Our love to all.*

Robin and Heather.

---

1. Workers' Educational Association.

LETTER 22

[17th May, 1935]

My dear long-suffering Cecil,

(How nice your writing is, with a good broad pen.)

It seems that you will not long continue in *your* distorted idealism of us, ungrateful wretches that we are. The sadly undeserved record arrived just when you said it would, and when we have listened to it I have said, 'I'll write to Cecil NOW,' but alas! it has got no further. And here we are, with a fire in the Studio – Heather covering books in chintz for our bedroom (to look well with a miraculous patchwork quilt we have just acquired) and I seated at my big work-window, with the cuckoo and blackbirds calling in the cold evening without. Thank you very very much for the beautiful Brahms continuation. It is a treasure. It works out just as I want it to. And you still haven't been given your watercolour, and your birthday passes by unsung. 'And yet I love thee till I die.' – At any rate, I hope you will. . . .

Won't it be amusing if I am stationed in Cambridgeshire next term? Smethwick and Wigan are thought by most people to be more likely spots, alas. But I shall not mind, with this haven to return to.

The garden now is beautiful, with hawthorn, lilac, and laburnum. In the South hedge there is a whitethroat's nest with five eggs. Our grass is long, and full of flowers, and Birds' Marsh is still purple with bluebells.

The R.A. turned down my two watercolours again, but hung the *Wren and Primroses* plate. It is very small, and Paul Drury tells me it is hung high in a dark corner. Now I am working at my tempera panel again. The hands are done. Also I have a design ready for a new large plate, called 'May', and am making studies for a plate called 'Hedge Flowers'. Heather has been distempering the stairway, ready to receive the William Morris curtains. She is also preparing lectures on Place Names for a Wiltshire Summer School at Cirencester. And the Matric marking comes fairly soon. We shall have a short holiday, so you must soon tell us when it is best for you to come, and we will fix it before anything else. . . .

Let me warn you that Leslie's multi-wooded bowls are dear. I'll discover the price before I order one for you. Leslie is having a smart Exhibition in Bristol next month.

We were extremely interested in your snapshots of Jubileed London. Do let us know how they developed.

Are you drawing again now? Tell me all about your kids' work. Are you going to Sweden? . . .

Dad isn't too well, but Mother amazes us all. We are going home tomorrow, for the first time for a long while. Cyril will probably take on some of my W.E.A. lecturing in Swindon next winter. He had a little article accepted in the 2nd Number (the current one) of *Family*, a new magazine which I think you'd agree is rather silly. The article isn't, though.

And now, Goodnight. We continue to labour happily under the delusion that you are one of our best friends, and offer our rustic love!

Robin and Heather.

LETTER 23

[19th May, 1935]

My dear Cecil,

It is, I know, very wicked of me, but when I came to address this letter to Charlie I found I had forgotten it and, moreover, lost your letter containing the address. So please forgive me, and post the letter for me.

What unutterably cold weather for May! Beeches, ashes, walnuts, and many hedge plants look very sick after the frost. I hope your pains have gone, and that the sun will soon shine for you. We are very glad of a good fire. Cyril, Grace, Helen Thomas and her wonderfully good-looking little grandson have been here to tea. All are well. Cyril behaved idiotically quietly, saying nothing practically – as is his wont when he comes here with other people – so that I wanted to shake him.

We are becoming Quakers very soon, because we find we have always believed just what they do, and we are eager to do any possible peace work with them.

Mother is very well, but Dad has neuritis in the right hand, badly. . . .

Now we must go to bed. Did I tell you we have acquired a lovely patchwork quilt?

Goodnight and our dear love to you.

Bruyère et Rougegorge.

LETTER 24

[undated, probably June 1935]

My dear Cecil,

We are returning the amazingly clever, very gruesome, most interesting masks by return, in case they are needed. I am assuming you are at Tunbridge Wells. Give our love to all your family.

I wasn't too far out, when I mentioned our probable sojourn in the Black Country. The Leeds district is to be our abode in term time for two years, at any rate. We shall only have a couple of rooms, we hope, furnished with our surplus from here; and the 200 miles from home must be put up with for a while. We are planning lovely excursions into the Dales of the West Riding, by way of compensation! And when we are more used to the idea we shall be quite happy. We might have been placed much worse, after all. Tell us all you can in favour of Yorkshire, please.

I shall love to hear all about the papier mâché business. These masks are most professional-looking.

No more now; – a great hurry.

Much love from us both.
Robin and Heather.

LETTER 25

[31st July, 1935]

My dear Cecil,

I am so sorry to have made you wrathful about the broken masks. They arrived in a sorry state, with the packing practically off them, Sir, and the whiskered mask smashed through the middle; and I took the precaution of adding a decent piece of paper to the meagre stuff you sent them in when I returned them to you; though I could have broken the masks to bits by shaking them ever so slightly. I'm very sorry indeed about it.

I hope you've had a good day in France with your Danish friend. We, too, are on the rocks, but we are very happy. Thanks for telling us about Yorkshire. Since writing to you I have had two very heartening letters concerning next term, one from the H.M.I. I shall work with, and the other from Green, the Art Inspector. I now feel quite happy about it all. We need not live *in* Leeds, but the H.M.I. has suggested a place quite close to open country, and within easy reach of the Dales and the Moors, so we are going to try for that. The man sounds so nice and friendly, and Green tells me of interesting work on the Art side that I have to do.

The nuisance is that we may have to go to Leeds during August, at short notice, to see rooms, if our advertisement brings some forth. So could you possibly be free during the period August 9–20th? We may have to go up in the early part of that time, in which case we should dare to ask you to postpone your visit for a day or two. In any case *our* visit should only be a weekend one. I have to try to catch the H.M.I. of the district before he goes on holiday; that is why the date has to be vague. It *may* be better for you to come earlier, but we'll endeavour to fix it all definitely soon. Bear with us, faithful creature that you are.

Take some photographs of our upstairs rooms for us when you come, please, so that we may gloat over them during the weeks when we are away.

Everything is beautiful this evening in the golden light. We have a goat tethered in our field. She is one Bluebell Wilkins of Sutton Benger, and belongs to the postman. She is at present bleating to me, and eating hawthorn at the same time. You shall meet Bluebell. She has ancient-looking horns and somewhat evil eyes, but has a mild and friendly temperament. Incidentally she is very fond of men, and lives close to the earth.

Heather has spent the day in Corsham, and is probably now cycling home. She would say, 'Give the dear creature my love, and tell him we value faithfulness more than anything these days,' if she were here. She is wonderfully well now.

Goodnight, and our love to your most dear and innocent parents, and to Daisy and all.

With much love to you.
Robin and Heather.

LETTER 26

[26th October, 1935]

My very dear Cecil,

I was so touched by your letter to Mother – which arrived on her birthday! – in which you said Wiltshire seemed very far away that I am moved to spend precious minutes in writing to you now, even though Heather wrote from Leeds last week. I hope you feel duly honoured, Sir. No; I'm only writing because I want to, and because it's lovely to be writing to you from home again.

I do so hope you are feeling better. Even here, in this beloved field, there is cold mist today, and I hope you are sitting by a warm fire. *Do wear enormously thick, long, woollen pants, and good honest long-sleeved vests.* I almost think Heather had better make you stream-lined, flannel body belts for Christmas, you poor creature! Even I have had a horrid cold.

I wish we could all live happily together, in close contact, with nothing enormous to bother about. You really *must* leave Soham as soon as you can. I must say that even Leeds seems very healthy. We have had six most interesting weeks, and this break – with next weekend here, too – is setting us up well for the remaining half of the term. I *love* the work, and should hate having to teach again. It seems so much more worth while, to me; and it is so satisfying to be *used* at last. I mean, all my resources are being called upon, and I feel I'm really having to go 'all out' to do the job well. It's a good feeling. Heather gets very keen about it all, too, and looks forward to my many tales!

Mother isn't really very well; she is up one minute and down the next. This blood pressure is frightful. But, oh, the immense relief to us that a cure is *possible*. . . . It is so kind of your mother to be so eager for our mother's good. Give her our love. I hope greatly that the 'slight operation' of Daisy's you referred to in Mother's letter was an early miscarriage or abortion, for everyone's sake. It is a queer strange world, isn't it?

Heather is extraordinarily well. So are all at Home. Poor Grace is mightily encumbered round about, but rejoicing, and extremely well. Dad looks absurdly small and thin. He had to work till midnight last night. The trees in the Dales were baring quickly: here the elms are thick and green.

Bluebell[1] has eaten quantities of grass. There are roses and many Michaelmas daisies in the garden, and I've just cut cabbage for dinner. Heather's mother and daddy are staying here with her next week while I am away. There are wonderful musical happenings in Leeds and Bradford. Down here one feels so deliciously cut off from the grim and active world. We gloat and gloat over every corner of the house, idle and sentimental children that we are. Our love and many yearnings.

Robin and Heather.

---

1. The postman's goat: see letter 25.

LETTER 27

Written from Far Headingley in Yorkshire; undated, probably late January 1936.

Sunday afternoon.

My very precious Cecil,
Forgive a scribbled letter in pencil. I am sprawled in front of the fire, – though we *ought* to be walking in Wharfedale on such a mild and Springlike day. We have had very wintry weather, but today a great tit is singing, and it would be good on the moors. But Heather is marking her Cambridge papers – mostly from Malaya and Ceylon – and I am trying to make up arrears in letterwriting. I can't remember who wrote last or when. It was a delicious holiday, and so nice and long. Mother stayed with us for several days, and the change seemed to benefit her. However, she has been very unwell again, and mystifies everyone. We are going home next Thursday week, and are greatly looking forward to seeing her. I have to lecture at a teachers' course – I think, yes I *did* tell you – at Stourbridge for the following week. Heather will spend it at O.C.F. with her Daddy and Mother, and I hope to get the second weekend as well, returning here on the Monday night, February 17th. Then follows a course at Densbury, almost immediately.

And, joy of joys, I am lecturing at the Board's Oxford course, from July 4th to 18th. That will be like a fortnight's holiday to me. Heather will be at O.C.F., of course. Now if it were Cambridge – but I may come your way yet. . . . The Board's History course is held in Cambridge, but the Art in Oxford, always.

Well, it has been an enjoyable term, so far. Your calendar comforts us, and we often turn up your lovely Kington Langley photographs. . . . I believe in photography, and would LOVE to have thousands of photographs of flowers, trees, even machines, architecture, paintings, objects, details of craftsmanship, and most of all the heavenly human body. We don't use photography enough. And processes of reproduction need to be cheaper so that books may be illustrated by photographs more lavishly. I'm having an awful time with the little book I did for Dryad. (It is due in March at 3/6 by the way.) They are doing the thing so meanly. It is all small and frugal and inadequate. It won't be at all a good book, – yet it *could* be, if 50, instead of 15, photographs could be included. However! By the way, Macmillan's are bringing out Heather's little *Exercises in Punctuation.* It is a sound scheme, Mister Crouch; tell all and sundry!

Did I tell you I'm doing . . . a booklet on *Lettering for Schools* for Dryad. *Please* give me your own idea of what you think the ordinary uninitiated teacher requires as a help – more especially the teacher in elementary schools. I should so much value your help here. . . .

I had to go to Wakefield to serve on a committee appointed to select pictures for schools. It was *great* fun. I wish you could have been there, and heard the scandalised old members . . . denounce the suggestion that nudity in pictures should most certainly be put into the schools! They even tried to stop us from admitting a lovely Virgin and Child, because the Infant Christ was naked at his mother's breast. Isn't it amazing?

By the way, you'd enjoy reading the late Prof. Lethaby's *Form in Civilisation* – unless you know it. We've also just bought *The Way of all Flesh* and *The Lonely Plough*, and I badly want D.P. Bliss' *History of Wood Engraving* which has – unhappily for Bliss – been remaindered at 12/6. It was 42/–, and, I believe, worth it.

Grace and Julian are progressing well. The latter is now being fed on cow's milk as he refused to thrive on his mother's. Cyril seems very busy – and successful – with his bird lectures. Heather's sister, Sylvia, is in Nassenheide (near Stettin) in Pommerania, having the time of her life in a glorious old country house, where she is helping a girl to learn English and French. It is a lovely job, and she's happier than we've known her for years.

We are hoping to hear Paul Robeson in Leeds on Tuesday – unless he is 'put off' because of George V's funeral. I'm so sorry about the old King. I think he must have been a decent and fairly innocent creature. I'm sorry for the 'Prince', too – with that bossy mother as his hostess. I should marry out of self-preservation instinct, I think, if I were he! There are some very good dinner hour chamber music concerts at the university this term. We heard Laurence Binyon there last week, on Chinese Painting. It was lovely – such perfect prose.

My day in York was good. What a minster it is! . . .

Goodbye, now, and our dearest love to you.

We often think and talk of you.

Robin and Heather.

LETTER 28

Far Headingley. [24th March, 1936]

My dear neglected Cecil,

Olive wrote today saying she had heard from you, and I am just wondering when I last wrote to you. Was it before I went to Stourbridge? – Your letter was merely dated 'Monday evening in the Fens', but it came ages ago. We loved it. Thank you in advance for the life drawing. I greatly wish I could join you at your classes. . . . Send me lots more of your photographs. And have you seen the new Studio book called *How to use your Miniature Camera* by Ivan Dmitri? I enclose the prospectus in case you haven't.

. . . Yes, I will come to Fenny Soham. In fact may I book a date now? It is probable, though, that you will have gone down for the long holiday; I shall be up here alone, probably, for the weekend of July 24th. Heather will be at home, so she would not be able to come with me, but if you could endure me alone here I am. Let me know.

The Dryad book is better than it might have been, after all. I am hoping to see it done fairly soon. Heather has in mind a really good book about the richer side of English language. We are seeing Prof. Weekley at Easter and are going to discuss it then.

Your ideas about lettering are most helpful and fresh. Thank you very much indeed. I should *love* to see your fabrics some day. They sound really alive. By the way, I bought a yard of lovely stuff last week (to show to teachers) designed by Adeney and printed in two blocks – black and red – on white. It is a wonderful design. Duncan Grant has been doing some good things, but they meander rather meaninglessly.

Paul Robeson was quite breath-taking. We saw the rep. company here do *Major Barbara* very well last week; but I think it is a foul waste of time to act such unsatisfactory, misguided stuff. Shaw[1] is a positive menace. Never has a man so misused good brains. I should like to shake him, hard! Last week, too, was the Festival of Song (by 800 Leeds children) but alas, as I have heard all the songs many times in many schools on many many days since September the affair was a little dull to me; but Heather thought it very good. She also loved the Pro Arte Quartet at the Univ. The Dinner Hour Concerts have finished for the Term.

Never a word from Am. But Olive tells us you mentioned the death of Am's father. What a tragic family. I am so sorry, but I suppose it's good, in a way. Our love and best wishes to Mop. People born in April are always lovely, tell her!

. . . By the way, do you like *The Way of All Flesh*? I have been reading it lately, and I've often thought of you. . . . Did the governors give you an Art Room and a radioGramophone?

Heather is busy marking Scottish scripts. She hopes to get them done by April 3rd when we go home. We have seen a lot of home this term. I got two long weekends through the Stourbridge affair (and H. the week between) and then again the week before last. A thrush had built by our back door, and now Olive reports that there are four eggs, so I hope we shall see young on Friday week. By the way, I am likely to be in London on April 6th and 7th. You'll not be going through just then? I start the term by lecturing for a week at Loughborough College and then I shall return to collect Heather.

Last Saturday Mary Glasgow (a colleague) went with us for a heavenly walk in Washburndale. We (three) drew a lovely old pack horse bridge and walked for miles over the moors. All day we heard the unbelievably beautiful, passionate, urgent and mournful call of the curlew. *What* a note! We had never heard it before, and I can't forget it.

Tomorrow I go to Wakefield to select pictures for West Riding schools: great fun. I've been inspecting Training College Students in their final School Prac. How I recalled Goldsmiths'!! These were a very level, dull 'C' crowd, giving painfully over-prepared lessons!

. . . Now I must write a report.

Goodnight and God bless you, and our dearest love to you.

Robin and Heather.

Love to all at Home.

---

1. Compare comments on page 37 of *Double Harness*.

LETTER 29

Far Headingley. [30th April, 1936; incomplete]

My dear Cecil,
I'm writing before breakfast; it is an exquisite morning, and even Leeds is putting up a good show of Spring. We left home on Monday afternoon and it seems like starting all over again here, as we had become so used to O.C.F. once more. We were very glad to hear of the arrival of your niece. How lovely for Daisy to have a change, at any rate. Give her our love.

Mother – whose sight has quite gone now – and Grace and Julian spent a week with us while Cyril went to Skokholm (an island off Wales) to watch birds. We had a very pleasant time. Julian is a bright person, and altogether lovable. The Loughborough course was very full and interesting. I spent some time at Dryad, and one memorable evening in Dryad's cottage in the Quorn country. My little book comes out on May 6th. They have made a mess of the dust cover – but the rest looks rather well, I think.

Heather's final proofs have gone through, so her little book won't be long in coming now.[1]

We travelled via London, and I went to the R.A. varnishing day. My *Hedge Flowers* is hung sky-high, as usual, though there are only three rows of pictures this year in the Etching Room so it *does just* show! Sanderson has something, but I couldn't find Am's name. It's not a very promising show. The best things I saw were Bateman's *Bull being auctioned*, Ethel Walker's miraculously lovely *Christ and the Woman at the Well*, and two Dod Procters – loose and Renoirish, and quite unlike her usual stuff. There are *very* few good watercolours, and the number of etchings is very small. . . .

---

1. *Exercises in Punctuation.*

Saturday. [probably 1937]

You poor creature! Your letter, record, and photographs have just come, and we are most touched that you should write to us when you are feeling so unwell. We greatly hope that this foul malady will soon subside and that you will be able to enjoy the remainder of your holiday. Our dear love and blessings to you. We hope all are well at home and that Michael is better.

The record is exquisite. Mother listened to it from her bed (in your room) and loved it, and soon we are going to hear the complete work. Thank you so very much for it. It is a treasured possession. All the photographs are lovely, and the one of Pinion 'holding a bell rope' quite marvellous. It is so kind of you to shower these fresh beautiful things on me. We do not deserve them. . . . You go from strength to strength. I should LOVE the set you promise me; but please do not bother to mount them for me as in any case I intend to make a complete collection of your nudes in a book I have prepared for the purpose. They give me enormous pleasure and I often use them for models for drawing. I hope you don't mind.

The Fen Floods picture is most romantic and beautiful – and quite unbelievable.

The boxer looks very good. What finely built shoulders he has!

. . . The Bach *Matthew Passion* was ravishing. I feel a different person, having lived through it. The recitative – which is usually ugly, I think – was almost the most natural and telling feature. I'm attempting to fix up a meeting in Leeds with C. soon and a weekend *here*. (But tell me if you would object to sharing our big bed with him; if so we could fix up a temporary affair in the 3rd bedroom. *Let us know, please.*)

. . . I'll do what I can about the Cambridge visit; I expect all will be well.

Now about the etchings:

1. Which would you like for Christmas? I think I have a *Hedge Flowers* in Leeds, but tell me *frankly* which you'd really like best.
2. Would you like *Wren and Primroses*? It is published at 2½ gn's, but if you promise to keep it to yourself you can have a print for whatever you can best afford – up to a max. of 10/6. But let me know. Maybe you'd prefer

another. It is extremely good of you to *want* my work, and I feel duly honoured.

The Dryad lettering book comes out in a week or two. It is 2/6. Our *Wiltshire Village* book is being published in the Autumn of 1938, by Collins. I hope you'll like it. Heather is beginning to get down to the substance of it, and it is thrilling her. We have been pumping Mother for old Langley news this week. She has been remarkably well, all things considered, and has spent a happy week here. She has more physical balance and can talk very coherently and has few 'bad turns'. I dare not wonder how long it will last.

The weather is delicious, and the 'dawn chorus' is quite stupendous these days. There are exciting nests in our hedges, our newest visitors being a pair of venomous Little Owls. We watch them wooing in a comical way in the evenings.

Primroses are at their best but not at their most plentiful stage. White violets were early. I long to paint a new tempera panel. I don't know whether I told you I was elected a member of the Society of Mural Decorators and Painters in Tempera (uneuphonious mouthful!) on the strength of the awful portrait panel I did.

This heavenly sunshine should do you much good.

The Board's work is still most thrilling and varied and absorbing. I don't somehow feel I do any job now – but travel about England to discover queer things about schools and colleges and to meet an extraordinary assortment of educationists! I wonder when it will come to an end?

Heather's sister Olive is going to spend a fortnight with us in June, in Yorkshire, when we hope to explore Swaledale and Wensleydale.

. . . Give our love to your Mother and Father and to 'Aunty G', and take our love and gratitude for yourself.

Rougegorge et Bruyère.

LETTER 31

A postcard to Cecil Crouch, written from Far Headingley, 17th July, 1937.

Saturday night.

It was most kind of you to write, and thank you very much, Cecil. I didn't at all expect to be elected.[1] I sent six prints up last month. People like John Farleigh are so much better than I am; but here is an impetus now to get on with a lot of new work. The worst of it is that one needs so many lives. The B. of E.[2] takes *one*, but a very pleasant one, I must say.

By the way, *entre nous*, my experience of 'S.'[3] insp. has shown me that your work is well above av. and you should earn praise next time. We feel very guilty about receiving a record from you. It must be for 1937 as well, please. . . . We hope you are free from influenza. Our room is gay with catkins from home. I should love a very long talk with you; there's so much to say. H. is buried in papers.

Much love from R. and H.

---

1. *Hedge Flowers* was chosen as Robin Tanner's diploma print on his election as Associate member of the Royal Society of Painter-Etchers and Engravers in 1936.
2. Board of Education.
3. Secondary.

LETTER 32

[12th June, 1938]

My dear Cecil,

It is quite disgraceful that you should have to wait so long for these two plates, and now you may no longer need them; so I shall not of course mind if you return them.

We wonder often how you are. I have not been to East Anglia for a long time and all my London visits happen during your term time. . . . One of these days we will certainly drive to Tunbridge Wells. My plans are a bit uncertain. The Board have just asked me if I will go out to the Gold Coast to inspect

Achimota College next term (2½ months in all), and I am debating whether to say Yes or No!

We got *Wiltshire Village* off to Collins in good time and we are hoping it will be published in the Autumn.

Our garden and field absorb so much of our time these days. There is an enormous crop of grass but we can't get anyone to cut it. I think I shall soon turn farmer. A robin, a wren, and a chaffinch have each hatched their young on the same day – all within a yard of one another on our porch! The babies keep blundering into the windows.

Heather begins marking next Saturday and we are going to have our fling in the Cotswolds before then. Gloucestershire is a lovely county to inspect.

Our many loves and greetings to you,
and I pray forgiveness for my sore neglect.
Robin.

LETTER 33

[16th December, 1938]

Our very dear Cecil,
This print of *Wren and Primroses* comes with our love and many warm thoughts. It is very kind of you to want to possess my work at a time when few care for such un-obvious things and it is a pleasure to share it with you. It is absurd, by the way, to say you do not give me your work: your photographs have always given us great joy, you know; and we shall look forward to seeing your latest. And as for the *Gill* book of Nudes – that is a flagrant extravagance which I don't think you ought to give us, much as we should love to have it! (There! that's nicely put!) No: you were ever too kind.

. . . We have been struggling for the last five weeks to get a visa for one Dietrich Hanff, a German Jew, aged 18½, who has to leave Germany and whom Heather's sister, Sylvia, (who still lives in Germany) has implored us to adopt temporarily. He was an engineering student in Prague but was not allowed to remain in his own home in Germany. I only hope he has not already been pushed into a camp. His parents wrote a sweet, sad letter, and he sent us his photograph – he is a good looking creature. I don't quite know what we shall do with him, but one can't not endeavour to save a life. Oh, it is a sad world; and we are so much the haves, aren't we?

Picture me probably *completing* my new plate during the holidays.

Our dear love to you.
Robin and Heather.

LETTER 34

[29th December, 1938]

My dear Cecil,
This is to wish you and all at home a happy 1939, to send our love and greetings to you, to say that, alas! we shall not be able to come to see you this holiday, and to thank you for the exquisite Gill Nudes and your greeting card and the quite remarkable photograph of the acrobatic bathers!

The Gill book is a great joy to us all; everyone loves it, and we *do* thank you enormously for it. Yes, I, too, hope he'll jolly well follow it up with 25 Males, for I know how powerfully he can make them. This is a book we shall always cherish, Cecil.

The School Magazine is always interesting. I like the portrait of Mr Crouch! Who *is* this new young artist of yours? Your two photographs are lovely, and we are very glad to have them. (By the way, you *did* receive the etching? I registered it, to Soham, early.) Please thank your home for the Christmas greetings.

Heather's mother is ill, with severe varicose veins among other troubles, so our plans have to be limited. Then we are preparing a room for Dietrich, too. And next week I simply *must* get down to my plate: oh, how I long for some free days in which to do the things one waits so long for.

Today is warm and springlike and green. We have many primroses and catkins, and the air is soft. I can feel the Spring beginning.

Heather sends her dear love with mine. Have a peaceful, happy holiday and then a good term.

Many, many thanks for all your kindness.

Robin.

LETTER 35

Sunday. [March 1939]

My dear Cecil,
There is only time for a hurried note to send with the long-awaited print of *Hedge Flowers*. . . .

It is a lovely windy, sunny day and we should like to be out but there is so much writing to be done. We are still battling for Dietrich against the Home Office regulations which become increasingly brutal and unreasonable week by week. We are now trying to get the poor wretch on the plea that agricultural workers are scarce; and we have got a farmer here to agree to let Dietrich work, unpaid, for him. That *might* expedite matters. Meanwhile the boy grows more and more desperate.

We are well and happy. Heather, having organised the Chippenham effort for the Peace Conference Petition, is extremely busy, and the house is like an office.

We hope your floods have gone and that there are celandines in bloom. The first primroses here are as great and lovely an event as they have ever been. *How* I love this time of year.

How does the photography progress?

Our warm love to you.
R. and H.

LETTER 36

Easter Saturday. [9th April, 1939]

My dear Cecil,
I hope all is well with you and all at home. We send warm greetings and love. Today is exquisitely springlike and we hope you are enjoying the sunshine.

This is not to be a long letter: there are so many to write, and my heart is so full I find it difficult to express much. And this is all because of our darling Dietrich who arrived in London in the small hours last Monday. I had an unbelievable time meeting him. We raced the Gestapo by 24 hours only! And what a grand little creature to throw away! He has won everyone's heart and you will love him. He has been through hell, and his poor brokenhearted parents are going through it still. We have him for at least a year, and probably more. We must emigrate him, and probably to U.S.A. But I cannot begin to tell you the story here. You must come down for a long weekend soon – or failing that, an ordinary weekend. Tell us when you could come this term, as early as you like. And when you come you must play to Dieti. Music is his greatest passion, and to see him transported by Beethoven is a revelation. I do not possess (and dare not at the moment afford) Beethoven's *Fifth* nor *Ninth Symphony*, and I wondered whether it would be asking too much of you to bring either or both if you came for the weekend, so that he could get soaked in them again? He longs for them. Beethoven is his greatest love.

Well, I must away. Our dear love to you.

Robin.

LETTER 37

[3rd May, 1939]

My dear Cecil,

I was caught up in such a rush of happenings after your letter came that it was quite impossible to arrange a meeting. But it was very good indeed of you to tell me all your plans; I'm afraid we shall have to wait until August – unless you are free for the Whitsun weekend. I long to see you, and so does Heather.

. . . The enlargements of Mother are the best you've done. I gave one to Leslie, who was most grateful. Thank you so much. You could not have given me anything I should have liked better. Dad is pretty well. Olive is, too, but she has had a bad winter. Leslie is developing wonderfully. He is much the best of all of us.

Yes: *how* we should love to come to see you. But HOW difficult it is! But we have not given up hope. Our love to all at home; I do hope they are reasonably well. . . .

Dietrich is a darling, and it will break our hearts ever to part with him. His

English improves daily. He was able to transfer from farm trainee work to Leslie's woodwork, if you please! So Leslie is teaching him (for nothing).

Our great problem now is to get Dr and Frau Hanff (Dieti's parents) out of Germany. Like him they have affidavits for U.S.A., but their waiting number is over 57,000, and life becomes less and less possible for them in Germany. I cannot tell you the indignity and privation to which they are being subjected. I am spending every penny we have and every penny we earn, but still I cannot afford to guarantee for the parents, so I am getting some friends to guarantee 6d. or 1/– per week for two years. Already I have secured an income of 12/– per week in this way, but I need £2 to do the thing at all reasonably. For Home Office purposes a friend is putting £400 India Stock in my name (as guarantee, only, of course). Now I know what tremendous commitments *you* have, but if you can think of *anyone* who would give me 6d. or more a week for a period up to two years do please ask them. . . . It seems to me that if one can save a few human souls it is about the most worthwhile thing to be done at this moment.

I do *not* despair of the world.

I am full of hope even now.

Excuse this outpouring.

With much love and many yearnings.

Robin.

LETTER 38

[1st October, 1939]

Yes, you poor creature, it *is* time I wrote to you. This is Sunday afternoon, and a lazy, sleepy, peaceful one, and not one for a long letter. It is difficult to believe in this war at all here, where rooks are cawing and nuts are ripe and the garden is ablaze with daisies, and we are all going normally about our peaceful occupations. And the queer thing is that inside I feel very calm; and I began a new etching on Wednesday. Dieti is amazingly brave and a great strength to us. He has worked wonders in our garden during the last month. Now he has gone all wine making – gallons of elderberry, casks of blackberry! On Friday there came a last brokenhearted letter from his parents, posted September 1st.

We have tried to get into touch, via your kind [Danish] friend, who also wrote to us. *Do* thank her warmly. There are many things to thank you for. All the photographs are *excellent.* Do send further copies when you can. Could the little one of D.'s room be enlarged one day? You are a dear kind creature, and we cling to you in these bewildering days. I could write much about the war, but you know just what we are thinking and what we feel is the right way out. Until Xmas, presumably, I am to work at my normal work. I can do that with a will (if I can get enough petrol!), but later on I do not know what foul ministry they may try to drag me into. Then I must be ready to stand, whatever may happen.

. . . Leslie is doing wonderful work. He will refuse to fight. He may go on the land, or he may continue his work if he can. Or he may even join the Friends' Ambulance Unit. . . . We are only at the beginning of all the misery if this war is going to be prolonged. Don't talk to me about 'the miracle of evacuation'! I will a tale unfold one day. My days are spent tackling queer jobs. It will be seen ultimately what a ghastly psychological mistake evacuation was. We have all much to answer for. How ashamed I am of 'Britain'. Our 3-year-old evacuee, Corinna, was a trial at first. . . . Now she is settled. She is extraordinarily clever and we are very happy, though she takes up much of Heather's time. Give them all at home our dear love. Dieti is a great light in our house. We are going on as usual just as long as ever we can. There is a peat fire burning and Heather is cosily knitting. I wish you were here. Write often. Take great care of yourself.

Much love from us all.
Robin.

LETTER 39

Sunday Morning. [May/June, 1940]

My dear Cecil,
It was reassuring to have your letter and to know that your return journey was not too horrible. Your visit did us a lot of good, and all three of us thank you for it. We only hope you'll be able to come in August. Many schools here are having regular long weekends throughout the Summer instead of any

continuous holidays. We greatly hope you have found your Mother much better this weekend, and that she is able to enjoy in some measure this glorious weather. Can there ever have been such a Spring and Summer? Dieti is hoeing his beloved garden at this moment – naked to the waist: Heather is marking scripts like mad before going up to London tonight (we having been descended upon by three long distance visitors yesterday, who stayed all day! – often poor Heather's ill-luck once marking starts!) And I am head cook and housewife today.

We saw a notice in one newspaper that every 'male alien' is to be interned, and that many are to go to a camp 'in the West country'. So we have packed Dieti up, all ready, in case; but we still hope he may not have to go yet. It is such a long time since we heard from his parents or his brother, that now we hardly expect to hear.

Annoyingly, 'the military' disappeared last Sunday just at the time you did, and nothing has been seen of them since, I'm glad to say. Though innocent Malmesbury and Corsham and the like are crowded with soldiers. It was wretched that our peace should have been so disturbed throughout your visit. The village has seemed hundreds of years older since the soldiers removed!

We are sorry you have had such a tiring week. We had a warning on Monday night, some 20 minutes after we had been awakened by two bombs which fell near a farm three miles away! So we spent an hour or two reading aloud to Dieti *Through the Looking Glass* in the hall. That has been our one experience so far, though last night we could hear very distant rumblings in the Bristol direction. Poor Bristol was badly hit twice last week, and we hear there was a daylight raid there very early yesterday morning. Most of our village slept through its warning and heard no bombs! One fell near Olive's village in the Cotswolds. Where *haven't* there been raids? Look after yourself and don't get cold o'nights! Cyril is feverishly excavating a shelter in his garden for his children.

I don't know what happened to your knitting pattern; there is no sign of it here. I spent the week still trying to establish some sort of teaching conditions out of chaos among our new evacuees. Never have I known anything so completely upsetting to normal life. I find it hard to look forward to any sort of system or stability again. Do you think that the Chamberlains and Hoares of

England will secure a fate like that of France for this country? In spite of violent assurances one cannot help wondering. In fact, the assurances are *so* violent that they seem untrue. . . . I don't think any of us here feel at all worried, except perhaps Grace, who was very shocked by the air raid warning; but she is calmer now. Do write to us from time to time, and let us often remember the good days we have shared. I feel full of faith, and the urge to 'create' is very strong in me these days, though the time for one's own work grows less and less.

God bless you: don't ever desert us.

We all three send our warm love.

Robin.

LETTER 40

Thursday lunch hour, in my car, on the Cotswolds.
[June 1940]

My very dear Cecil,
Just as I was leaving home there came a wire from the Board, telling me to receive evacuees at Cirencester on Friday night. Presumably that will mean I shall be kept busy on Saturday and Sunday – as I was a fortnight ago when Clacton-on-Sea descended on me. That is why I feel it wise to wire you. I hope, though, that in any case if this is your only weekend for a while you'll come in spite of my wire. We long to see you again and to have a happy talk and share many things. I hope and think you will find us unhysterical and calm. My heart bleeds, but I haven't lost my faith. It would be easy for me to point a finger to governments and say 'I told you so.' But that would do no good. Now, as long as I am able, I must work to keep worried people sane and to preserve human standards and decent ideals. Strongly as I hold to my peace testimony I cannot separate myself from the nation of which I am a part and to which I owe so much. And I must therefore constantly endeavour not to fail of understanding and respect for those who are risking all in response to the call to arms. I am sure that a true peace is to be won only through a power that owes nothing to violence. That is where we stand, and at present there is much that we can do in our small way to help.

. . . Up to the present Dieti is with us, and presumably we are out of the restricted area for the moment. Dieti's Plymouth friends are interned and his Bristol friends (2) have to leave Bristol by tonight. They don't know where to go, and we don't know how to help them. It is all a tragic business – to have fallen from being 'refugee guests' to 'enemy aliens' in so short a space. Dieti is a great comfort to us. So are you. I wish you were here with me to enjoy this exquisite hilltop breeze, these orchids, and the rolling woods that run down to the gray roofs of Painswick, two miles away.

My very dear love,
Robin.

LETTER 41

Late on Thursday night.
[3rd July, 1940?]

My dear Cecil,
The blow has fallen: I returned from work this afternoon to find they had taken our beloved Dieti to the internment camp. Heather says the detective and policeman were very kind – though they searched the house for bombs!! and thought a most innocent paperweight was a military sextant! We two feel desolate tonight, and it is a most heartbreaking loss. I condemn the system of interning those people who have been declared entirely innocent – the 'C' Class, to which Dieti belongs. And it is unutterable folly to force Dieti to idleness now, when here are his bees and garden and woodwork. It is silly to say the innocent must suffer for the guilty; are we such mugs that we cannot discover which is which? The little creature was very brave, of course, and we cannot fear for him. I suppose it is only selfish of us to mourn his loss, but it feels like a great open wound tonight, and we long to have you here to comfort us. Heather says Dieti *would* take a photograph of you with him – that cut-out one. It was awkward to fit in the space allotted to it, but he would take it, and said, 'Tell Cecil I was determined to take him with me.'

And how did you find your mother? . . .

We've heard nothing of air raids since the Monday after your visit, except that gunfire in the Bristol area is occasionally audible. Marlott is to have an anti-tank point in its front garden! That is today's news. Even the S.W. is going all anti-invasion, though there isn't a sign in this village so far.

Heather is deep in 1200 exam. scripts. I'm glad she has something she *must* do quickly, because it keeps her mind a little off the desolation we feel. . . . Have you had a quiet time in Soham lately? Poor Bristol has caught it rather badly. I am still evacuating children, but somehow my job seems rather worth doing, in spite of everything. Goodnight now, and God bless you, you dear faithful creature.

Much love.
Robin and Heather.

LETTER 42

Wednesday. [July 1940]

Dear comforting Cecil,
Your letter was balm to our tired spirits. We could bear the awful parting better if internment were more humane. As it is we have only had an official card from Dieti – just stating: Dietrich Hanff, 43535, Warner's Camp, Seaton, Devon. He is no longer a person but a number. We write, of course, and I hope you will, but there is no reply. I writhe impotently and angrily at all this foulness. The Society of Friends is making a bold stand for better treatment in the camps, and we pray they may succeed. My heart is very sick and heavy, but I shall not give way to misery. I must go on, and I will.

Soldiers have returned to the village, but then they are everywhere. I am battling today with a major who wants to take my garage. He will win, I suppose. He merely scoffed at the Board of Education and said it counted for nothing now.

Meanwhile a blessed rain descends and the world is drenched in vivid green. And, remarkably, the cuckoo is still calling, ten days later than we have ever known it to. Dieti's vegetable garden is a miracle of abundance, but how can one enjoy the fruits of his innocent labours, and he not here to share?

Now about your parents. At the moment we are still free. If only they could decide that they *will* come, even if they don't come at once, it will make it quite possible for us to refuse others. But one does not know any day when our accommodation may be snatched up. I would rather help your parents than most people, and it would be so awful if we had to refuse them. So *do* do what you can, and let us know as soon as possible. Then we will keep room for them at all costs.

As for you, come when you will, and stay as long as you will. Heather's marking (which wouldn't, of course, stop your parents' coming) does not end till July 25th. After that we are free, and we have no holiday arrangements at all this year. So do stay longer than usual.

We have more or less quiet nights, though we sometimes 'hear them go over', very high up. I arrived at a school near Bristol the other morning to find a raid 'on' – English and German aeroplanes fighting like mad over our heads. Oh how I hate the look of this country – which is now being buttressed up with sandbags and concrete. My beloved Malmesbury looks more medieval than ever! Leslie's work continues in a desultory way. No one wants him on a farm. . . . I must now do some housework before Leslie comes to help me check marks.

Thank you, you dear, dear Cecil, for all your love and understanding. The darker the days become the more we yearn after those we love and who love us.

Robin and Heather.

LETTER 43

[1st September, 1940]

My dear Cecil,

. . . We are only half a home without Dieti. His life at Warth Mills, Bury was much worse than we had imagined. Can you picture 3000 men in a windowless mill with the oily machines still standing, and *nowhere* at all to lie down, and *no* furniture and *no lavatories* and no belongings and very little food? We have exposed it all most thoroughly and are assured it shall be closed quickly. I know now what the assurances of Home Office and War Office mean, alas! Dieti has *told all* to Heather who, after constant pressure, was allowed to visit him at House 26, Peveril Internment Camp, Peel, I.O.M. She had an awful crossing, but it was worth it. Dieti is more or less well again after his bitter taste of English Concentration Camps, but he craves for freedom. The new White

Paper shows *no* change of policy, however, and our application for his release (we found four specific jobs of national importance for him!) has already been turned down. You mention that conditions in our army are very bad. That is a disgrace, too, but it has nothing to do with internment conditions: there should be no comparison. These innocent refugees (declared innocent by our own judges only last October, after searching tribunals) should not be herded together *at all*. They should be living freely and in no way like any army. Heather and I are using all our energies to try to get this disgusting stain on England's reputation removed. If I had time to tell you all I know about our treatment of 'aliens' you would be as ashamed as we are.

No, I'm afraid we aren't likely to be in London for a long while. I wish I could go to 'Thunder Rock' with you! I've done no drawing for two months, but I long to. It is hard to feel settled when I know my little foster-son is in such distress and when I think of all the sadness everywhere. Dieti loved his letter 'from dear Cecil': do write to him again (remembering your letter will be censored). People generally are so disappointingly smug, aren't they? We are fast losing friends because we dare to fight against English treatment of refugees. Well: let us lose them all but we shall not mind. That is a lesser thing than joining with obvious wrong. I can see that we are in for a lonely time for years to come. We are thankful, though, for all the resource we have been given, and we are happy. Your love of us is a great consolation, Cecil. Don't drop us if you can help it!

With much love from us both.

Robin.

LETTER 44

Sunday. [late December 1940]

My very dear Cecil,

Heather is most desperately ill in Chippenham and I cannot write much now. Dieti was released last month and is working with Leslie at market gardening at Sir Staff. Cripps' old home at Filkins, *very* happily, as he cannot live here owing to this being a 'protected' area! We set off gaily to spend Christmas there, when a terrifying haemorrhage overtook my little Darling and we had to rush her to hospital. In spite of transfusion there is no progress. If we can save her life she must have her womb removed, as it is filled with a fibroid growth. The present struggle is to *save* her – which fine doctors and specialists are working hard to do. I have some hope, still, and Heather is amazingly brave and wonderfully determined.

Thank you so much for your dear letters and the record tokens. I could do nothing about Christmas at all, of course, and we had planned to do so much. When I have a minute I should love to choose some records for H. She badly wants the new recording of Bach's *Sheep may graze*. It *is* kind of you. It is difficult, actually, to think of anything but saving Heather's life at present. I've just seen her and she has had another bad night, but she could just speak to me.

Dieti has been allowed to come to see her. Leslie is still hoping they may use his blood for her.

I'm *so* sorry you've been so unwell. Take care of yourself, dear Cecil.

Much love to all.
Great hurry.
Robin.

LETTER 45

Late on Thursday. [2nd January, 1941]

My very dear Cecil,

It was comforting to read your characteristically warm and loving message. Your love and the love of so many friends is helping my little Darling so much. At last, after an almost hopeless week, there is REAL PROGRESS, and I feel a changed man. I have even *fed* Heather today with grapes and tomatoes! And she is hungry! Isn't it wonderful! The doctors are very pleased and almost surprised. Heather and I somehow know that all will be well and we are summoning up all the courage we know to help us in the coming dark months.

You sweet, dear creature, to suggest coming down to me. I shall never forget that thought. Actually I have had that darling Dieti with me since Saturday, and he returns to Goodfellows on Sunday, when Leslie comes to fetch him. And Sylvia, Heather's sister, is going to live here for a while. And our evacuees have

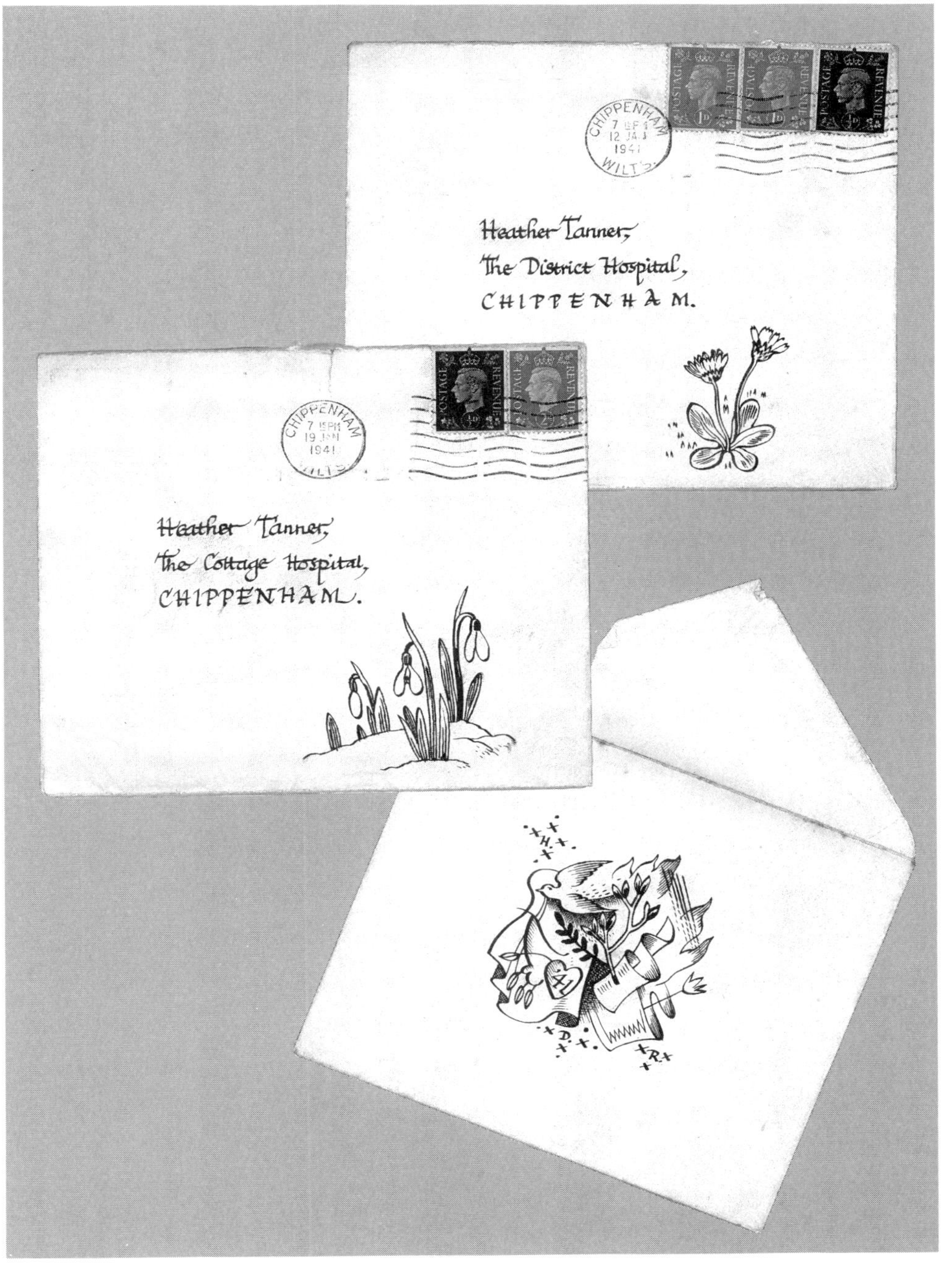

Heather Tanner,
The District Hospital,
CHIPPENHAM.
Heather Tanner,
The Cottage Hospital,
CHIPPENHAM.

mercifully gone. (We had intended to have a changing stream of tired people from bombed areas for short periods, now, but that must go.)

Heather would love a line from you. By the time it reaches her she will be able to read it, I feel sure. Oh, if only we can get her well! . . .

Give my love to all at home. I pray you are all safe and well. I expect we shall get Bach's *Sheep may safely graze* with your record tokens. Goodnight and God bless you.

Much love.
Your own Robin.

LETTER 46

Sunday. [October 1941]

You poor longsuffering Cecil!
Even this isn't going to be a proper letter: there is so much official stuff to be done. It has been lovely to hear from you and to know that all is more or less well. I haven't been to London for two years, and as the Board is in Bournemouth I'm not likely to visit London often. Heather's Examiners' Meetings there are only brief visits. It was good to hear all your news. . . . Let me report our news in brief:

Heather is very well, fatter I expect than when you last saw her. . . . She cannot do all she would like yet and tires rather easily, but all is extremely well with her. She did two lots of marking in the summer, has written some lovely pieces for 'Woodland Flowers'[1] (for which I have finished fourteen drawings and made studies for 60 others). She has preserved masses of fruit and vegetables. We both deserve medals from Lord Woolton. We kept goats for a while, but an idiotic government which allows winter rations for race horses and hunters, foxhounds and grayhounds, refuses to allow any rations for goats. So we had to get rid of them, especially as Leslie let us down over the building of a house for them. Picture me returning with Elfenbein (large white Saanen milkgoat) and Heidi (one of her daughters – adorably pure white and without blemish and biblical and holy, with tassels at her throat) in the backseat spaces of my car + R.A.F. boy who asked for a lift, from Southampton on the hottest day of the year! I found milking very easy, and Elfenbein gave five pints daily.

We wallowed in butter and cheese. We loved the creatures for their beauty, cleanliness, affection and intelligence, and it was heartbreaking to part with them. In a better world we shall certainly keep goats!

I have never done so much gardening as now. And oh, what endless labour! The outdoor tomatoes have been a great success. I gathered in pears and nuts yesterday. Dieti comes for a weekend about once a month, bless him. He is an enormous success at Goodfellows and loves the work. He is a great comfort to us and is developing finely. He listens to a lot of music, having access to the Cripps' gramophone and library of recordings. We have a few very good new records you must hear. There is a silly law here that no one may stay for more than three nights (without permission, which is rarely granted) as we are reserved for war workers. I have protested, as you may imagine. So come for your three days, Sir, whenever you may. We greatly missed seeing you during August. I had only one week's holiday.

At the moment I am all war-nurseries for Bristol, but for the most part I do a good deal of very normal work in the country districts. I now spend ½ time in Bristol. . . .

I've spring-cleaned my etching and tempera apparatus, and mean to do some work this winter. Just keeping up with the odd jobs of merely living takes so much of my time. Leslie is now doing forestry and lives in my old studio, now placed at the bottom of Cyril's garden. He has made it very beautiful within. Cyril mellows. Susan, the new baby, is a most interesting and vital child! You would find her extremely engaging: we all do. David is at the priggish-little-boy stage: a bit unbearable. . . . Olive's evacuee family of five have just left, after 1½ years, and she and lonely Dad are the sole occupants of Marlott. It is a sad, dead place. Dad is young and well, but he misses Mother dreadfully.

Heather's parents are well and happy, living mostly in a world of their own, very sensibly. We become more and more a bureau for lost C.O.s[2] and refugees and what not. There is endless work. We sometimes feel it would be pleasant and easy to be in the swim, supporting 'the war effort' by collecting bones and agreeing with our propaganda, etc. But we must be true to what we believe to be right, wherever that may lead us. I've bought a lot of books since you were here – old ones mostly, and textbooks and museum catalogues – which give us most pleasure. At a wonderful junk shop, in Chippenham, of all places, we have found some lovely things. Dieti is very keen on Architecture, and we are helping him with it. I'm making what I think are beautiful portfolio collections of good fabrics, good woven textiles, good lettering, etc., as a nucleus for the kind of work I think we ought to be doing if there is ever a sensible world again. The Board seem pleased.

Our dear love and warm thoughts.
Ever your Robin.

---

1. Published in 1981 by Robin Garton as *Woodland Plants*.
2. Conscientious objectors.

LETTER 47

[1st November, 1942]

My dear Cecil,
I bought a little C18 writing box at the Bristol Red Cross Shop recently and have spent this incredibly wet Sunday scraping off 200 years' dirt, putting new handles on the two little secret drawers, relining the writing board, polishing the beautiful hinges and handles and refitting the three compartments with writing materials. Now it is finished. I can feel the shade of some C18 gent. here in the room with me. I have his sand-sprinkler and his seals. And now I'm sitting at the box at the table, while Heather does her German lesson in a chair by the fire; and yours shall be the first letter to be written at it. I wonder whose was the last.

I don't think I ever replied to your letter of August 2nd, which you were pleased to write from the Royal Air Force, Mildenhall! What the world has come to! Your friend never turned up and nor did you; but I hope you had a good holiday and that your Mother and Father are well, and that an austerity-half-term in the Fens hasn't given you your old aches and pains. All I ask for that I haven't got is a lemon – lots of yellow lemons, full of healing juice! We are very well and incredibly busy – as you seem to be. I expect you advised the use of size with powder-colour for the murals in the W.A.A.F. rest room you mentioned?

Yes, I managed to needle and bite a small plate and paint a rather large watercolour and do two more drawings for Heather's book during my two weeks' holiday. We took Dieti to *The Merry Wives* and the last-but-one Albert Hall Prom. Concert (mainly Beethoven); and we squeezed in a very good lunch hour concert (Stratton Quartet) at the National Gallery and that quite remarkable show of war paintings. *The Merry Wives* was superb! As for that Cockney charwoman of a Mistress Quickly! Heather and I stole a day and went up to the Sadlers Wells Ballet – but I expect she told you? *The Wise Virgins*, *Comus*, *Hamlet*. How we loved it. Did you see the Penguin New Writing about the S.W. Ballet? Last week in Chippenham we heard the Jacques Orchestra (C.E.M.A.) – Boyce, Holst, Mozart, Handel, Elgar, Dvorak; and I heard the Czech Trio in Bristol recently. Also we saw the Old Vic *Othello* in Bath; Bernard Miles, as Iago, was completely perfect: Valk, as Othello, fell very short of the part, alas. Oh, there is so much I should love to share with you, tell you, ask you, show you. Will the war ever end and people become sensible again? Hanging on to decent standards and love is very difficult. I am thankful for my work, because, in a very small and limited way I feel I can help constructively. But, oh, the difficulties!

Our happiest news is that, after long application, the Chief Constable has allowed Dieti to live in this holy of holies, and he comes next Friday!! We three are walking on air. Dieti, we hope, will be allowed to work this field for Friends' War Relief, and we want to get him through Matric in his spare time. His brother has been deported from Wiesbaden to Poland, and we fear the worst about his parents. . . . Grace expects a baby next Spring. Leslie – I never know what he's up to; I believe he's still doing forestry! Olive[1] is very, very farmy. Dad is well and young. Heather's Mother and Father are old and tottery, and she spends two days a week with them. . . .

We've bought rather a lot of records (mainly Bach and Beethoven) since you were last here. Our warm love and warm thoughts.

– always your Robin and Heather.

1. Robin Tanner's sister.

[13th November, 1943]

Dear Cecil,
It was very good to hear from you. I was away in Birmingham when your letter came, and now Heather is busy spring cleaning Rose Cottage – while her parents are away for a week or two with Olive[1] – so I am writing for us all three. Heather's mother has pernicious anaemia, and is a great worry. Both parents are in their 80th year, and we simply cannot get any kind of domestic help, so Heather cycles home for three long days a week. But for the marvellous cooperation of our beloved Dieti – who will surely go up in a chariot of fire if he grows much more saintly – I don't quite see how we should manage, life is so absurdly full. We were very relieved to hear that there is some improvement in your mother's health. Give her our love and tell her we often go over our idyllic last holiday before the war, and thank her for it.

The war brings out the worst in nearly everybody – not the best, as our propagandists would have us believe. I see disintegration, instability, insincerity, laziness, stupidity, ignorance, ugliness, obstructiveness, blind evil everywhere: and everything grows steadily worse. Less and less do I put my trust in princes – or white papers; and when the P.M. declares his lifelong battle against socialism I merely despise still more the masses of people who suck in so readily the man's bombast and toryism. I see no hope at all for a real progressive age. None of which makes me really miserable. We are happy at heart, and more sure of our beliefs that ever before. As for this religious education business! I cry with old George Fox. 'Down with your steeple houses!' . . . We are as nationalist as the Germans, and our smuggery is appalling. What do we *care* about the Bengal famine, which we ourselves created? What do we care about the Beveridge and Uthwatt Reports? Who really desires education? How often I long to retire, and remain within these four hedges, to etch and paint and garden at peace! Which reminds me: we had a day printing etchings a few weeks ago, the first time since Dieti's arrival!

. . . Yes, Bristol had six 'W.V.'s[2] last week. Collins has had a few more bound up and distributed, but I think they'll be the last. I've done a lot of work for 'Woodland Flowers' but Heather has been too absorbed with parents to make any progress at all.

. . . Now about Leslie: he is back from N. Ireland, and is in the R.A.S.C. as a driver, in Derbyshire. He wrote an amazing letter this week, denouncing with great vigour everything in his new life and what it stands for, and saying that at last he finds he is an absolute pacifist and that he feels an utter stranger. He is seeking advice about how to act. At the best he expects military imprisonment for the duration, but he seems determined on his course. We knew this would come: it was inevitable. . . .

Dad spent last Sunday here. He is well and active. He doesn't think much, and it is hard work trying to get any idea into him! We haven't seen anyone else for many months, but I think Cyril may be coming soon for help with his new job. He's going to run a new temporary council school just erected to serve the vast 'estate' working at Corsham. . . . He was too weak to resist the Home Guard, even though he utterly despises it and thinks it all wrong.

Dieti is working hard in his garden, and has sent off masses of parcels of vegetables to needy people this season. He's working for Matric in his spare time. Heather lectures – mainly about anti-Semitism and the refugee problem, but also occasionally on English subjects for the W.E.A., to the W.L.A.[3] etc. – from time to time, and has done a heavy load of marking this year. . . .

I've nearly finished a new etching, *Lesser Celandine*. I've greatly enjoyed doing it. . . .

Our dear love to you.
H., D., Robin.

P.S. Please mention Leslie to no one.

---

1. Heather Tanner's sister, also known as Faith.
2. Copies of *Wiltshire Village* (all the stocks and blocks had been bombed in a Glasgow warehouse).
3. Women's Land Army.

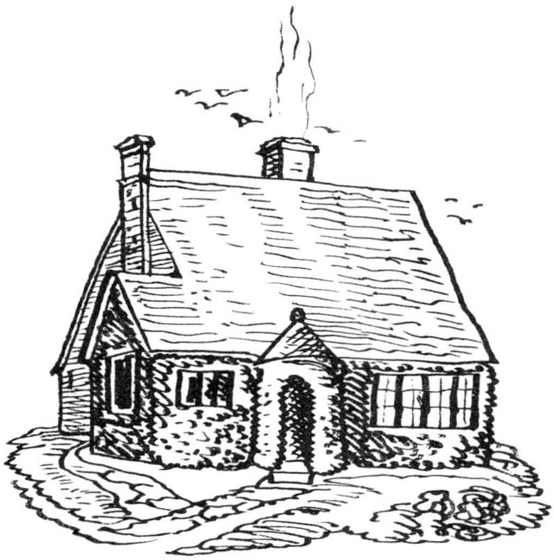

3

1946–1956

This section spans the post-war years from 1946 to 1956. Robin Tanner was working in Bristol and Gloucestershire, but his commitments, in particular to primary courses, all over the country, increased. Chapter 8 of *Double Harness* describes this period.

LETTER 49

[21st December, 1946]

My dear Cecil,
Pardon this mere note: the whole house is like a junk store, and I can hardly find space in which to write, as we have become an unofficial receiving centre for clothes for Europe. Oh, the weary cleaning, darning, mending and packing! Oh, the casual standards of people who magnanimously part with their old vests and pullovers! However, we've got off more than 2 cwts. of warm stuff, and Leslie has been able to take more to people we know in Belgium and Holland who have nothing. The frustration at not being allowed to share one's rations with people on the Continent must be felt by you as keenly as by us; what, if any, news have you of your friends? Otto Schwartz, the anti-Nazi, Aryan German from Stettin who saved Dieti[1] is still alive but starving, and so far we have been unable to help him.

We hope so much that all is well at home, and that you will have a cosy fireside holiday. I go to a course on the 3rd, alas, but hope to take a holiday when schools re-open.

Dieti is hedging and ditching, and is delighting in all the signs of Spring that are here already. Heather cannot 'get over' her mother's death, and I don't think she ever will: one just doesn't, and I don't believe in the nonsense of 'Time, the great healer'. Her father is still lost and bewildered . . .

I still cannot find a steel-facer, so still cannot print my etchings, – so your last year's Xmas gift is still not ready! The enclosed comes with our love as a small contribution towards a record or a book.

– Now to the old clothes again!

Love from us all three,
– in great haste.
Robin.

1. By swiftly reporting his predicament to Heather's sister Sylvia.

LETTER 50

[30th August, 1950]

Dear Harry[1] (and Edward, too),

I was very delighted to have your letter; it arrived when I was in the throes of painting a picture and it served to remind me – as I painted – of those days in S.E. London a quarter of a century ago when painting seemed a much easier business to me than it does now! I was so glad to hear all your news. It is reassuring and heartening to know that you two are earning your livings in such sensibly constructive ways. I have sometimes wondered whether you might both have become schoolmasters, under the Emergency Training Scheme – a job you would both have done well.

Yes, of course I remember you, vividly; and I well remember your Mother, who always seemed to me so gentle and kind; and your sister I always thought beautiful; and somewhere in the background I remember a much older brother, don't I? and your father, too. I'm ashamed to say I've forgotten most of the boys I taught at Blackheath Road; your letter has reminded me of Victor Bostock (large and intelligent and a policeman's son, I expect), Victor Mallett (tiny and very bright), Whittenstall (. . . poor boy, and living in a tenement building somewhere near the Broadway), Tommy Atkins and a boy called Blackmore (dirty but nice, I thought!) and a bright eyed creature called Dymond. Now I wonder if you remember any of those? Only last year, when I was directing a teachers' course at Goldsmith's College (during the summer vacation) I drove my car back to the old haunts. I stopped and hesitated outside Barclays Bank; I went down the High Street; into Evelyn Street again and Creek Road; was surprised to find what a really grim prison 'our' school looks; drove over the Heath and to the top of the Old Dover Road where I used to live; and finally got down to the noisy lower road and the river – where I had some teachers painting. I was horrified at so much bombing in those parts. I must say I felt a warm affection for Deptford and Blackheath again, and I still think of those early days with much pleasure.

Yes, I should like to talk of music and books to you both and about painting and sculpture. Shall I lose marks if I confess a great liking for a good deal that is being done in the Arts today? I would say, for example, to name one from each of the three Arts I have mentioned, that Dylan Thomas, Benjamin Britten and Henry Moore are all three first rate. But perhaps one day you will come and see us here, and then we will discuss this!

I forgot to say that I heard from old Mr Nunn[2] a few months ago, after many years. He is happy and active.

. . . Perhaps we could meet, one of these days. I'm trying to remember how old you two must be. 26? In a year or two I shall be 50! and the years have stolen a lot of my hair but increased my girth!

Heather does some examining for various universities, in addition to all the work of the home. We are both keen gardeners, and so is Dietrich, whom we adopted in 1938. We are Quakers – as perhaps you know – and when the ghastly persecution of the Jewish people of Germany began we worked to save all we could. One of Heather's sisters who was teaching in Germany implored us to try to rescue this 18-year-old boy, and after a long struggle we did. We were too late to rescue his family, all of whom were brutally murdered. We cannot think it was chance that brought Dietrich here to us. He shares our way of life completely and were he our own son we could not love him more. He has experienced awful horrors (even, I am ashamed to say, in English internment camps) but he is now a magnificently balanced, happy, sensitive schoolmaster. His greatest passions are the violin, Bach, architecture, beekeeping and languages. He and Heather have motored down to the Haute Savoie during this month and relished hearing French again.

We are doing another book together, but it moves slowly. My work – which I otherwise love – involves a lot of travelling (mainly by road) and absence from home. I should like much more time for my etching and for my garden; I'm always hoping to retire early, though I don't know what we should live on!

If Teddy will tell me which Library he works in I will certainly stroll in and have a talk with him one day, and if you are ever in this part of England we hope very much that you will come to see us.

Warm greetings to you both and to your family.

Robin Tanner.

---

1. See Harry Coles in list of correspondents.
2. Headmaster of the Deptford school where Robin Tanner first taught.

LETTER 51

To Sam Black, HMI, shortly leaving for Canada.

[17th August, 1949?]

My dear Sam,

You said my letters came at the right moment and so did yours yesterday, for I had simply had to go to bed and here I still am – laid out with what must be lumbago! It happened suddenly, paralysing me, so that I've had to leave my poor little Heather to paint the studio (2 coats) all alone, most maddeningly; for I *feel* extremely well and active, but I can't move about. I'm a lot surer of myself this morning, though, and I'm still hoping I shall be able to go to Devon for the Course on Friday. This has never happened to me before, and I feel much chastened. What is so very wretched is that we two had so carefully planned this working time together and had just got the studio dismantled and shrouded for painting – and then this: and no Dieti to come to the rescue. . . .

So here I lie and think, and count my many blessings and try to be patient; I plan an address I have to give next month at a Conference of training college tutors, on Infant Art. Tell me whether you think this is a possible line to take: I'll talk about the things children collect around them, of their OWN choice. Do you know that moving poem by Coventry Patmore, called 'The Toys'? I shall use that. His little son has been sent to bed by him, in disgrace, and he goes to visit him, to see if all is well, and he is moved to pity and remorse when he finds that –

'On a table, drawn beside his head,
He had put, within his reach,
A box of counters and a red-vein'd stone,
A piece of glass abraded by the beach,
And six or seven shells,
A bottle with bluebells,
And two French copper coins, ranged there with careful art,
To comfort his sad heart.'

And I shall reminisce about my own childhood: how I used to play a game of 'Pin To See The Peep Show', the latter being a sort of collage of petals and leaves. And so I'll lead on to this elemental need in children to make articulate their love of shape and texture, colour and pattern. I think one mustn't, at this stage in our educational history, narrow 'Art' down to 'Painting'. I wonder if you agree? This power to select, this business of choice, of discrimination, seems to me one of the most neglected and most important elements in aesthetic education.

Your dear letter was (and is) an enormous comfort. Yes, I keep telling myself that if our friendship is founded aright – as I know it is – then mere physical distance will not hamper its growth; and I even think that if we both want it badly enough then by imaginative and careful planning we shall be able actually to meet sometimes. Nothing is really impossible.

Your descriptions of life at home and with your jigsaw puzzle landlady delighted us. It is very good to picture Myra and Hazel and Betty resuming the old life with the old familiar faces. These last weeks in Liverpool will be odd for you, so frequent letters may not come amiss.

The cat is much concerned at my being in bed, but when brought to see me he walks out of the window and explores the steep roof instead. Dietrich returns from Honfleur with his student friend Alain on Monday, and A. will stay here for six weeks. Bill, a delightful college friend, will come too, so once more we shall be a houseful. When do you and Betty go to Paris, Sam?

Put up with this lying-down writing. It comes with warm love from a distemper-bespattered Heather and an exasperatedly-immobilised Robin.

[9th September, 1950]

Dear Harry [Coles],
Your long and very absorbing letter has certainly filled up the gap, and it is nice to be well informed again about those twins whom I remember more vividly than any other boys of my London days. And what is so interesting to me is that by your letters you and Edward sound as acutely different as you certainly were when you were eight-year-olds! I am especially glad that over such a major problem as your attitude to war, however, you share a common view – which Heather, Dietrich and I share, and I am proud that you took up the difficult pacifist position. Except for salary (which, since I am, technically, a Civil Servant was 'frozen' throughout the war because I dared to register my objection!) I suppose I really suffered but little for my belief; indeed, so very understanding was the M. of Ed.[1] that it used to ask me specially to look after the welfare of C.O. schoolmasters in difficult positions. Our cottage provided shelter in turn for many persecuted people – by no means all English – and of course we knew a great deal about the F.O.R.[2] I hope you came to like many of those Poplar bargees with whom you had to work?

I was most interested in your music comments. Alas, I remain a non-performer though I am a keen listener. The Bath and Cheltenham Festivals are our special pleasure, and next month in Bath a remarkable Bach Festival is planned. (I am almost ashamed to confess to you that the Three Choirs Festival happening at the moment in Gloucester, only 33 miles away, is not a very vital attraction for me.) I wish I liked the sound of the human voice! Apart from that brief gift from heaven, the sexless voice of a boy, and then the voices of a very few mature people like Eric Greene, Peter Pears and Kathleen Ferrier, I am not much moved, I'm afraid. Nor does a full orchestra ever give me quite the satisfaction I get from chamber music; and if I had to try to answer the ridiculous question – What particular music means most to you? – I should have, I think, to answer The Later Quartets of Beethoven.

I'm glad you like Tippett and Britten. No: I haven't yet been to St Matthew's, Northampton, though I must. Graham Sutherland was at

Goldsmith's College of Art with me and I want very much to see his *Crucifixion* there – unpromising and derivative as it looks in reproduction.

It is a nice thought that you sometimes get practice on the Goldsmiths' organ. In my day old Dr White used to extract a pretty rich and colourful juice out of it! but I don't know who plays it now.

If you ever make a pilgrimage to the South-West – and I think that Gloucester, Bath, Malmesbury, Glastonbury, Wells and Exeter – to say nothing of the innumerable rich and unspoilt village churches – would greatly interest you, I hope you will let us know.

Please thank your Mother and Betty for their kind greetings, and please give them mine.

With warm good wishes.
Robin Tanner.

---

1. Ministry of Education.
2. Fellowship of Reconciliation.

LETTER 53

[3rd July, 1952]

My dear accommodating Cecil,
It was very kind of you to reply so promptly. . . We will hope to see you on Thursday, Sept. 11th. We shall look forward to that reunion immensely. I shan't be here much myself before then! Now I'm off to Hull to run a Training College conference, and then I go to Dartington Hall for ten days, and so it goes on! I wish I could be with you in London on the 16th. . . .

I've just returned from a strange world: Dartmoor and Exeter Prisons and the two remarkable 'open' prisons at Leyhill and Falfield. I've been selecting work for the prisoners' art exhibition at S. Ken. I met some amazing men. I found I had a lot in common with most of the 'dangerous criminals' I sat and talked with. At Leyhill, particularly, I met the 'homosexual criminal', (sic!) – a sad young ballet dancer with a tremendous hero-worship for the governor! – a danceband leader, schoolmasters, and so on. Always I found myself saying, 'There but for the grace of God go I.' I talked immensely freely to the governors about this unsolved, mishandled, savagely-treated problem; and what heartened me was their enlightened dissatisfaction. But we must talk when we meet. The more I see of people and the world the less I understand either, alas.

I have had a young Cypriot with me this week: a Turk, actually, with a point of view so unlike my own.

Pardon this scrap.

I must pack.
Love from us three.
Robin.

LETTER 54

Sunday night. [18th July, 1954]

My dear Cecil,

We were delighted with your letter: the most settled and happy you have written for a long time, in spite of your endless responsibilities and cares. You have certainly undertaken a great deal, and no doubt the more you do the more 'they' will expect; it is easy to see the whole focus of your family shifting Girtonwards! Yet I'm sure the new cares also bring a new freedom, and it is good to find you putting your money in your own purse (rather than the Soham one, that is) at last. With good neighbours, and your father contented, . . . life should surely look up a little. But it is sad that you cannot even have the relief of a holiday. I am losing all mine this year. I have to sit and write instead, as the Ministry of Education is pressing for earlier publication of the thing I'm slowly doing than was expected. Next Thursday Dieti sails for U.S.A. (until mid Sept.). Heather is marking Cambridge papers. So here the two of us will sit, with occasional excursions into the garden to gather fruit and vegetables or to mow grass. This lamentably uncharitable summer fails to invite us far, in any case! We have had hot sun today, and roses are quite phenomenal, but wind and rain and cloud have sickened us. OBVIOUSLY the world's weather is being upset by all this crazy and revolting Hydrogen bomb business: nothing could be clearer. Why need we be surprised?

It would be lovely to come to see you, bless you. One day we shall. It is a warming thought to nurse. Thank you so much. Dieti would love it too. You, by the way, would love his latest, vastly improved photography; he goes from strength to strength. He 'suffered' a full inspection . . . last term, and my colleagues wrote to tell me he was absolutely brilliant and quite exceptional.

My work never seems to take me East, I'm afraid. I see a great deal of London while this present job is on. There are certain compensations. I have not been to the Ballet since I last went with you. Tell me about David Blair – and your American friends.

I do hope your father's foot has recovered now? Give him our warm greetings. We last met on that visit we paid you when war was imminent, do you remember? What a long age ago that was! What another world!

No, we haven't read Douglas Brown's book on Hardy. Anyone who loves Hardy so much must be a good person – though he might well be humourless, of course.

I hope your garden is taking shape now. I think you will see pleasant developments when you next come here; the shrubs and trees have put on a sudden spurt, and everything looks mature at last. I think I love gardening as much as anything I do in my absurdly various life. If only I could retire!

Bath Academy (at Corsham Court) had a remarkable open day last week. Heather and I went, and I wished you could see the work: all so fresh and alive and sensible. Cuthbert Bates (my music colleague, who runs the Bach Festival in Bath every autumn) is to move to your parts soon. I hope you meet him. We have booked for six concerts at his last festival in October!

Percy's Lacock house is very pleasant indeed, and he and Lena spend their time planning their garden. My Oxford brother has been very ill and I thought he looked a sadly sick person when I called recently. The rest of the family are silent. The Rice children haven't been here this year. David is in the army!

Edward Thomas, our American friend, comes in late September, I don't know for how long. It will be good to hear from him and Dieti the truth about life in U.S.A. at the moment.

I am conscious that this is a very dull letter. I have been writing all day, mostly brown envelope ones, and I'm afraid you've come in for the last half hour; but I wanted you just to know you and your Father are very often in our thoughts, that we look forward to a leisurely time with you one day, and that all goes well with us. Our love to you both.

Heather, Dieti and Robin.

LETTER 55

[2nd January, 1955]

My dear Cecil,

I'm afraid we always picture you coping with some family crisis or other, so we weren't surprised to hear your poor father had had bronchitis; we greatly hope he is better now, though this sudden cold wind after the delicious December Spring is hardly good for him. How lovely it is to have flowering currant, wych hazel, cherry, jasmine and viburnum fragrans and heathers all in bloom at this comfortless season; thirty years ago, only, a winter garden was a much less exciting venture. The first yellow crocuses are opening and little cyclamen, and a sprinkling of celandines and aconites in the hazel copse. I long for nothing beyond these four hedges; if only I could have the rash courage to retire and somehow eke out a living without ever having to face the public world any more! . . .

Seriously, though, it becomes increasingly hard to be optimistic. At the same time I am convinced there have never been so many essentially good people in the world; they are our hope, even though they are leading quiet lives. . . . I am also convinced that in the Arts today there is *much* that is very good. Quality is still the concern of a few.

We are going all high fidelity, at the moment; the affair, when complete, will be built into the corner where our hopeless old gramophone still stands. You must come and be critical when it is done.

Your very kind gift has already been used for Edwin Muir's Autobiography – a book we have wanted badly. It was a sweet thought of yours to send to us at all when so encumbered. Our grateful thanks.

Dieti's photographs of U.S.A. are astounding. He has taken some wonderful ones, too, of house and garden – and especially of flowers. Percy and Lena come today. They and my Oxford brother are all we continue to see of my quaint family . . .

Heather is in the throes of Cambridge (overseas) marking and I in the throes of Ministry of Education writing, still.

Our very dear love to you, as always.

Robin.

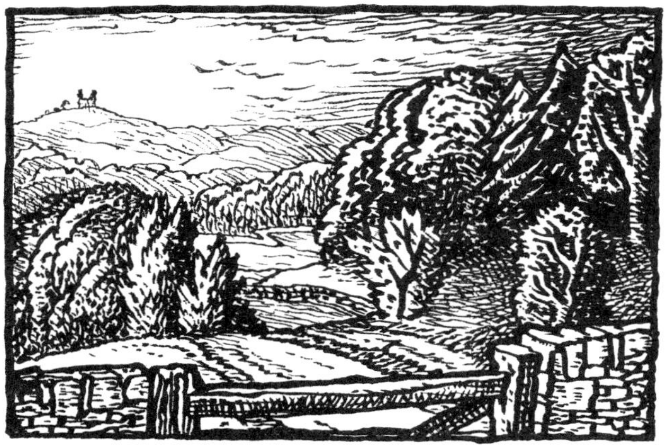

4

1957–1964

This section is dominated by Robin Tanner's work with Edith Moorhouse in primary schools in Oxfordshire and with courses for primary teachers. He wrote about 350 letters to her between 1959 and 1988; it is inevitable that selection has had to be severe so that other correspondents' letters could also be included.

LETTER 56

[21st May, 1959]

My dear Cecil,
Heather sent your letter to me to Yorkshire, whence I have just returned after running a fortnight's course. . . .

We are very distressed at your eye operation and only hope all goes well now. Will the result be permanent and satisfactory? How I wish we lived nearer, for with increased pressure on us from all sides our hope of leading a life of civilised and leisurely friendship diminishes. But in less than five years' time . . . I live for April 1964. This has been a shocking year for hard work. Heather and Dieti marched from Aldermaston to Trafalgar Square, and we set up and ran an anti-Nuclear Exhibition in Chippenham Town Hall. (I would have marched too, but was lecturing.) Then came Dartington. Heather helped and was brilliant. How I wish you hadn't dismissed it but had come. It happened to be my 200th Course, and I made it a banquet for friends from everywhere. I can never be so lavish again nor expect such help from so many fine people. Everything fell into our laps, and I don't think any one of the 40 will forget it.

. . . I saw *West Side Story* with Dietrich, and I MARVELLED. It bowled me over completely. You see, it is the West Riding primary schools (where Movement as an art is more highly developed than anywhere in the whole world!) grown up! Only last week, in a mining village, I saw droves of ten-year-old boys, stripped to the waist, dance and move like gods. I saw a pit accident, with incredible compassion shown to the wounded, and then a glorious rejoicing at the end. I saw these boys go 'teddy', and mutiny over a football referee's wrong decision. It was incredible – and all of the same remarkable genius as *West Side Story*.

Because H. still lectures at Corsham and my work is now so far off, and because commitments (such as the implementation-of-Wolfenden Society) involve us in so much labour, we never seem to be alone and idle. . . . It is so long since you were here. We're none of us getting a summer holiday, *but we are very cosy in winter if you would come then*. Our L.P. records are many, and D. has some superb photography to show you. I draw, but never etch, and must really wait till I retire. Then I have great plans. . . .

Take care of those eyes, dear Cecil. Go on thinking kindly of us. We have loved you for well over 30 years! and our love is strong and good. Forgive our apparent slacknesses.

You are very much in our thoughts.
Heather and Robin.

LETTER 57

Saturday. [20th June, 1959]

Dear Edith,
Heather sits marking her London 'Advanced Level' Literature papers in a bower of Albertine and Van Fleet roses, after our meal (proudly prepared and cooked by me!) of our own peas, carrots, asparagus and potatoes, and raspberries and strawberries; and, as I am afraid of marring the brilliant green of the lawn by mowing it, I can now begin a pile of letters. The first must be to you for your very generous, very understanding, far too humble, but happy and inspired letter to me after our wonderful day together. How the ears of all those dear people in our schools must have burned! It was a curiously beautiful thing for us two who care so much about them to be hovering about them that day, yet seeing none of them; planning and plotting on their behalf in dogrosy lanes and by stone walls; discussing them in ancient naves and chancels! and drinking their healths in The Bay Tree! Of course we aren't 'soft' about those teachers; they will be as good as we let them be. James Fairbairn wrote to say: 'I hopped down to Oxford on Friday on the chance of seeing Miss Moorhouse,

but was told she was "with Mr Tanner". I thought, how splendid! And I hope you "spoiled" her, for that's what we all need and thrive on!' I sat in The Shaven Crown on Wednesday night, drinking coffee with my colleague, and with Mr J., just after we had enjoyed the latter's excellent roses. I said, 'Has Miss Moorhouse ever seen them?' He replied, 'She's seen a few, because I took her some last Saturday!' That did me good. And yesterday young C. said to me, 'You see, none of us want to try to hide anything, because we know you and Miss Moorhouse will see it, anyway! But you don't let us have any fears, so we don't mind what we say or ask. I find it so easy to say all that is in my mind to you.'

Those are the things that really matter, and our reward is that these men and women let us help them to be their best selves. I count that an enormous privilege – as I know you do.

Yes: I must have been born under a kind star! And nothing could have given me greater happiness nor a deeper sense of fulfilment than to come to Oxfordshire. . . . Do not think, ever, that the gain is all on the side of Oxfordshire, for the satisfaction and pleasure that come to me from sharing common problems with you are tremendous. If the Dartington Course, for example, really was as rich as you say it was, then that was possible only because of the great stimulus I get from working in a group of schools that are largely of *your* creating. . . .

Blessings from
Robin.

LETTER 58

To Nan and David Evans and their children, Margaret and Sandy.

11.30 p.m. [2nd July, 1959]

My dear Both,

Before I retire to bed I must tell you that all the way home (and how beautiful a drive it was through those empty lanes, with an unwonted view of familiar places in my headlights!) I thought of you four in your idyllic valley, in what must be one of the most beautiful settings in England; and I felt happy and inspired after that peaceful evening with you in your beautiful house and garden. It rounded off my visit to Langford perfectly, and I thank you deeply for such a charitable and kindly thought. I like to think that my first sight of your haven has been on this particular day; I shall always remember it with swans and roses, and the light fading along the valley, and our quiet talk about sensible, ordinary things in those well-loved old rooms.

Have an easy weekend, David, after the turmoil of this week! I only hope I haven't (albeit unwittingly) aggravated the aches and pains that have assailed you lately.

The white rose near your entrance is one of the famous old Rugosas, and its name is 'Blanc double de Coubert'. The two with rather grayish leaves, near the house wall, are Alba, 'Maiden's Blush' and Alba, 'Céleste'. I wonder what sensitive, kindly people planted them there? I wonder if you agree with me that all houses carry a 'feeling' (I don't know what else to call it) with them – of being lived in with misery or happiness, turbulence or serenity? 'Waterloo' [1] has such a deep sense of peace about it that I am sure it has always been lived in by kind, hospitable people; long may the tradition continue!

My warm thanks and wishes.

Robin.

---

1. David and Nan Evans' house.

LETTER 59

[12th July, 1959]

Dear David [Evans],

When I met Miss Moorhouse at the Royal Show she said you had left the tent but a minute earlier. That was sad. Apart from hoping to find you on the top of your form again I had also wanted you and Leslie Horner to meet; he is the Head of that remarkable West Riding school of 400 miners' sons, which I have often told you about, – where the boys move and play games and dance like young classical Athenians!

I think you would have been proud of a bunch of your children, though. Leslie Horner and Geoffrey Elsmore were both amazed at them. I was standing there, bewildered and wondering where the Education tent might be when they saw me; they came up eagerly to greet me, then took me along to the plan of the Show, showed me just where we were, and where I had to go, adding, 'What a pity we can't find Mr Evans, so that you could talk to him.' As L.H. and G.E. put it, 'Well: those kids might have known you all your life, the way they met you, and you and he might be members of one family!' (In the broad sense, I rather hope we are, anyhow.)

Miss Moorhouse spent yesterday here with us, and I was delighted to learn that she is going at last to find her way down to your idyllic valley. That is very good. . . .

I like to think that a friendship which began nearly three years ago, when you were so immediately kind to the stranger in your midst, has been only strengthened by the 'event' of the 1st and 2nd July. If I know you and your school the better because of it, then surely you know me better too, though I realise that for you the picture won't be quite complete until you have crossed our threshold.

My love to you all at 'Waterloo'.
Robin.

LETTER 60

[22nd July, 1959]

Dear Nan and David [Evans],
Words are a poor vehicle for thought and feeling – yet they are all we have, so I must somehow try to use them to communicate to you the deep peace and happiness I felt under your roof. You two have an immense amount to share with your friends, and it warms my heart to witness hospitality so freely given and so gladly taken.

That harmonious supper party will take its place among a few others in my memory that have about them a quality that can sustain one through times of disheartenment; as we sat there, enjoying one another and Nan's superb food, I could hear Edith Evans, in Christopher Fry's *The Dark is Light Enough*, saying 'We must value this evening as the one Tuesday in the universe, for the rest have gone, and no more may come; and we should be on our most immortal behaviour!'

That is what I find so wonderful about Oxfordshire: we seize the moment, have it, enjoy it. This 'living immortally', as Fry would call it, is desperately important; and I bless you and all my other friends for it. It is that that makes your schools so alive and on tiptoe.

To you, David, I would offer very special thanks for letting me be part of the circle – instead of being merely someone pleasant enough but outside it. I count it a privilege to be allowed to be an ordinary fallible creature, able to cultivate friendships without having to hold back or to fear he may only embarrass by giving of himself. And I know how much of the ease and warmth among those friends we have in common is due to you. Among the many things that you and I have in common is an attitude of having nothing to lose (and therefore everything to gain!) and that, of course, is why we are able to know each other so honestly. I know I must not expect everyone to be as uncalculating: but let *us* at any rate rejoice in our own good fortune.

I hope that neither of you thinks that any small detail of kindliness and understanding and comfort passed me by during what seemed like a long holiday with you. That exquisitely comfortable bed, the peaceful ripple of the brook, your lovely hot water, the views from those two deep windows, Sandy's trusting chatter with me and his very lefthanded drawings of cows!, Margaret's gentle praising of her daddy's skill with paint; that memorable late walk and all of us talking in the garden and later over our good port; all the business of setting off in the morning, and the happy postponement of my parting with 'Waterloo' until 1 p.m. . . .

It was all very good; and very right that it should happen just now, when I have three weeks of very exacting work to do – work that I know I am not good enough for. Sometimes, in the throes of lecturing or discussing or teaching, my mind will leave London . . . to smell your roses or contemplate the valley from your western windows. Have a restful holiday. (If pain can be willed away, then I can assure you yours must go soon, David.) Forget about your school for a while; and one day before Christmas let us get down to making books together or pursuing anything else you would like help with.

It makes me very happy to think of Miss Moorhouse and Miss Robinson visiting you tonight, and I can well imagine the impact upon Miss Moorhouse that this first entry into your family will make. I must confess that, for me, returning to 'Waterloo' on Tuesday seemed as natural as returning home; and I found that my memory of it and the description I gave as part of my lecture in Bristol were both an *under*estimate. I am glad, though, that I was alone when I came the first time: on Tuesday it was lovely in another way, seeing the house full of relaxed and happy people. . . .

My thanks and my love to all four of you.

Robin.

LETTER 61

Dartington: very early on Monday morning. [undated: 1959?]

My dearest Nan [Evans],

Heather and I hope you will like this pot, made by a good potter friend of ours here at Dartington. Her husband, Sam Haile, was a superb potter too, but very tragically he was killed in a motor bicycle accident – and we lost a great genius. I always love a white pot for flowers, especially for really bright ones; and I am longing to see this one in 'Waterloo'. Don't you like the way the 'profile' of it – and the indented lines on it – suggest quite a wide fanning out of the flowers? It comes to you with very great love from us, and as a memory for David of the extraordinarily wonderful time we are having here together. To me there is something strangely significant in the fact that of all the hundreds of Courses I have run there has *never* been one as easy and blessed as this one; and this is the first that David has attended – and cast his influence upon. Small wonder that the entire community knows him and seeks him out; he melts the hardest and cheers the saddest wherever he goes. Small wonder that I – who had thought I could love no friend more deeply – find myself loving him still more. It is wonderful to see him relishing each succeeding course of the Banquet that Dartington is; and it is a very special joy to be sharing this particular course with him because it is the best I can *ever* offer, and it will go on yielding worth and happiness for years, I am sure. We must have an evening, Nan, when we can sit quietly together (the five of us, for Dietrich is a large part of all this – although I only now mention his name) and describe the course in detail with you. And maybe we can have last night's poetry again one day; and there will be many photographs of our exhibitions to show you.

Forgive this hurried note. This morning is a great festival of Costume, and I have to fit Heather into a busted dress with a 20″ waist!

I can never tell David how great a part he is playing here – yet I think you can guess.

Warmest love from us three.
Robin.

LETTER 62

[23rd July, 1959]

Dear Edith,
Before I become completely submerged in preparing and packing for the National Infant Course let me offer you our warmest good wishes for a wonderful holiday. If anyone deserves a perfect one, that is you. I hope you will forget all the rebuffs, setbacks and disappointments, and go off for your holiday with a deep and satisfying sense of being instrumental in revolutionising the education of children over a whole countryside. You could not have failed to feel the strength of the lead you have given Oxfordshire teachers, surely, at that rather moving gathering on Tuesday; of course you will have gone home feeling sad and bereaved, but also, I hope, proud and sure and privileged. How beautifully managed the whole meeting was! And as for the table: I have seldom seen one so utterly perfect, timeless, beautiful. I shall always remember it.

So shall I always remember that equally perfect, timeless, beautiful lunch hour at Chadlington. That was an inspired choice of yours; thank you so much for a lovely experience.

And tonight you will be enchanted and enthralled by that perfect haven at Sherborne. Can there be another schoolmaster in all England so favoured? I am sure there is no need for me to describe Tuesday night's party there: *good* news (never the occasional bad) travels quickly in Oxfordshire! I can only say it was quite wonderful, and staying the night seemed completely inevitable; that appeared to give as much pleasure to the Crippses and the Johns as to anyone.

Heather and I have just been working out next term's Saturday or Sunday visits of Oxfordshire teachers here, and it looks as though we can entertain 26 in all before Christmas! If only weekends were longer!

Think of us, from August 12th onwards, happily re-decorating our house. In addition, I've promised to give the Bath Bach Choir a new cover for its 1960 Festival programme and a new design for its unique 'Carols by Candlelight' concerts; and I've promised a lot of new drawings for Scott's catalogue,[1] – so it will be a busy holiday.

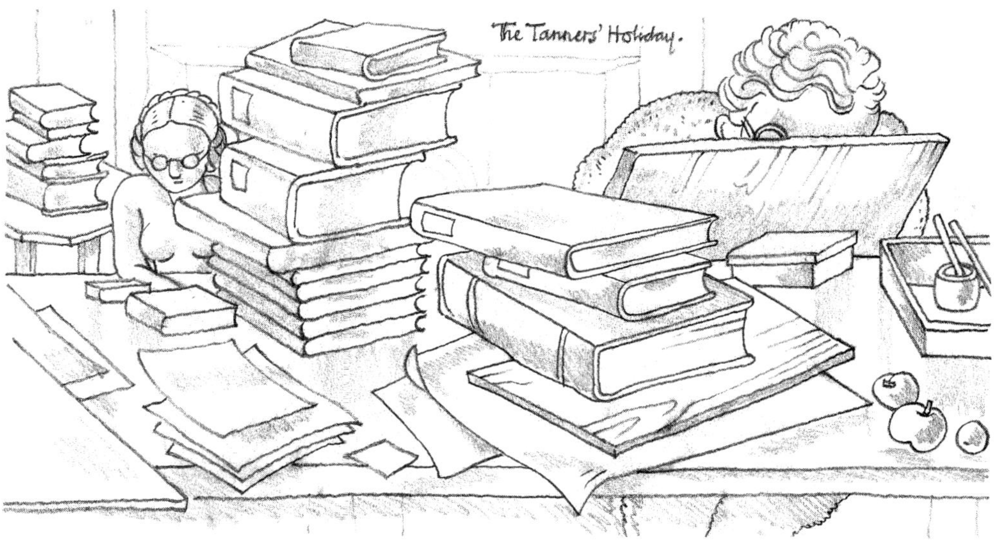

Blessings on you; and may we have a good autumn term.
Our love and all good thoughts.
Robin.

1. Robin Tanner had a bartering arrangement with Mr Scott, a Somerset nurseryman. The former made drawings and in return was sent plants for the garden.

LETTER 63

Written from the Ministry of Education, Curzon Street, London.

[30th September, 1959]

My dear David [Evans],

When I join the staff as your assistant master on October 12 I should like to give whatever you need most, so these are only very tentative suggestions:

From, say, 10.30ish until 12 would it be a good idea to make simple books, with your own class? I would show traditional methods of folding, stitching, and the making of a patterned cover. Each child would need a darning needle (I will bring thread), one large sheet of paper (which will become the pages of an octavo book), and a smallish piece for the cover. A few potatoes, some white wax crayons, a few brushes of any kind, a few pots to hold colour (I will bring the colour), and a penknife or two would be useful.

Then let us have a quiet chat in the lunch hour. In the afternoon would you like me to teach the boys of the two top classes? If each would bring something he has collected – such as a lichened stone, horse chestnuts in their case, an apple or pear, a shell, branch, plant, feather, any object at all, not necessarily a 'natural' one, that will make an admirable starting point for a picture. Any sort of paper you happen to possess, and any sort of paint and brushes, will suit. Actually, I should like to use a variety of media, so I will supplement yours. I should like to mount and display the work before the day is over, so that everyone goes home feeling proud of what has been achieved. I hope I don't fail you. I will give you my best. If what I've suggested is not what you have in mind let us change. I am game for anything!

. . . I hope you all enjoyed Sunday as much as we did. It was wonderful to have you all with us and for you to meet Heather and Dietrich at last. Time went so fast that we did little of what we intended. But there will be many more such days. Next time I will show you my Pembroke drawings and the alpine ones that set Edith M. going.

Our united love to you all.

Robin.

LETTER 64

[8th October, 1959; unfinished]

Dear David [Evans],
Your letter finds me in retreat from the world on election day, and about to tackle no less than 50 Min. of Ed. letters; I have neglected them for days, and, as you see, I would rather write civilised notes to my friends!

. . . On Monday afternoon I finished a job I was doing at Idbury school unexpectedly early and, as is my wont, returned home via your valley. So I visited your strangely feudal church first (and learnt incidentally that Mr D. J. Evans will be transporting Mr Dadge – was that the name? – on such and such dates). I found the white marble sculptures most entertaining and I enjoyed the fine C18 lettering. I must take some rubbings. Then I gave myself 40 minutes, sitting on the stone bridge, drawing that dreaming, sun-drenched, reposeful, timeless, well-loved, hospitable house called Waterloo. The door to the garden was open, and an occasional white chicken filtered into the lane, so Nan may have been about; but it seemed wrong to invade her afternoon. It wasn't a good drawing, either, so I had to destroy it; but I enjoyed attacking the problems it presented. One doesn't really know anything until one tries to draw it.

Don't bother overmuch about meeting my comic needs for next Monday at school, David.[1] I look forward to teaching your kids. I've been getting my hand in; I taught a little school to write on Tuesday, and we got quite a long way.

1. See letter 63.

LETTER 65

To David Evans.

Curzon Steet, LONDON. W.1.
[17th December, 1959]

It feels strange, David, to be writing to you from here – the Inspectors' Common Room at the Ministry, with its uniformed messengers and stale air, and all London surging below at Christmas shopping. Yet I should love to share with you and Nan 'my' London, which I have known since Heather and I were students in this University: tonight, for instance, I exchange the anonymity of my hotel for the quiet beauty of a little Mews house (only five minutes from Marble Arch) where two very dear friends, who are the finest potters in the land – Lucie Rie and Hans Coper – live and work; and last night I was deeply moved by Michael Redgrave's, Flora Robson's and Beatrix Lehmann's acting in *The Aspern Papers*; and tomorrow I spend in my beloved V. & A. Museum – before returning home on a late train. That is my sort of London, and it is full of wonderful friends.

But this note is really to tell you what a triumph I thought the entire celebration on Tuesday was. Everything about it was appropriate and good: your unerring wit and humour, your perfect intuitive mastery of the human situation; the feeling. You are wonderful to your staff and children, David, and I love and honour you for it. It was a privilege to be allowed to be one of the family, and I shall always remember it with a glow.

But bless you for much more. When I am away from home I tend to sit back and look at the passing year. Usually it seems a bit silly to ask oneself what – of so much that has been good – has been the greatest thing in all the year, but not so at the end of 1959.

Nothing can compare with the maturing of our friendship. For me that has been by far the greatest inspiration, and I thank you both from my heart. To be worthy of friendship is my constant care. I crave that in 1960 I can do something towards that.

I shall write again before the end of the month.

Till then, take all you will of the love I offer all four of you.

Robin.

LETTER 66

[19th December, 1959]

My dear Edith,

I was just about to sit down to write to you when your magnificently full and glowing and positive letter arrived, so pulsing with your vivid impressions of festivities and parties! You took me to them all as you described them, bless you; and I feel like you about the strange lapses people show at Christmastime. . . . I wonder if, as early as next October, you would let me give a talk, with a little exhibition, a reading, and perhaps even a few demonstrations, called 'Anticipating Christmas'? I should love to try to help in this way. . . .

The 'Carols by Candlelight' concert was a wonderful evening, and the party after it, in a splendid room overlooking the million lights of Bath, was 'out of this world'. I expect I am becoming far, far too perfectionist. Yet seeing that glorious performance of *The Aspern Papers* on Wednesday, followed by a marvellous night with my beloved friends, Lucie Rie and Hans Coper, in their pottery near Marble Arch on Thursday, has only confirmed me. Hans and Lucie have *both* agreed to come to Dartington! I am beside myself with happiness. It will be an amazing show of their work; and their astringent wisdom and their immense humility you will find astounding. We talked of this very thing: innate good standards and good sense. Oh if I could help raise those with you in Oxon! . . .

I must give a lot of thought to the plan for David's Sherborne day. I'll send you some suggestions first. We must certainly read some poetry, of course. But I wonder whether a bit of simple talk about the meaning of Art – and some gentle discussion about standards and values, about discipline and freedom, and about our own native powers, is what we are really most needing. In David's home and with his exceptional, intuitive understanding, I believe we might get a very long way in our thinking. Let us face it: only inasmuch as we can cause teachers to go on educating themselves shall we get good education in the schools. Although I think I never lose faith and rarely lose heart I am often impatient at the zigzag graph of progress; and it is usually at Christmastime – when I am exposed to such an onrush of ugliness and undisciplined excess everywhere – and at the end of the year, anyhow, when some sort of stocktaking seems inevitable, that I see how small a thing I have accomplished. What I can say this year, of all years, is that I have never enjoyed my work so much; and you must surely know, without my telling you, that a very large part of this happiness and zest has sprung out of the maturing of our friendship. I wear your friendship as I wear that onyx pin on my lapel! I hope everyone can see that I am happy and eager. I hold our friendship dear.

There are wonderfully happy days ahead and much to share. 1959 will always be for me 'the start' in Oxfordshire. . . . Your devotion to the schools is itself an inspiration. I constantly remind myself of my immense good fortune in being able to join in the renaissance you are bringing about. . . .

. . . Even this letter has had to be curtailed because the room has suddenly filled with unexpected guests. So forgive it. It brings, even so, our dear love and warmest thoughts. . . .

Heather, Dietrich and Robin.

LETTER 67

[28th December, 1959]

My dear Edith,

Before I attack a monstrously heavy Ministry of Education post I must send earnest and loving wishes from us all three that this wretched Thing that has laid you low will have gone by the time this reaches you. We are SO sad that you were sipping your tinned mushroom soup when we were drinking your health in claret! We are, of course, all of us, vulnerable at this time of year. (Even my usually rude health has not prevented a revolting head cold from sitting upon me for days, so that I feel leaden and stupid.) But who, of all our countless friends but you would have had the fortitude and guts and imagination to enjoy vicariously the family festival of Christmas Day? This year I was so filled with longing to make contact with many friends on Christmas Day, in the flesh as well as in spirit, that only by stern self-discipline was I able to stop myself from making a grand tour! First, I should have gone down into Somerset, up to Bath and on to the Downs, out to Malmesbury, Cirencester, and all that Cotswold seam; then up to Headington by way of Kidlington – where I should, alas, have found you prostrate – and home again via friends in Berkshire and Marlborough! Instead, like you, I did it in my imagination. In my imagination, too, I flew to those I am in love with in New York, Seattle, Vancouver, Auckland, Wellington, Tokyo, Ghana, Zurich, Paris, Edinburgh – to name a few. . . . We looked at the nearly 300 greeting cards, and read and re-read letters, and felt that heartbreaking movedness that comes from love – such as yours that makes you draw that spray of ivy and yew; and David's that made him letter his fine poem and write a letter more full of condensed wisdom and charity and feeling than I can say; and Susan Bosence's that led her to make a wonderful straw star . . . And I could go on and on. I feel all unworthy, and am determined to do more in 1960 for everyone.

You asked about our Decorations: On the front door a wreath of berried evergreen sprays from the garden, with a modelled white star in the centre. Our long table filled with flowers: four bowls of white Roman hyacinths (we bring these on in succession for three months), two white cyclamen, and a pot of flowering things from the garden – jasmine, viburnum fragrans, wych hazel, heathers, etc. On the low table in front of the fire, three wooden carved trees from Germany – white curled pine: fabulously beautiful. And all along the oak lintel of the fireplace, stars and stars and stars – a collection we have amassed from Denmark, Norway, Germany, Finland, and East Anglia, with some of our own. Most were hung (invisibly) so that they twirled in the heat. The whole room was white and straw and wood: I should say 'is', for we shall not disturb it until I leave for Whitelands [Training College] on Sunday.

David is all agog to get on with plans for January 30! He has asked H. and D. to come, and they would love to, but only on condition that we be allowed to share substantially in the material provision for that great concourse. Tentatively, I have suggested a poetry reading (by a group of us) called 'Art Without Epoch', followed by a chat and discussion on values and criteria in looking at Art generally: the simple common denominator of the Arts, what we look for, and what we must learn to bring to them. I would bring a fine painting and if, as you say, we each brought our two best Xmas greetings, that would be excellent common ground. I believe our 'chairman' for our roundtable talk ought to be Heather: what do you think? She has a simple clarity and the knack of keeping everyone active. . . .

Our dearest wishes for you and our deep love as always.

Robin.

The following six extracts from letters to Edith Moorhouse give an insight into the careful planning and preparation for courses: in particular at Dartington Hall.

[24th February, 1960]

. . . I've just finished the Programme [for Dartington]. It is a staggering banquet! At 9.15 on the last night – after my final lecture – we are having a wonderful concert by the now internationally famous Dartington String Quartet and also by a soprano and a guitarist; and during that afternoon those who wish may watch and listen to the rehearsal! . . .

[19th March, 1960]

. . . I regard 'Dartington' as my major attempt to offer them ['these wonderful people in the schools'] something I have had to go through labour and birthpangs for; and I am applying my very best thought and effort to those ten days. (I hope, by the way, that the A to Z set of Questions I've sent out this weekend will strike most members as a mild little 'textbook' on the ways in which young children learn. Will they see that connection, d'you think? Does the Programme whet your appetite?)

. . . There's no reason why you shouldn't invent a Question of your own for your work at Dartington, by the way!

I'm not going to allow you to keep to the notion that you do not do one single thing really well, Edith. What about your Oxfordshire Dream and Thing? (How I blessed that visionary Edwin Muir last evening, by the way!) . . .

[27th March, 1960]

. . . Another substantial batch of letters came yesterday from frightened Dartingtonians, terrified of my Questions. Only dear Leslie Horner (to whom I had sent them out of interest) wrote eagerly about them, distressed at what he would be missing. I assume and expect too much, I suppose. Sometimes I think I must be all wrong. You and David comforted me very much by your insistence that this preparatory work for Dartington is right. Oh thank you for your noble support. . . .

[10th April, 1960]

. . . Now I feel I must go into retreat, so to speak, and put on the habit – even the hair shirt – of dedicated preparation for Dartington. This is the greatest gift I have to offer, and I must try harder than ever before to make my gift worthy of all you, my dear, my very dear, my dearest friends, whose trust and support and love are a wonderful inspiration and discipline and challenge to me. I am deeply happy but sobered: not anxious but eager: not in any way apprehensive but profoundly aware of my great responsibility. Wonderful advance is made possible by Dartington, and my difficult task is to make myself the right agent of the experience and the subsequent advance. I crave to be equal to the job. I shall need all your loving involvement and charity. I know how wonderfully fortunate it is to be surrounded by people I love and who love me; but there will be, too, those who are 'uncommitted', who have not 'surrendered'; we don't want to 'convert' them, but we do want to help them to know themselves better. I hope you know, my dear Edith, what joy and security and fortification your sharing of the Course with me will be. I only hope that for you there will be some gain too. . . .

[1st May, 1960]

. . . If Dartington has fortified and encouraged us all – as it certainly has me – then I am deeply grateful to have been the agent (so to speak) through whom the experience was made possible. I take – and indeed want to take – no more credit than that. You must know that I have friends more countless in number and marvellous in kind that I deserve: I have never consciously sought them: having them humbles me, and sharing a few of them with others of my dear friends, like you, lessens my sense of having so much more than my share of love and life. My hope is that we shall all find this ultimate singleness and aloneness which I tried to speak of in my last talk less difficult to meet and master; I crave that you, dear Edith, who give so magnificently, will find 'a house within' when you need care, 'a guard within' when you need rest, and say like Rilke 'The love that I have had! Upon my breast / The beauty of the world clings, to weep there.' That was the thought that was most strongly present in me as people sped away with their pot plants and all their lovely work from A to Z. Your own work was fine, liberal and outgoing; and I know you tasted of so much that was great and noble and savoured such good fellowship that Oxfordshire will see a fresh fire burning in you – and you and I together will accomplish more. Do not be discouraged. Rejoice, and feed on the Banquet. Oh I hope I did not fail you badly at any point; I wanted to make the offering perfect, yet even at this distance I begin to see the pitiful flaws. I shall do better next time. . . .

[18th September, 1961]

This week I'm giving Poole teachers the first Course they've ever had; my car is high with an exhibition of Junior School craftwork (which I have never been able to show you and which contains only Langford work from Oxon.) and an exhibition of 'Ultimate Standards'. I have yet to prepare two addresses, but at least I can pause to answer your letter of a week ago. . . .

. . . David and I spent a long time on the Comber weekend arrangements. I think, after all, we must let him and Nan carry out their wish to give us supper on the Saturday night, though I feel very strongly that you should cause everyone to contribute say five or six shillings (all unknown to N. and D. of course) and present them with a cheque afterwards. Feeding some 20 people is costly. Don't you agree? I've told David *I* could only co-operate in the plan if he allows me to share the cost.

Heather has prepared her talk on Placenames and Surnames, and if she hasn't been sent to prison before we meet I think it will be good.

I'm prepared to take anyone who wishes to Windrush and/or Northleach churches. Given at all reasonable weather I think we could get through a great deal of interesting work.

We spent an evening on the William-Morris-day plan, and we agreed to offer this – if you agree – to a personally invited group of teachers only: Visit Kelmscott Manor on a Saturday morning after half term : Picnic lunch : See an exhibition at David's school of his children's work : A conversation-description-exposition (scripted) between David and me. He is prepared and happy to do this, and I think it might be a memorable day. Let me know your reaction, Edith. . . .

LETTER 74

The Tanner's holidays on the Continent feature in this and the following two letters.

[7th September, 1960]

My dear Cecil,
Yes, I cling to Provençal notepaper even though we have left that eternal hot sun. This damp coolth is a poor exchange, and in spite of our good neighbour's care we are swamped in jungular growth. Yet of course it is good to be home; and of all the 100+ letters awaiting us very few were as welcome as yours. It was good, too, to have your card yesterday, and hearing your news and your pungent (and often perversely wayward!) reactions to life is always a treat! While you continue to write with wit and punch we shall certainly never have a moment's worry about you! Few people can be so surrounded by friends, surely; and having your house to yourself must be a lasting solace – as well, of course, as a perpetual drain and worry, as ours is.

The death of 'Aunty' is another sad break with that happy past, alas. How vividly, and with what gratitude, I remember those good Tunbridge Wells holidays, when Mop was a carefree pretty girl and your house was filled with early golden-rod. . . .

I was in London (but at work) until August 8th, but I only went to Art shows. Picasso is, I am sure, 'great', but I can't truly say I should ever want to *possess* anything of his. And he earned no respect from us when we saw at Arles that he is pleased to preside over and foster bull-fighting. Musically, we have had no treats since the Bath Festival in May, which was perfect. The autumn Bach Festival is our next event. (Later I will send you the brochure I designed for it.)

Our three weeks in Tuscany and Umbria and Provence were perfect. I expect you know most of it? At Ostend we put ourselves and our car on the night-sleeper-express (with a sleeping compartment for three) and woke up in Milan. We loved the place. The greatest surprise was to find Leonardo's *Last Supper* far less faded and 'gone' than we were led to suppose. Next day we drove down to Florence, by way of mountain country exactly like all those heavenly backgrounds in Florentine paintings. For a week we spent enchanting days down in the blazing city and cool nights in our hilltop convent-hotel at Fiesole. What painting, what sculpture, what architecture! But we loved the modern life, too, being lived in ancient places: the gentle policemen in white from head to foot, and such beautiful, proud, courteous people everywhere. Arezzo, San Sepolcro, Assisi, Perugia, Siena, San Gimignano: they were all amazing, and it was hard to leave them. Pisa and the Carrara Mountains thrilled us, and a Mediterranean night at Sestri Levante and alpine nights at Pinerolo and Grenoble were wonderful. The Côtes du Rhone vineyards, down to Avignon, and at last to Arles and that strange Camargue – with its rice fields and flamingoes – occupied our last four days. That country just IS Van Gogh, isn't it? It is all there, just as he saw and loved and left it. . . .

This hurried scribble bears our warm love, as always.

Robin.

LETTER 75

[begun 10th September, 1961]

My dear Cecil,

Yes: your letter found us drunk with the beauties of Romanesque S.W. France, still reeling from the splendid terrors of the Lascaux paintings, and in love with so much – with a man and his family who sold us natural wools in Sarlat market and who a few days later entertained us to their own walnut wine in their remote and beautiful home; with those old time forgotten villages and traffic-free flowery lanes of the Brionnais; with the rosé wines and fine cheeses of Périgord; with the young man in Conques who was washing out his wine casks in readiness for the new harvest and who took us down into his stone cellar to taste his precious vintage; with the painted medieval wooden figures, unrecorded, in church after church, that D. photographed; and with the utter tranquillity and emptiness and unconcern and hospitality and timelessness everywhere. The customs officer at Dover cast a kindly, almost understanding eye on our roof-high loot of brooms, pots, dried plants, wool, baskets, cheeses, wines, books, drawings, bulbs, cooking pots and the rest! All that was a week ago, and now we are miserably immersed in the fight to bring some sanity to the present nuclear-hysteria, the fight to bring that monstrous bounder, Eccles, to his senses, and the mundane fight against the tide of weeds in our tropical-looking garden! H. and D. have gone up to London today to the C.N.D. meeting in Trafalgar Square. The world situation can never have been so perilous; the industrial situation in England can never have been so bad and depressing; and the education of children is deliberately put in peril by a Government that thinks NOTHING of education and chooses to persecute the teaching profession. I have to give two public lectures next week, one in Winchester and one in Oxford; if you hear of my dismissal and imprisonment don't be surprised, Cecil! . . .

I spend the last week of the month at Curzon Street, when I must catch up with a little of what is on in London.

I hope Brighton proved a refreshment, and that your redecoration pleases you. We're very glad most of your cuttings survived. Apart from cool, white, wild lacecap hydrangeas and a few belated roses and white autumn crocuses and little white cyclamen under the hazels and some heathers, our garden is a level and uninteresting green. I planted 1,300 bulbs last week, however.

Our warm love, as always.

Robin.

LETTER 76

[18th September, 1962]

My dear Cecil,

We were delighted with your letter and thrilled that you had been to Italy. Surely you didn't go alone? We long to hear more. For the most part, I think we saw and stayed at rather different places from you, and when we return we must fill in gaps with your help. We took our car by train from Ostend to Milan. We loved Milan, even (I nearly said *especially*) the Pirelli and another skyscraper. The journey down to Florence – mainly on that skilful autostrada –

was memorable. In Fiesole we stayed in the Convent of San Girolomo! Those blue nuns run a sort of combination of nursing home and hotel. It was refreshing each evening to come up to their cool olive grove and vineyard and see the Duomo and Campanile still sizzling below in the heat.

We stayed, too, in Arezzo, Perugia and – best of all, even dearer to me than San Sepolchro or San Gimignano – Siena. It is Siena I long to return to. On our way back (over the Alps and into Provence) we went via Genoa and Pisa, staying in an old backwater of Sestri Levante. And of course we never reached Ravenna nor Venice. We should love to see your transparencies. Yes: D. took some amazingly sensitive and skilful ones on the positively fabulous journey we had through Romanesque France – Rouen, Chartes, Autun, Cluny, Tournus. But his most remarkable (and our most remarkable experiences) came out of the remote cul de sac in Haute Tarentaise, where we spent the latter half of our holiday. Eagles soared, marmots called from virgin forests and 'rare' high-alpine flowers were common. Our host also acted as mountain guide. I drew like mad. We drank heavenly sparkling wines (unhappily they don't travel well), ate *escargots*, jugged marmot, bilberries, wild raspberries and strawberries, mysterious terrines, unspeakable cheeses! and glorious fruit. It was all out of this world and we shall never be the same again!! . . .

Our warm love to you.

Robin.

LETTER 77

[9th July, 1962]

My dear Charlie [Naylor],

Since the 20th of June, when that vividly Charlie-ish letter arrived, I have been on my travels, lecturing, setting up exhibitions and 'damaging' people – in London, Herts, the Isle of Wight and in Hampshire. . . . Heather is glad you found her talks of interest and it is nice that you shared them with Freda. (And if what you say about Freda's intellectual grasp being stronger than your own is true – which I doubt – then you'll understand that Heather has a finer intellect than I have: at school she was always top of the form and I was always second, and I had to suffer the humiliation often of being 'beaten' by her at Art!)

We were delighted to read about your Men's Discussion Group, and full of admiration, too. We only cannot see why religion and politics (both so inseparable from life) should be taboo. As very left-wing Quakers – members of C.N.D., pacifists, anti-bloodsports, anti-colour bar, anti-Establishment and Socialists – we find that strange. . . .

You ask if I write poetry. I would rather practise that art than any other, but I am sadly inept at it. The verses I enclose were published last summer in *The Countryman* and because they gave friends . . . pleasure, you may possibly like to have them, though maybe you'll dismiss them as being merely 'Georgian'.

Congratulations on so quickly passing your driving test! Let me know as soon as you decide on your Southern tour. I have been looking at my official diary, and I find that my last Course ends on August Bank Holiday, and that I shall only be at home from then until the 9th, when we escape for three weeks to Burgundy and the Haute Savoie. However, we are all three at home again on September 5th.

I know exactly what you mean, Charlie, when you say that what Woolley gave you, above all, was – and you put it perfectly – 'the insight promised through seeing life through poetry and as poetry'. That is exactly as I see it. Life lived 'poetically', so to speak, is life lived with a quickened awareness, with sharpened sensibilities, and always inspired by the power of human love. Poetry can say the unsayable, make possible the impossible! I would almost assert that it can reconcile the irreconcilable!

Those poems by John . . . and Kathryn . . . are a great tribute to their sense of security with you. Those two kids have poured out their very life blood for you, bless them. Go on with the good work. Show these boys and girls the good life.

I wish I could write at length, but I have to pack my car and set off for Derby. Yes: I shan't be very far off for the rest of the week, so feel my love reaching you.

Always your friend,
Robin.

The following extracts from letters to Edith Moorhouse deal with a holiday in France and an over-full national programme, which meant that Robin Tanner was spending less time in Oxfordshire.

[5th August, 1962]

You see I am back to my French notepaper! We set off on the 14th (August). We drove first to Rouen, then we went on to Chartres for two or three days. Then, via Sancerre, we reached Autun, where dear Barron joined us. We spent several days there and then away up into the Haute Savoie to the remote, high cul-de-sac at Peisey-Nancroix, near the Italian border, for a week. Then, on September 3, back to Lyons and home on the car night express, via Boulogne. . . .

[8th September, 1962]

Oh, how painful is the process of putting on one's harness again after those weeks off the lead! We reached here safely, disgorged the heterogenous collection from our car, lodged Barron overnight; and have spent every waking hour since then trying to cope with the waves of growth in the garden, C.N.D. affairs, correspondence, unexpected guests and just getting ourselves straight again.

That last week in the lonely Tarentaise – eagles soaring over the Mont Blanc skyline, and marmots calling from those virgin flowery mountainsides, and waterfalls crashing, and a kindly community pouring their all out before us four foreigners – was so memorable and moving that we all feel we have left a part of ourselves behind. I drew red gentians, soldanellas, and snowline treasures I had never seen before. I drew curious chimney pots, glacier formations, and a full dress cemetery-scene with the mountains as background! Our hotel was French beyond belief, with fabulous food and wines; and we soon became part of the family. One daughter, Colette, – a beautiful, artless, unmade-up creature who waited on us – is coming, au pair, to England, and we look forward to having her for a weekend. You will be enchanted by D.'s photographs of her and of others in the village wearing their *frontières* of black and gold, looking like portraits by Holbein . . .

But I must come to my senses and answer your kind letters:

It was sweet of you to send us a Welcome Home. The year is going to be a very, very full one. The other parts I work in, particularly Dorset, Poole, Bournemouth, and Hampshire, are waking up to new possibilities and will rightly lay claim to my help; and of course my allegiance has to be distributed as equally as possible. But I feel sure you understand that, Edith, I shall in no way desert my beloved diocese: you know that. (And even after retirement I'll give you time if you still need me.) But the Ministry of Education sees it like this: Through your Honour I've got recognition for the pioneer work you've established, and in a lot of ways I've put the county on the map, so to speak, and got proper understanding (through my Reports) of the widespread good work done. But that is only part of the whole. I am constantly being pressed by the Min. of Ed. to spread this feeling wider. That is why I have to spend time next term in Liverpool, London, Nottingham, Sussex . . .

I expect that sometimes when you feel a bit under-keyed or over-tired you take all this personally. I beg you not to. Always, please, know that I share your problems deeply and with love. If I appear to 'neglect' or 'overlook' or 'omit', do please tell yourself that I do so only because the larger situation demands it. There is never any *personal* thing in all this. My body is being torn limb from limb by SO many needy people outside the county I shall always love best. And my influence would be a poor thing indeed if it failed to grow without me. I am human enough to recognise that 'Much wants More', yet I have to see my work largely and clearsightedly. In the last few years of my official work I do assure you I shall continue to give you ALL I possibly can. Change is inevitable, and . . . it comes upon us because our life and work are so GOOD!

Of course, we are all going to miss dear G. – but a wider, thirsting world is going to have him. We can't possess him, anyhow, can we? . . . I naturally am glad that the Min. of Ed. . . . has taken him; but that is unimportant beside the fact that when I have gone he will be there for many years to carry the torch. This is poetic justice, Edith, isn't it, if ever we have seen it? Nor shall we *lose* him. We shan't feel hurt if we hear and see little of him, for we shall know he sprang from us and is still a part of us.

I thought I would let you know my timetable till November 23. After that I have to be away until December 5, when Ruth W. will help me in Oxon. for three days. Then I'm all over the country till Christmas.

So do please believe that any long silence does NOT 'mean more than busyness', although once it never prevented me from writing. Now, alas, it does. Even with only five hours' sleep and neglecting H. and D. and my own private life and interests shamefully, I just can't keep up as I once did. The pressure is fantastic. So I beg you not to feel personally hurt, ever, but to understand. . . .

My love to you as always.
Robin.

LETTER 80

[7th October, 1962]

My dear Charlie,
Yes: I feel I've left such a large part of myself behind in France that I must continue to use this comic notepaper I bought in Burgundy. I cannot remember from what region I sent you a greeting. First we had a fabulous feast of Romanesque sculpture, all the way down from Rouen and Chartres, along the Loire with its forgotten villages, to Autun (where one marvellous Gislebertus – as you probably know – devoted his life to carving in stone for the Cathedral, in C12), Cluny and Tournus. Then we crossed the Juras, into Savoie; and our best days were spent in a remote hamlet in the Haute Tarentaise, a few miles from the Italian border, and with Mont Blanc eternally glittering white in the sun about fifteen miles north of us. The English are shy of this very indigenously French, untouristic village. . . . 'Les Anglais' were, in fact, a great novelty; we became part of our host's family, and the village turned out to bid us goodbye! . . . One day I'll show you my drawing of the quite fantastic village-churchyard, with white 'sepulchres' all round it – each with its figure of a saint within; and a wonderful litter of beaded-wire funeral ornaments; and the whole seen against distant glaciers and blue black forests . . .

Your poem, 'This Day' gave me a lot of pleasure. What I specially admire is your gift – which I don't possess – of terse, spare, economical expression. My naturally extravagant and excessive nature gets in the way when I try to write: I am too much in love with words.

You ask about my 'left-wing-Quaker beliefs'. Put in a sentence or two they are, I suppose, these: I believe that 'God' is that of *good* in every human being. I must try to find and answer this good. I myself am responsible to God, and must manage without a 'priest' or 'minister'; I need no intermediary, so to speak. I believe I must act according to my own 'inner light'; my obedience must be to that, not necessarily to 'my country', 'the state', etc. (Indeed, at this moment we three are fighting hard *against* our government's wanton leading us into nuclear war and world suicide. We have protested against the slogan – which everyone knows is a hoax and a lie – 'Civil Defence is Common Sense' – that is being stamped on our letters. We march from Aldermaston. We attack the death penalty. We are of course Socialists, because we know that the reverse only means exploitation and the perpetuation of 'class'.)

I recognise no hierarchy. Charlie Naylor and Robin Tanner and 'Prince Philip' and your friend Edwin and the children you teach are equal members of a world society. I recognise no titles, not even 'Mr' or 'Esq.'! I refuse honours. I am not aware of class, colour, creed, age, background, seniority, juniority! I have nothing to lose. For me, Jesus was divine only in the sense that we all are. I count his example a supreme one, though, and wish to follow it.

I reverence life, and under no circumstances will I therefore take it. That is why I renounce war and all war preparation. (History shows all too clearly the utter futility of war; and we all know what any future 'war' would do to the world.) I believe in the force of love. . . .

If you don't already know the poems of Yevtushenko, please accept them, with my love. Those I have marked are my favourites. They have moved and heartened me tremendously, and I believe you will love them.

It is a day of mellow sunshine, and we are about to harvest our apples, which hang heavy from the trees. The autumn crocuses under the hazels remind me poignantly of the alpine meadows of Savoy . . .

I hope this term is going well for you both.

My love, as always.
Robin.

Kington Langley.
New Year's Day.
1963.

My dear Edith,

First: A Happy New Year to you from us all three; & all good wishes for 1963.

And what an entry into it! I hope that the unbelievably disastrous & annihilating blizzard that smote us on Saturday had spent itself before reaching as far north as Oxford. Our garden is a shambles. Cherished evergreens such as eucalyptus, arbutus, tree heaths & brooms are maimed and broken. Our fruit cage is smashed. And still it snows! It took D. & me some hours to dig a narrow way through to our front gate: now we must begin again!

LETTER 81

New Year's Day [1963]

My dear Edith,

First: A Happy New Year to you from us all three; and all good wishes for 1963.

And what an entry into it! I hope that the unbelievably disastrous and annihilating blizzard that smote us on Saturday had spent itself before reaching as far north as Oxford. Our garden is a shambles. Cherished evergreens such as eucalyptus, arbutus, tree heaths and brooms are maimed and broken. Our fruit cage is smashed. And still it snows! It took D. and me some hours to dig a narrow way through to our front gate: now we must begin again!

Never in our 32 years here have we known anything like this. We really *are* marooned! The silence of white isolation is strange and not without its peculiar pleasure. And in the blessedly even and constant warmth of this cottage, cyclamen, hyacinths and cacti are flowering; and with the fine flowering sprays of wych hazel, jasmine and viburnum fragrans we fortunately cut on Christmas Eve we have created our own illusion of spring.

Heather is deep in marking; I have immense arrears of writing to make up; and D. spends a lot of time digging out and fuelling and feeding our ancient and lonely neighbours in the cottages nearby.

If I can reach Chippenham (by 7.45 a.m.) next Monday I should arrive at Oxford by 9.30 a.m., and I'll come straight to your office. I must return by the 2.20 from Oxford, I'm afraid. Not that these arctic conditions look as though they will *ever* yield!

Your beautiful 'Traveller's Joy' drawing took five days to reach us! but what pleasure and admiration we felt on seeing it! The whole conception is fine – colour, texture, form, tone and feeling. Strangely, Philip Best sent a pen drawing of the same plant, which I must show you one day, for it is quite the most masterly he has ever done. . . .

Yes, your prediction was right: close on 300 greeting cards and 150 letters at Christmas make a real problem, especially as Heather has to co-ordinate the work of a team of examiners, . . . in addition to usual chores. Her 94-year-old aunt played our piano lustily on Christmas Day, by the way! . . .

Now I'll lunge and plunge as far as our beleaguered post box! It is hard to find the lane, and one sinks in the snow up to the tops of one's wellingtons! We all three send our dear love; and may 1963 bring countless joys and blessings to you.

Robin.

LETTER 82

To Charlie Naylor.

[20th May, 1963]

A wave of the hand before I leave this paradise-garden for the coast, Charlie. I thought you might like to have this new edition – published only last week; some of your kids may show an interest, perhaps.

I had one of my 'ideal' dreams last night; it is the only dream I ever have; it is always the same; but alas! I only dream it very rarely – usually when I have been made supremely happy or have gone on to some new height in life.

I was in an exquisite, windless garden under a perfect blue and white sky: flowering trees, faultless flowers. My very dearest friends were there, just lying or talking and drinking wine and laughing – but quietly: Sam, Ewart, Edward, John, Margaret, Mary, Ruth, Barron, Tom, Cyprian, Jane, Hans, Lucie, Paul, three more Johns, two Leslies, two Davids, Olive, Frances . . . oh, and many more, and, for the first time, my beloved Charlie. You seemed to know all the others. Your hair was longer than life, and needless to say you were the life and soul of the party! It was wonderful that you have come into this absurd recurring dream at last!

I read this utterance of Michelangelo's yesterday, from his notebook:

> 'You must know that I am, of all men who were ever born, the most inclined to love persons. Whenever I behold man or woman lovely of mind, or one who possesses great talent or dexterity of mind, or can do or say something more appropriately than the rest of the world, or wounds me with his goodness, I am compelled to fall in love with him; and then I almost give

myself up to him, so that I am no longer my own property but his, and he in part mine.'

Robin.

LETTER 83

To Charlie Naylor.

Gloucester Hotel, Weymouth. [20th May, 1963]

Don't think I shall continue to 'persecute' you with letters at this rate, Charlie! This is my only means of protest against distance, and a way of attempting to share with you this very curious, various and absorbing life that earns me my bread and butter. You see, the sobering thought comes to me sometimes that by the time you are a man of fifty I may well be dead: we may only have another twenty years of each other's friendship – or possibly less. So let us postpone nothing, lose no opportunity, not fritter away any chances or waste any, either. . . .

A letter is a poor substitute for meeting, yet I never cease to marvel that a few black marks on paper can be made to communicate deep feeling. I suffer intolerable anguish at parting, (leaving Heather and Dietrich today was hell) and perhaps that is why I go to more extreme lengths than many to attempt to minimise it through writing.

Early this morning I drove over the ancient Wiltshire Downs – their long and round barrows stark on the skyline – to the Saxon hilltop town of Shaftesbury, where I posted the lettering book to you. Then I tumbled down into the incredibly fertile Blackmore Vale – the land of *Tess of the D'Urbervilles*. I've never seen more apple blossom, lilac and laburnum in one morning, and the deep Dorset lanes were white with wild garlic and parsley. At Blandford Forum I called to see a show of pottery by McNally, who teaches at the Royal College of Art, and I bought a small addition to your gray collection – I'll send it next weekend. Then on through Hardy's Dorchester to comic, dotty old George III's Weymouth! This hotel is his original house. I sit writing at a window looking out at a deep blue-green sea. The boat for the Channel Isles is just leaving. If you were here we'd walk out to Portland Bill or the Chesil

Beach tonight, Charlie. As it is I shall write a report on the Art I've inspected; I stepped straight into a delicate human situation, but I hope I've left both teachers – a man and a woman and neither much at ease in a classroom and both with most unfortunate taste and a strident commercial taint to their work – feeling happier and a bit more confident. It wasn't an easy day. And what will Bournemouth give me tomorrow, I wonder? . . .

The sea grows milky and misty now and lights are coming out along the pier. The white edges of the waves make the whole scene look like a wax-resist painting. And so goodnight, my dearest Charlie. . . .

Robin.

LETTER 84

To David Evans.

[13th April, 1964]

Dearest Ally of them all,
Although there was little chance to talk together alone, you were aware, I know, how much I depended on you at Dartington – as indeed I have over all these years in this venture. And to thank you seems indecent, irrelevant, almost absurd. I would rather say how much I love and honour you for all your incredible involvement, your silent ministrations, for the masterly and subtle therapy you do, your fearless and impassioned convictions, your magnificently generous social example, your patience and forbearance (especially with me), and your glorious zest and bonhomie! Bless you for all these wonderful qualities and for your unique contribution to the Course.

Your Langford session seemed the natural culmination to all you had already done for that fine community of men and women; and it was, without doubt, your very best, David – though you must have known that. To say I felt proud might sound patronising. I certainly felt proud to be your friend.

That last night – which was easily the best we have ever had – owed a lot to you; and it is wonderful of you and Nan to cope with Independence Day!

Barron left last night, in fine fettle. She had been very touched by you and Nan.

I haven't yet unpacked my car, as there has been a continuous Dartington-extension-party since Geo. and Avery and I reached home! I feel very, very tired – yet not weary. I will confess to you that although the Course didn't quite reach my conception, yet I do feel some sense of fulfilment. And what makes me happy is the thought that my dear younger colleagues, in a year or two, will be ready to run better courses than I have done.

I look forward to seeing you at The Lamb for dinner on Wednesday the 22nd.

My dear love to you all four.
Your deeply grateful Robin.

LETTER 85

[undated, probably just subsequent to letter 84]

My dearest David and Nan,
. . . I must say again for us all what is really unsayable: yesterday was supreme: perfect: quite unsurpassable: never to be forgotten; and we bless and love you for it. Although the day was, in a sense, an experiment, it immediately became so inevitable and so obviously right that no one seemed a stranger, and this might have been the 100th such meeting instead of the first. I hope you both feel as deep a sense of satisfaction and fulfilment as we three do. Nothing could have been more lovely than the whole feeling of yesterday and every detail of it; and it was all owed to the genius and love and care and preparation and fabulous generosity of you two. I am thankful that we meet next Friday, David, when we'll contrive a half hour's peace together in which to talk about the glory of yesterday. For glory it was. I shall never forget the wonderful arrival of car upon car, with bottle upon bottle! in that beautiful haven; and dear Sandy and Margaret playing their parts, and everyone looking dazed with delight; and then forming quiet little groups among the flowers and in those hallowed rooms. Oh, what a moving gathering it was! – And few of those dear people realised that it marked, too, a third significant anniversary! Can it be true that

there was ever a time before then? before we knew one another? before life was so highly charged, so quickened, so sacramental?

Be wonderfully happy, both of you.
We send abiding love and gratitude.
Heather, Dieti and Robin.

LETTER 86

[undated, probably June 1964]

. . . My dear Edith, if you are really sure you want to make this change you contemplate, then I hope it happens. I'm bound to say I believe there is far more satisfaction to be found in your present work – especially as a Vice-Principal under the new epoch is the unfortunate administrator who sees little of the really educational life of the college. I feel, from what I see, that I would far rather be a lecturer. But in any case . . . I hope you won't lightly leave Oxon. I'm afraid I think it would be a mortal blow to Primary Education, since you wouldn't be replaced. Bless them, the schools couldn't continue long without a leader, good as they are. If they can have you for the next eight vital years, then I think they might be surer.

But I mustn't try to influence you, for I know you will do nothing without a great deal of thought. You and I know, of course, that this is Oxfordshire's heyday. The schools know it. If you continue I shall count it only a privilege to continue to offer you help if you need it. You know that December 31, 1964, doesn't mean an end for me – only a new beginning. I shan't desert!

Your wondering about the future only makes the dazzling present seem even brighter. But whatever happens, always be assured of my love and sharing and admiration.

Robin.

LETTER 87

[28th July, 1964]

. . . Oh, thank you for your generous letter, dear Edith. Yes: it was, absolutely unreservedly, a marvellous weekend and one I shall always feed upon. It was not only quite flawless: it showed how good and great men and women all are when they obey the best in them and take flight – miles behind all the pretty lines drawn for and by them! I loved everybody. It was all inspired. Nothing quite like that can happen again, since it was the inevitable culmination of years of association, working and thinking together, and of a group of harmonising minds and hearts. The glorious thing is that it has happened – before it was too late.

It is so difficult to talk of Newbold Revel,[1] since I was the central victim of it. . . . (The toasting and the tributes to me, and the spoiling and the kindness were all so much, much more than I had bargained for that I feel a fraud, and I feel emotionally bruised, having run such a gauntlet. Percy Wilson,[2] by the way, entreated me to stay till next July – assuring me I could do and go just where I liked! – but I have held to my decision.)

I will tell you this, Edith: NEVER have I had such a chance to communicate to colleagues from the whole of England and Wales not only the spirit and quality of Oxfordshire but of H.M.I. relationships with teachers and the L.E.A. I spoke openly about the force of H.M.I.'s involvement and the dire need for him to teach, to originate ideas and to nourish growth. This was all new ground (or, rather, thin ice!), but it proved right to dare to tread it. I prepared the central lecture very carefully, and this was to have been taped; however, it will be distributed to all colleagues, and if one would interest you, you shall have one.

The Tower Hill (Basil's class only) exhibition was set up by Geoffrey, and it was marvellous. I put up Langford, and it shook people to the core. As text to my lecture I put up a large, cool exhibition entirely after my own heart. One could call it 'The English Idiom'. It was touching to see how *excited* H.M.I.s were to see what Oxfordshire now almost takes for granted!

We had a wonderful session looking at transparencies of North and West Oxon. schools – indoors and outdoors – and of dozens of Dartington and other exhibitions I have put up for teachers.

We rejoiced at the wonderfully genuine original music and verse of Ted Haycroft's and Basil's children. I hope the tape will be lent for next week's National Music Course.

I had to say a long piece about you and the advisory teachers, and the physical provision, and my relationship with you all, and what goes on at The Lamb and O.C.F. and Waterloo and many other places!

Of opposition there was *none*: rather, if I must be absolutely truthful, of movedness at the whole story – the story of children transcending their 'innate intelligence' (sic!), of happy teachers who know where they are in a world where there is no sense of 'us' and 'them', of men and women developing their own gifts and living kindly and beautifully and non-competitively. Your ears must have burned! Oxfordshire is for it! . . .

It really was a tremendously significant week, a chance of a lifetime. . . . The work involved was tremendous. (We were taking down exhibitions at 5.30 a.m. on Friday! Geoffrey was wonderfully good at wangling difficult display problems. We had to roll up a vast pink and blue and mauve carpet because we couldn't stand it! but Rev. Mother forgave us – and even for removing a crucifix!)

But I feel so glad I've been able to tell the story of what we stand for that I'm not tired. Inside I find myself almost sobbing, yet I feel inspired to go further at Woolley and Liverpool. The weight of physical labour alone in the next three weeks is going to be heavy – but those magical hill towns of Umbria and the shining profile of Mont Blanc loom in the distance and goad me on. A blessed holiday to you, dear Edith. Always staunchly at your side, and with love.

Robin.

---

1. A teachers' training college where courses and conferences for serving teachers and for HMIs were held.
2. HMI, Senior Chief Inspector.

LETTER 88

To David Evans.

Peisey-Nancroix, Haute Tarentaise, Savoie.
[30th August, 1964]

Picture the scene, David. We arrived in the evening of the 27th, hot (and I somewhat alarmed!) after the hazardous journey over the little St Bernard Pass (why has no one told us there is a fine wild Botanic Garden at the top of the Pass, on the French side?), and Colette greeted us with kisses and handed me your letter. 'Who is it from?' I asked. 'Ees it vrom Dehveede?' she instantly exclaimed; and when during dinner I showed her your message she was delighted and asked me to give you all her love. It is good to be back. The 'roaring peace' of the river below; the great white hulk of Mont Blanc; the ice-cold dry wine called Apremont, and the marvellous rough velvety red *vin du pays* . . . and the figs and peaches and melons; *les escargots*, the amazingly varied cheeses; the women in *frontière* headdresses (like haloes) scything steep hillsides; the goats and their bells; all the casual, happy life of this untidy precipitous village – the old enchantment has flooded back after two years most abundantly. Here we can re-think our Italian adventures, which really were incredible – largely because we chose the little used, unsurfaced white roads that took us up and up, into a biblical rocky land of olives and cypresses – settings for the Good Samaritan and the Garden of Gethsemane. Lizards – transparent in the sun – would dart across the track. We would meet women carrying loads of fodder on their heads, and good-looking almost naked men working among the vines and melons and maize. We searched for one of the greatest pictures in the world – Piero della Francesca's memorial to his mother (he took her name because his father died before he was born). At last we found the lonely cemetery chapel that holds it and nothing else – high up a baked hillside at the end of a grove of cypresses – and a young brown country boy stood on guard while we adored this great classically beautiful woman, her right hand pointing to her pregnant womb through a vent in her skirt. It was worth all our deviations and adventures to find it. We have seen remarkably beautiful paintings by Fra Angelico, Fra Lippo Lippi, Duccio, Lorinzetti, Raphael, Sodoma and many other of my loves. And we have got to know incredibly fine buildings such as Spoleto cathedral – Spoleto (next to Siena) I love most, I think, of all the towns we visited. But you would have loved the walled hill towns, such as Todi, Gubbio and Montepulciano, too. Yes: one day we *must* all see Italy together! . . .

It is the *human* situations I share very specially with you, for you more than anyone else would 'get' them. Picture this one, for instance: Yesterday we followed a properly marked route (red paint spots on rocks, *à la* Hansel and Gretel) which gave us a wonderful day on the heights. We gathered marvellous flowers and ate a heavenly lunch, in full sun because the breeze kept the air cool and sweet. But the descent was shocking; it was nearly perpendicular, with a terrible gorge below! So when at last the ordeal was over we went to a primitive cottage 'café' to buy Vichy. The woman (in *frontière* headdress) brought us into the cool, dark interior, and her son – a brown chamois of a young man – joined us. He said he was our postman; and sure enough, there among the aubergines being prepared for the evening meal on the bench where we sat lay a letter from George! He wouldn't give it to us then; it had to be duly delivered. He talked of his rounds in the mountains, and told us of a hermit – a man of 40 only, 'with big blue eyes' – who refuses to see anyone at all except in the winter, and even then he rarely speaks. Our postman said he keeps bees and grinds his own flour, and 'lives on that'. Conversation turned to headdress, and a mentally defective woman was sent to unearth an old, treasured *frontière*, which we duly admired. Our postman (wearing only the barest of briefs) rummaged among cupboards for old photographs of relatives in Tarentaise costume. Two old men now joined the party. We were cross-examined, and had to tell our whole life histories. Even the brown, belled goats appeared to listen. It was difficult to get away. Clearly this had been for these folk the event of the day. Just as we were going the naked postman ran out to ask what I was carrying under my arm, and I was forced to show him the drawing I had done a few hours before of silver Mont Blanc with our perilous zig zag Pass before it, and the black peaks all round. He nearly went mad with pleasure, and we had to go inside again, and everyone in the place gathered round to see! . . . At night, after a fabulous dinner, our host gave us all a hot infusion of Génépi – a rare, woolly herb that grows alongside edelweiss, and which is used for the local liqueur. He had gathered the plants two days before, among the snow. The scent and taste were wonderful, native, wild and compelling. We felt at last that we were real, genuine Savoyards! . . .

The parting at Christmas – there is no finality in it for us. True, I can no longer share my own growth and foster yours, in the same official way; and I must leave the field open and clear for my successor anyhow. But what you and I have built up together we can – albeit subtly – continue to build on. Thirty full years as an H.M.I. have left me in need of a tremendous spring clean – both physical and spiritual! And that will take a month or so. But soon I shall be ready for all that comes. And if you and I continue to have need of each other – as is certain – fresh ways of meeting that need will show themselves. (I have never believed, even, in 'till Death do us part'. Not even death can make final what has been *really* alive.) So you and I need never worry, David. The marvellous day-to-day contact and involvement in school has to go; but I shall use all the art I can muster to contrive frequent meetings – days at O.C.F., with more poetry and music, Sherborne visits, courses, joint excursions and . . . occasional nights again at The Lamb. . . .

It would be a great satisfaction to me – as I think it would be to you – if, next term, we could escape together for an evening alone; then we could talk over, at leisure, plans for next year – and the next – and the next . . . Sometimes I protest at the accident of chronology that places me sixteen or so years ahead (I shall be nearly 80, I suppose, when you retire!), but yet I see that even *that* is right. Out of just that difference of generation has come the very quality we call 'Dartington' or 'Oxfordshire', which I like to think has brought about a bigger revolution among us all than any other factor. So instead of really protesting I rejoice and am thankful. . . .

Heather, Diet and Faith send their love to you all, with mine.

A sundrenched and happy Robin!

LETTER 89

Undated; written just before Robin Tanner's retirement in December 1964.

Royal Oxford Hotel.

Dearest Nan and David [Evans],

Together, you have done so much to make my last days as an H.M.I. rich and easy and full of hope for the future that you must be the first I write to today. Staying those two nights with you did much to soften the blow for me, and I shall always look back on them with a sense of warm comfort and peace. These last weeks have unfolded very beautifully – just as I had dared to hope they might; and you must know how deeply I realise that behind much of the subtle planning is your kindly, imaginative thought. In fact, over the years – these wonderful vintage years – always you two have been at the very centre, and I love and honour you for your steadfast care and generosity of spirit and your unsurpassable hospitality. I could never repay you, though in the good years ahead I shall try to.

I expect Bill will tell you of the dreadfully difficult drive to Edie's, and of the very happy gathering there afterwards. The house and surroundings one couldn't see, of course; but it is splendidly planned, extremely spacious (far too much room for one person, really), gracious, carefully worked out, and altogether delightful. You will like it very much – especially the large central room, with its 'sun room' attached.

All the 'Office' people were there, and after drinks and modest 'eats' we sang carols by candlelight round Edward Barnsley's perfect table. Then the Chairman of the Education Committee said nice things about me and presented me with an extravagant bunch of record tokens – to my utter amazement! I felt rather a fraud, and that they ought to have gone to Edith! They shall buy, among other things, Britten's *War Requiem*.

The exotic 'Home Sweet Home' nearby provided an excellent dinner, ending with lemon syllabubs! And a moonlight night greeted us afterwards – though it became foggy again near Oxford. I only hope Bill got home safely. It pours with rain at the moment. . . .

All my love.
Robin.

The following piece of verse is a tribute to the teachers Robin Tanner worked with and, though not a letter, a fitting conclusion to this section.

OXFORDSHIRE TEACHERS

They came together by no particular plan,
From Pembroke, Yorkshire, Sidcup, Glamorgan,
And Midland England, to man the schools of these villages –
Langford, in the flat and elmy country of William Morris,

Its church amazing with Saxon sculpture;
And Cotswold Filkins, more Gloucestershire than Oxford,
Compact and grey, about its winding roadways;
Leafield, with a still lingering sinister gypsy feeling –
A grey encampment in the Forest clearing –
The Forest of Wychwood, long since denuded;
Milton-under-Wychwood and Shipton-under-Wychwood,
Poetically perfect as their names.

No particular plan: and yet I dare to think
Some strange design brought these young men together;
Some common bond beyond the accidental,
Their five acutely different personalities
Sharing a common purpose and reaching to the same ideals.

Pembroke gave one a voice all will stop to hear,
Whether in church or inn or on the cricket field;
Founded him on a rock, steady and serene
Gave him an unquenchable love of poetry.

The Riding left its mark upon another –
Tough, yet compassionate, with Pennine hospitality;
Warm and spontaneous, full of affection.

The man from Glamorgan would have you believe
He is just an easy, jocular fellow: popular everywhere,
'The life and soul of the party'.
He was born under a kind star; he is plumbing still
His own depths, and finding still his own gifts –
Though his hobby is finding them in others.

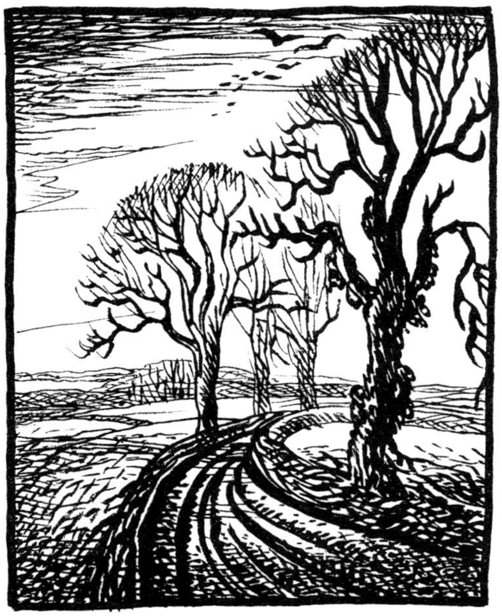

5

1965–1987

This section covers, roughly, the period from Robin Tanner's retirement at the end of 1964 to the publication of *Double Harness* in 1987. Because of the large number of letters, they have been arranged thematically under six headings – etching, calligraphy, primary education, natural history, exhibitions and art galleries, the Crafts Study Centre, and poetry.

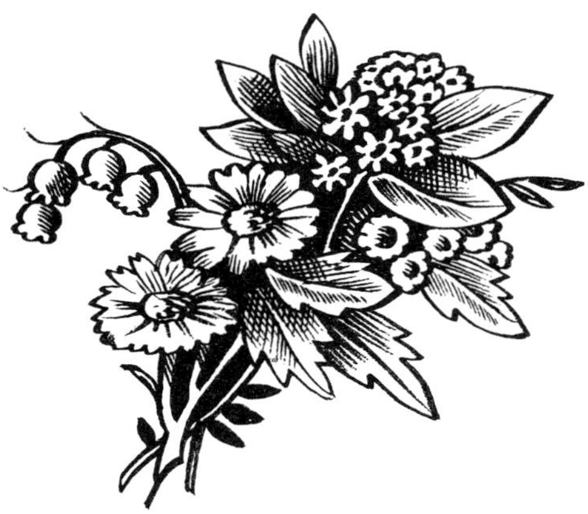

Etching

LETTER 90

[13th March, 1972]

Dear Cecil,
The man who wants to buy my complete etched work is one Raymond Lister. On the dust cover of a book on Craftsmen in Metal which he has written and given to me, he is described as 'a director of GEO. LISTER & SONS, architectural metalworkers, of Cambridge'. He must wait till the autumn for my work, I'm afraid, as demands on our time are terrific. . . .

LETTER 91

This and the following six letters are all to Raymond Lister.

[3rd March, 1972]

Dear Mr Lister,
Your kind letter gives me the opportunity to thank you for writing *Samuel Palmer and his Etchings*, which I always hope has gone a long way to correct the notion that after Shoreham, Palmer petered out. I shall never quite recover from the tremendous impact the etchings made on me when I saw them first – with the Shoreham drawings – at the V. & A. Exhibition in 1926. True, they haven't the exuberant, daring, impassioned feel of the earlier work, but to me they are the perfect, deep, mellow flowering of S.P.'s maturity. (We only possess *Opening the Fold* and *The Homeward Star* which A.H.P. completed – both printed at Campden, but the former was considered by F.L.G.[1] to be the best impression printed, according to his marginal note.) It is good to hear from David Gould that you are preparing Palmer's letters for publication.

I have only etched seventeen plates, and am working on the eighteenth now. You see, from 1935 to 1964, when I retired, I worked as an H.M.I., which was a most enjoyable and creative job but was too absorbing to allow of much etching. Now again I etch obsessively, though my way of working is necessarily slow, and, I am afraid there will be only one print of mine in the R.P.-E.[2] show this month. . . .

I think it would be best for you perhaps to come here one day in the autumn – if that is not too far off – to look at my small opus at leisure.

Yours sincerely,
Robin Tanner.

---

1. F.L. Griggs.
2. Royal Society of Painter-Etchers and Engravers.

LETTER 92

[5th January, 1973]

Dear Raymond – if I may so address you,
We returned to find your letter last evening from spending the day with Nina Griggs, looking at F.L.G.'s Campden drawings, his tender watercolours, his own commonplace book and many other inspiring treasures. I had taken Nina a print of my little *June* plate, which she particularly likes; and we fell to thinking about 1976 – the centenary of Fred's birth – and hoping there will be a great exhibition of his work that year. She rightly feels the R.A. would be the place. These occasions demand long and careful preparation. I wonder if anyone has the idea in mind?

Your encouraging letter made me very happy. . . . I was sure our Bath project would greatly interest you. All those craftsmen you mention are friends of ours, and in textiles and pots the Collection is quite exceptionally rich. So far, the only examples of metal, wood and fine printing we possess are those listed in the catalogue. . . .

How good to hear of your craftsman background: your manifold activities and interests and achievements confound and shame me! I've just ordered your *Calvert* monograph and *British Romantic Art*, both of which we greatly look forward to.

Do you know, I was re-reading the vivid, arrogant, prejudiced but captivating Cobbett just when you were! He still holds me.

But please remove our ignorance: I'm ashamed to say we do not know Jas. Smetham's letters and memoranda. About F. Kilvert we are prejudiced, of course, since every lane and meadow here is recorded in his diary. We little knew, when we built our cottage 42 years ago, just where we were placing it.

Yes: Kilvert's preoccupation with flagellation and little girls has to be reckoned with, though it must be said that Wm. Plomer's selection from the original MSS probably gives an unbalanced view of the diarist. Regrettably, when W.P. had returned the original to its owner he burnt his own full typescript copy – little knowing that nearly all of the original diary (in 24 notebooks) would soon be destroyed also. Heather and I have read the only notebook that escaped, and it is full of marvellous passages that W.P. did not use. And the odd tendencies are entirely absent. . . .

We send you both our warm greetings for 1973, and it will be good to see you here in Spring.

Robin.

LETTER 93

[23rd January, 1973]

Dear Raymond,

Only a word to thank you for your kind letter. We pulled a proof of *White Violets* – the P.C.C.[1] plate – yesterday. This etching has been as straightforward as *The Clapper Bridge* was awkward; I shan't even need to lay a second ground; I must add a few pecks and tiny lines with a graver, and lightly reduce one small passage with a burnisher, and that is all. It is an enormous relief!

All you say about 'feel' and 'scent' is very close to me; maybe my sense of smell is a bit over-developed! for my family and friends tease me when I speak of the scent of so-called scentless things like glass, rice, paper, china, silver, blades of grass, dandelion leaves, shells . . . Yes, indeed: all the needling, biting, stopping out and printing of etchings I love as part of the whole strange experience. When mixing my ink yesterday I realised with acute pleasure that Frankfurt Black has a different smell from heavy French Black, and Venetian Red (of which I always add a pinch) has its own odour too. I may be mad! but in this rather harmful world mine is at least a harmless delight.

We, too, love Paul Drury's early work, and I wish I could persuade him to return to the pastoral theme. He comes here every year, and we talk about this, but he always seems too preoccupied to start again. He has a brilliant mind, and could have been as fine a musician as he is an artist. We have his pastoral plates, the most moving of which I think is *September*, which you reproduced in your Palmer book. We have a few of the portraits, too, which I find quite marvellous.

Robin.

---

1. Print Collectors' Club.

LETTER 94

[4th April, 1975]

My dear Raymond,

I like to think that your letter was travelling from east to west while mine was travelling from west to east: it's nice that each was thinking of the other at the same time. Letters that 'cross' give me a special kind of pleasure.

I am so glad that, by and large, the reviews of your Palmer biography have been so understanding and encouraging. . . . Geoffrey Grigson must often feel single and alone, for so often his is the only bitter and punishing review of a book. . . . Yet if you met G.G. you would find him warm and easy and compelling and entirely delightful. Let me know if you've not been able to get hold of Alethea Hayter's review, and I will send you ours. Her *Opium and the Romantic Imagination* is on our list: we look forward to reading it.

I wish I felt I lived up to the kind things you say about my etchings. I'm afraid I again felt at the Painter-Etchers' show like an old-fashioned countryman among smart, sophisticated, up-to-the-minute city dwellers. Yes, indeed, Raymond: my brothers are Bloomfield and Clare and that Wiltshireman Stephen Duck, and Hudson and Hardy and Edward Thomas and dear Wm. Barnes, and even our odd Richard Jefferies. And I revere the Georgics; and *The Land* Heather and I have loved and known almost by heart ever since we bought it when it was first published 49 years ago. It is a sadly under-rated book. We love *The Garden* too (which penetrates deeper, in some ways), but not quite as we love *The Land.* Reading V.S-W.'s son's *Portrait of a Marriage* in no way upset our judgement either.

Oddly, several people who bought my *November* at the R.P.–E. said they linked it with some of my blood-brothers I've just named! And I suppose that as we grow older we grow more like ourselves, so heaven knows what my future plates will be like!

We expect to print again this month. I hope you won't mind waiting for your prints. Perhaps we can bring them to you, we should love to come to see you one day, as you suggest. . . .

Yes: if I ever finish celebrating the months it would be good to do the seasons in the way you suggest – but only for the sake of doing it, I'm afraid: very few people would buy such a book. I am of course fortunate in that, apart from helping our Bath project forward, I have no desire to earn money by my work, and this makes me feel free to etch exactly what and as I please. We prefer to live simply, as you found us. . . . So it would never greatly worry me if I produced work which no one would buy!

It interests me – and I think this will interest you – that some of our avant garde and fashionable young painters are coming to view traditional work with warm feelings. For example, . . . Peter Blake, who lives near, actually bought one of the sets of my etchings and declares they mean a lot to him! This was a huge surprise! . . .

LETTER 95

[4th April, 1976]

Dear Raymond,
It was good to have your letter and it was lovely to see you both at that great gathering at the Ashmolean. It is a memorable exhibition, yet it has left me with three disappointments. First, I had expected to see a case containing some of F.L.G.'s letters, his beautiful commonplace book, even his handsome account book – all in his marvellous handwriting – and perhaps one or two of his exquisite silver-point drawings. Then, surely, for a great etcher's centenary exhibition the University could have afforded a worthy catalogue instead of a typed list. Lastly, how nice it would have been if the gathering could have

opened with a tribute to Griggs, spoken by, say, Francis Comstock or you or Ian Lowe.

Robin.

LETTER 96

[10th March, 1978]

My dear Raymond,
Many thanks for your letter and cheque. You cannot know how much your and Pamela's encouragement and understanding of what I try to say on copper mean to me. Etching is essentially a solitary job, though for me there is always Heather's wonderful sympathy. For the most part, though, one is alone with one's idea and an intimidating sheet of copper; and one knows that one's skill can never match one's vision. So, in a sense, every new plate is another failure! But you and other friends, because of the warmth of your appreciation, goad me on, and I am happy!

Robin Garton wishes I would do some plates for Gray's *Elegy*, which he would like to publish as a choice piece of typography with the original etchings. Actually I have often thought I should like to illustrate the *Elegy* – perhaps an etching epitomising it, and three or four smaller plates relative to particular stanzas. So perhaps after etching *December* I'll have a try.

All the reviews I've read of the Blake exhibition excite me, and we are planning to have *an entire day* at the Tate! As you say, such a marvellous venture is not likely to happen again for many a long day. So few people, I find, can 'take' Blake as he longed to be taken: I hope this great display will establish him more universally. I suppose he is the most essentially *English* of all our artists! I long to see the temperas. . . .

Our warm love to you both, and my special gratitude for all your understanding.

Robin.

LETTER 97

[24th December, 1978]

My dear Raymond,

. . . On Tuesday I took my plate to the Dickensian, unique establishment, Thos. Ross & Son, at East Putney, to be steel-faced, but first I went to the V. & A., reaching it at opening time. For the first half hour I was alone with Samuel Palmer, and even when I left an hour later only a small sprinkling of people were there. Raymond, I was overwhelmed, amazed and deeply moved. It is a far more telling and convincing exhibition (and exposition too) than even I had expected. No one can be in doubt any more. Let people now unlearn what Geoffrey Grigson has taught them and, instead, come face to face with the mature, mellowed and marvellously inspired Palmer! Those large watercolour and gouache paintings amazed and shook me. And to see so much of the inner workings of S.P.'s mind was a great experience. And to read those letters and to pore over the portrait drawings and photographs was good. And what a catalogue! And what facsimiles! I'm afraid I bought extravagantly.

I have a vivid memory of the 1926 exhibition: this is far more beautiful and more convincing. . . . I came away from it exalted but chastened. Here am I, an old and obscure etcher, with only 29 mostly indifferent plates to show for my long life of loving England. What an example this genius set me! I really must use my last years to produce something better. S.P.'s dogged singlemindedness and perfectionism shame me. *I* have too many interests, and I nearly said too many friends – but that would be ungrateful and ungenerous. (More than 300 have written recently, and of course I shall reply to every one. But a day is a mere nothing, yet I can't work more quickly.) I don't grumble, however: I just tell myself I'm fortunate, and I must regard etching as just one of my interests. . . .

Kind Robin Garton drove me from Lancashire Court to East Putney and on to Paddington through a London *solid* with cars!

Our love to you both,
Robin.

The next group of letters (98–102) are all to Michael Blaker.

LETTER 98

[3rd October, 1983]

Dear Michael,
Many thanks for your letter, which was waiting for me on our return from Pembrokeshire. Living in a silent, empty countryside, with deep ferny lanes, cromlechs, wild untamed coast, marvellously green hills and valleys, and 'old-fashioned' ways, made us feel we were back in 1923! It was a perfect holiday.

Yes, indeed: the death of the Elms was an appalling disaster.* The regeneration here is quite astonishing; some young trees are already 12–14 feet high. Will they, I wonder, prove resistant? I hope the etching will give you some pleasure. I usually print on a warmer paper, but this particular plate responds better to a stark white.

With good wishes for your work on Suffolk.

Robin.

Your Caravan delights everyone who sees it.

* Friends who live in France (Lot et Garonne) say their elms are now rapidly dying, alas.

LETTER 99

[7th October, 1983]

Dear Michael,
Although I know your very kind letter needs no reply, there are one or two things I should like to tell you before 'this correspondence is closed', as they say!

I'm so glad that *December* is giving you and Catriona pleasure, but more than that I find your sensitive understanding of it most heartwarming. We all thrive on praise, and praise from a fellow etcher is particularly encouraging. You have got right inside that *December* design; it took me nearly a year to realise it, and none of my work has been wasted on you. My grateful thanks.

Because I work slowly, and because Etching is but one of my many activities, I have nothing to send to the autumn R.P.-E. show, but I hope to have two small plates ready by next spring. . . .

LETTER 100

[14th February, 1985]

Dear Michael,

Your zest and youthful creative energy fill me with admiration! It was MOST kind of you virtually to take me to the R.E. show, and I'm very grateful. I must confess that I expected no one to 'get' what I was trying so hard to say in *January* and *April*, so it astounds, delights, and reassures and heartens me that you have. It is quite uncanny. Heather and Dietrich were as glad as I when I read your reactions. I shall be very glad to print an impression of *April* for you both – though it may be many months before I get round to it, the days and weeks and months are so full. But I shall not forget. . . .

It is splendid that the Beresford House Press is being born. I find the tradition of the English Private Press most endearing. If we three were half our age I think one called The Old Chapel Field Press might well come into being! And the Monograph of your work which you propose seems most appropriate. . . .

Robin Garton has given me that vast Catalogue Raisonné of Seymour Haden's work by Robert Schneidermann. What a man he was! We owe more to men like him and Cameron than we care to admit. I shall look forward to the next issue of the Journal. . . .

We send greetings and best wishes to you both.

Robin.

[19th June, 1985]

Dear Michael,

Your book is a delight from start to finish. We three are greatly enjoying it. Your versatility is amazing. So is your freshness and your spontaneity. Men like Whistler and S.H. would give you high praise, surely. It is your ready response to your experiences that you convey so convincingly. 'What a *happy* life this etcher must be having!' remarked a neighbour on turning over the pages of your book. In a sense it is, of course, a self-portrait, and a very telling one too.

The portraits (which are new to us) are lovely. I didn't know this was one of your interests. Nor did I know that Brighton meant so much to you. Your ability to record truthfully is something I should like to possess, for however hard I try I always seem to 'tannerise' everything I draw! I could never be relied on, typographically, I'm afraid: there is something lacking in me.

I found your Introduction so absorbing and vital that I was disappointed when it ended after three pages: I should have liked thirty-three.

Anyhow, Michael, it's a splendid record of a fine, dedicated etcher, and I hope many people will buy it. More etchers should follow your example, though I can well understand why they shrink from facing the vagaries of printers and the uncertainty of sales.

I rejoiced to find you honour Méryon so highly. I absolutely agree with you. *Le Stryge* was the first work of his I saw (when I was a student), and it knocked me out! Then I met *La Galerie de Notre Dame*, which I loved even more, then that odd little *Rue des Mauvais Garçons* and finally *La Morgue*. I feel exactly as you do about that immortal masterpiece. Strangely, few people have ever heard of Charles Méryon! It is a curious world! . . .

We all three send deep thanks and Loving Greetings to you both.

Robin.

We loved hearing about C20 Victorian Rochester! We can clearly visualise you both, dressed for the occasion, and making music. What an unusually happy community spirit for a *town* to achieve! It's easy enough in a village. *David Copperfield* will always be one of my favourite books.

As you may imagine, I was particularly delighted to find your group of what people are pleased to call pastoral etchings – *Amberley Cottages*, *Kentish Oast-house in August*, and the Flatford and Sudbury ones, and the delicious *Morning in the Weald*. I find them most evocative, true to the real 'English' feeling, and therefore very moving.

R.

LETTER 102

[31st July, 1985]

Dear Michael and Catriona,
Your exciting package arrived when Heather was making jelly with the last of our redcurrants, Dietrich was extracting honey from his bees, and I was working at the ninth of the 26 designs for our new book; so we waited until lunch-time for a celebratory opening.

I shall always have a special admiration for what I know I couldn't possibly do myself. The swift and delightful spontaneity and sense of *joie de vivre* conveyed in *Oast-house in August* immediately struck us, and already the print has given us *great* pleasure. I love that outrageously Blakerised tree! You are becoming as naughty as Robin Tanner! I think the way in which you let it embrace the entire composition is quite masterly. The gentle washes are perfect. The feeling of quiet peace is deeply realised. We've examined it carefully and talked about it a great deal. Thank you so much for sharing the experience with us.

One of my keenest pleasures is to sit with an old solander case, in which we keep our small collection of etchings. We frame very few, preferring to enjoy each one, individually and at close quarters – often, in fact, under a lens. . . . Your work is part of that dearly loved collection, and it will often be taken out and enjoyed by us and our friends.

Watching that marvellous flotilla of old ships must have been a stirring experience, and I hope some extraordinary plates will emerge as a result. We are so inland and leafy here that Chatham feels like another world. As a student I once stayed there with a fellow student called Friend, whose father (in the early 20s) was a well known Ship's Chandler. (That name for a grocer fascinated me.) . . .

Again, our warmest thanks, and Loving Greetings to you both.

Robin.

The remaining letters in this sub-section are to various correspondents.

LETTER 103

[begun 5th May, 1971]

My dear Cecil,

. . . How very sweet (and noble) of you to go to the R.P.-E. show! I was very touched. If you would like to have it Heather and I would be very pleased to pull a print of *The Meadow Stile* for you, i.e. as soon as we are vouchsafed a clear week for printing. It doesn't happen to be many people's favourite. Three people bought *June*, two wanted to buy *Wiltshire Rickyard*, but the plate wore badly, and I wasn't able to print more than six decent impressions. It was *Easter* that called forth most comment, and gave me quite a 'fan mail'! Though one person found it 'a bit claustrophobic' – which it is, of course! I always remember first reading those magical words in The Song of Solomon:

'A garden enclosed is my sister, my spouse . . .'

– And A Garden Enclosed is my paradise, my pastoral England! Not for me the wind on the heath, the great open spaces! I abhor a vacuum. All must be clothed and bosky and rich and perfect, with not a space at all!! My next plates (if I live to complete them!) will be even more so! A lot of people quite unknown to me wrote to say my things gave them pleasure: a bank manager at Blackheath, for example, and a strange person at Sotheby's . . . It was encouraging. Boston (Mass.) art gallery acquired two prints of each plate for their collection. I wish I could get started again, but we have had a weary succession of interruptions and unexpected, timetaking happenings. . . .

[29th February, 1972]

Dear David [Gould],
I have Raymond Lister's book on Palmer's etched work, and was of course grateful to him for going some way to counter G.G.'s arrogant assertion that after Shoreham Palmer was 'dead'. I feel that those plates – while less exuberant and impassioned than the marvellous early work – are a unique flowering of his genius at its mature height. But then: I am what is called old and square!

It touches me that you and Raymond Lister and the Ashmolean and Boston and a lot of friends should care about my work. No: *The Print Collector's Quarterly* only carried occasional advertisement reproductions of my earliest etchings! And the only complete collections will be at Oxford and Boston.

It is fine to be able to look forward to Sam. Palmer's letters; these too, I hope, will help to correct the oddly wrong impression generally held about the man.

I'm afraid *Wiltshire Village* is very hard to come by now. Ian Lowe has just told us of his frantic pursuit of a nice copy listed by an antiquarian bookseller; six other people had written for it, but he had also sent a telegram, and that was opened first! I still have the drawings, and shall give them to the Ashmolean. For 30 years Heather and I have been working at a book on the wild woodland plants of England: with so many other interests and demands on us it is still far from complete, but one day you might care to see the 60 drawings I've done towards it. I've 25 more to do, and Heather has written only about a quarter of the book.

I've forced myself at last to make a detailed catalogue of my etchings; they are very few; I'm working on the eighteenth only at the moment, and am taking one I've just finished up to the R.P.-E. show tomorrow. Then there are two more designs which I'm longing to work out, but I see no leisure ahead until September. . . .

I will enclose a list of my plates, and I'm sure it would be best for you to look at them at leisure at some time. We used different names for two we used in *Wiltshire Village*: Kington Borel is *Christmas* and Maslin Farm Chapel is *Alington in Wiltshire.* If you could wait until early autumn I could be certain to have decent prints of all the plates for you and Raymond Lister to see. . . .

LETTER 105

[10th January, 1973]

My dear Edith,

At last here is your print of *Flowers of May.* I had hoped we might meet here so that you could take it with you, but I am plunged in urgent work for some weeks. The Royal Society of Painter-Etchers has for 100 years run the Print Collectors' Club; you pay an annual subscription which entitles you to attend lectures and exhibitions, and every year an artist is chosen to etch the presentation plate. Each member is given one, and the artist himself must print this limited edition of 150 impressions. Alas! just before Christmas the blow fell on me. The etching has to be exhibited in the annual R.P.-E. exhibition in March, so although my design is only 5″ × 4″ it is a full-time job. Heather and I rather dread printing the entire edition. Oh for a life of ease and leisure! However, I'm well, and I love the work, and I hope my white violets (with a path beyond through a beech wood) will give some pleasure. When the job's done we'll celebrate! We really will! . . .

Please forgive this scrap of a letter. I must get back to needling little fronds of moss dipping into water: very tricky indeed.

We all three send warm love and every splendid kind of wish for 1973. Think of it! In eleven or twelve weeks your swallows will return! We are all owls, pheasants and barking foxes at the moment.

Much love,
Heather, Dietrich, Robin.

LETTER 106

[24th February, 1973]

Dear David [Gould],
Please forgive my long delay; Heather and I are up to our eyes in printing, drying and pressing proofs off the little Print Collectors' Club plate; we're almost halfway through the 170 required, but a lot of work still lies ahead.

First, about the prints you asked for. I'll try to find *Alington in Wiltshire* (syn. 'Maslin Farm Chapel') and *Martin's Hovel* among my meagre collection of those very early etchings, though I can't be certain that I still have perfect prints left. I have *Hedge Flowers* ready for you.

You asked about early states of *White Violets* (i.e. the P.C.C. plate). By some strange good fortune there was no need to lay a second ground: apart from a few pecks with a graver it seemed as satisfactory as I could make it, so there is virtually only one state. Such luck has never come my way before! . . .

Heather and I find it quite impossible to print with someone else present. I'm afraid we bolt the doors and put out notices against all comers when we are at it! Our kitchen, printing room and two bedrooms have to be used, and any third person would be a great hindrance.

When we've finished this huge job, you must come and see us. I'll write again as soon as I see a chance.

Greetings from us both.
Robin.

LETTER 107

[28th October, 1973]

My dear Cecil,
. . . I'm so glad Simon liked *Flowers of May*. I'm working at another flower-piece at the moment, but it's very difficult. It sounds simple enough. A cup filled with firstlings – aconites, snowdrops, the first primrose, and so on – stands on a wooden window sill. Outside the tempest rages, with rain and worse. It will be called *February*. That is, if I can get the copper for it! There is a world famine, and the price is now little less than for silver!! A great

bombshell has just been delivered by my etching suppliers: all the materials I use have been raised by from 33⅓% to 50% in price, and handmade linen rag papers (I only use these) are actually doubled! (*Flowers of May* uses a piece that now costs 60p, and as few prints are perfect enough to sell that sometimes means as much as £2.40 for one print!) All my powders and the fish oil I use to make my printing ink, and the various degrees of wiping canvas, and the wax grounds and acids and stopping-out varnish and sponges and pumice powder and the like have rocketed in price. So alas! Cecil, I am forced to increase the price of my work by 25%. . . .

The Holburne Museum in Bath wants a show one day, and I'm often asked to lend a work, but rarely have ready anything decently framed. I've a good and biddable framer nearby . . .

And now to work again – this time burnishing out a piece of over-bitten sky in my gypsy caravan etching: a slow, subtle job which I have never mastered properly.

My love as always. We still laugh together about our easy, satisfying Cambridge reunion.

Robin.

LETTER 108

[7th November, 1973]

My dear Jim [Fairbairn],
I used to think that in old age I should no longer need the stimulus of praise or appreciation of my work; yet I find I still thrive on it! And the quite extraordinary understanding that you show of my old-fashioned, bucolic etchings is most warming and encouraging. You say about them exactly what I hoped people might say – though they rarely do. And it makes me so happy if, by some lines scratched on copper, I am able to communicate and share what I feel and live for. I've just finished *Full Moon*, which apparently people think is my best – or most 'heavily charged' plate yet. If you find you like it when next you are here I should like to give you an impression. *The Plough* (a gypsy caravan under the seven stars) is nearly finished, too; and I'm working obsessively at designs for *January* and *November*. (Last year I was elected a

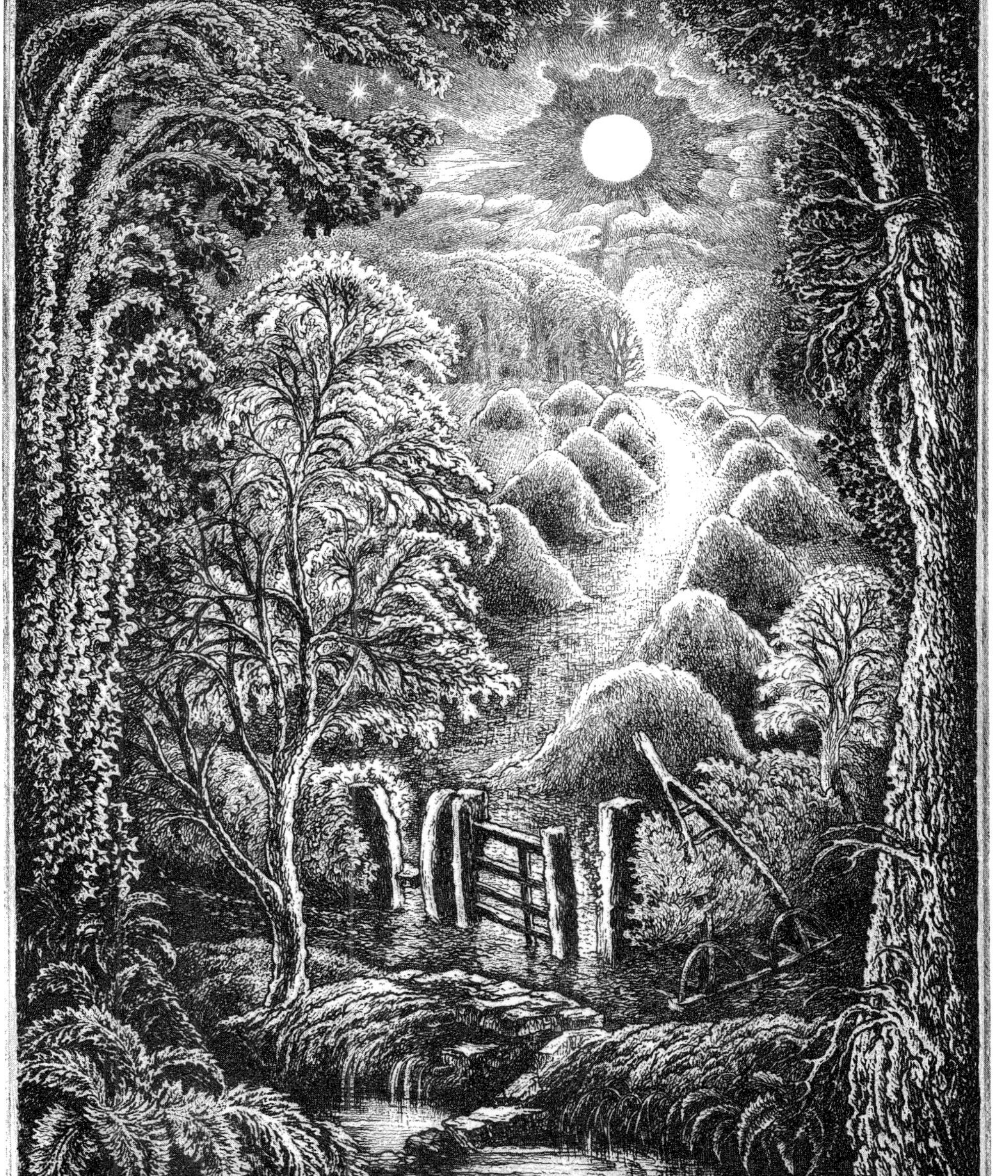

Full Moon, 1973.

Senior Fellow of the Royal Society of Painter-Etchers, and I feel I must try to justify such approval by producing freely, at any rate!)

The flowers in *Flowers of May* – all of which are wild, and some of which are rare – are Oxlip, Burnet Rose, Lily-of-the-Valley, Snowflake (Leucojum), Snakeshead Fritillary, Cathartic Flax, Germander Speedwell and Daisy. The violin-like coils are Hartstongue Ferns. . . .

LETTER 109

[15th January, 1974]

My dear Cecil,

. . . After a good deal of pressure, I'm afraid, I've agreed to Joe Graffy's proposal to publish my etchings and to let there be a full catalogue (as it is called) of my work. This book is intended to be the first in a series on English etchers. (Joe, who first read English at Oxford . . . now runs the Penn Print Room. He deals in English etchings and rare books. He is a generous friend of the Ashmolean. We three like him and his wife very much.) The plan seems to be to have, first, an exhibition of work from about 1820 onwards – in various good provincial museums, notably Kendal, York and Norwich and Bristol and Bath. Then Joe, rather grandly, wants to issue sets of, say, twelve of my etchings, each set in a solander case made specially for them, and with a catalogue. But single prints would also be available. It is only an *idea* at present. In any case, a good printer would have to be found for the large plates. H. and I could only cope with the small ones. At our age, and in this small house, printing editions is no joke. Whatever happens, I fear my wish to be anonymous and unknown is going to be shattered. My *only* reason for etching is because I must: I can't help it. But I'm being assailed on all sides. Nicholas Lott of Hampshire has just bought a few of my prints (at daft, astronomical prices in Albemarle Street) and wants information about them for a show of Romantic Art. Every week or so now, someone or other writes – or appears on the doorstep. It is time we both bought a telly, voted Tory, put our feet up, dozed every afternoon and did no work! But we're both cast in a totally different mould. Heather's last job before leaving for Burford was to address a (very intelligent and surprisingly sane) 'Women's Lib.' group in Chippenham on the wrongness and utter stupidity of war and on the sensible alternatives to it. What with fighting factory farming, the anti-abortionists, bloodsports, anti-Semitism, . . . demolition-fiends, closures of bridle ways, and for other pressing causes, there isn't much time for putting our feet up! We all three send loving greetings. We hope you are enjoying the first (but really rather late) snowdrops.

With love from Robin.

LETTER 110

[15th February, 1974]

Dear Joe [Graffy],
It was good to see you and hear of your always exciting adventures. I only wish I could be more useful. Your daffodils, which I grouped with ferns and willow in one of Bernard Leach's tenmoku-glaze pots, light up the room and give everyone great pleasure. (Bernard and Hamada are to appear on B.B.C.1 on Sunday afternoon, I believe.)

I've made a great drive towards material for R.T.'s catalogue,[1] and here it is. *I have no copy, by the way*. I gave you sheets about *Alington in Wiltshire* and *Martin's Hovel* earlier: now the set is complete. I realise, of course, that you may wish to use all this data differently; what I have done is to give the facts and try to clothe them just sufficiently personally to keep the reader's interest. But let us talk about this next time we meet, Joe.

If Paul[2] *could* be persuaded to write the Introduction – or whatever – he would certainly do it far better than anyone else. (I think he would feel pleased, too, to have a reproduction of that portrait head he drew, which he sold to the Ashmolean, in the catalogue. I think he must have drawn it in about '33 or '34, but the date is on it.)

– Not that Paul has ever seen some of my plates! I think he would need to look at all 21, and also to read the matter of the catalogue, before writing, don't you?

I'm remembering the Crafts Study Centre material, and also the set of 21 perfect prints in readiness for reproduction. They shall come next!

With loving greetings from us three to you all – and admiration and wonderment at your energy and dynamism!

Robin.

---

1. Twelve of Robin Tanner's etchings were included in the 'Exhibition of English Pastoral Etchings' organised by Joe Graffy.
2. Paul Drury.

LETTER 111

[22nd January, 1975]

Dear John [Parr] (and Betty, of course),
How very kind of you to write! It was reassuring to see your firm and youthful handwriting; surely your eyes must be excellent again? Before I forget it: your greeting at Christmas gave, and continues to give, great pleasure; we keep a special folio for these fine reproductions, and we owe a lot of them to you. What you say about etchings is true, of course. Those mighty, coarse zinc plates of Brangwyn 'tell' on a wall – but that is because they lack the subtle qualities which to me are inherent in etching. However, a lot of people (and some museums, notably the Ashmolean – which has a complete collection of my work on copper) quarrel with me, insisting that plates like my *Harvest Festival*, *Easter* and *Flowers of May* hold their own on a wall. I don't know. I only know that when I start engraving I never think I'm making a wall decoration but rather something to be dwelt upon intimately, and kept in a portfolio. Unfortunately, the only bearable reproduction of an etching is as a book.

I am sending you the smallest etching I have ever done. It has never been published, so it cannot be bought – except when an impression comes up for sale and fetches an absurd price. *White Violets* was commissioned by the Print Collectors' Club of the Royal Society of Painter-Etchers; and Heather and I printed all the impressions for the members on this delicious C18 paper. I was allowed to keep just a few and yours is one of them.

We hope you'll like it. My instructions were to etch 'a small wild plant in its natural setting'. I had drawn so many white violets that I dared to etch direct on to the copper, without any preliminary planning. I had no idea then how much it would be sought after. The plate is the possession of the Royal Society of Painter-Etchers, so there will be no more prints. As it needs to be looked at rather closely you might decide to frame it like a photograph, to stand up somewhere.

We all three send tremendous thanks, with our love.

Robin.

LETTER 112

[11th February, 1975]

Dear Jim [Fairbairn],

Your letters convey your vitality in a quite extraordinary way! We have all three been picturing your exodus, and are very glad you are now beautifully established in your new home. It sounds splendid. And if your mother approves so highly of your kitchen, it must be perfect. We send our warmest wishes to you for supremely happy years in Arncliffe Mews.

Warmth is almost more important than food, I think, and it is the surest way of keeping your possessions in good condition.

About hanging etchings: As long as one keeps the TOPS level all is well, e.g.

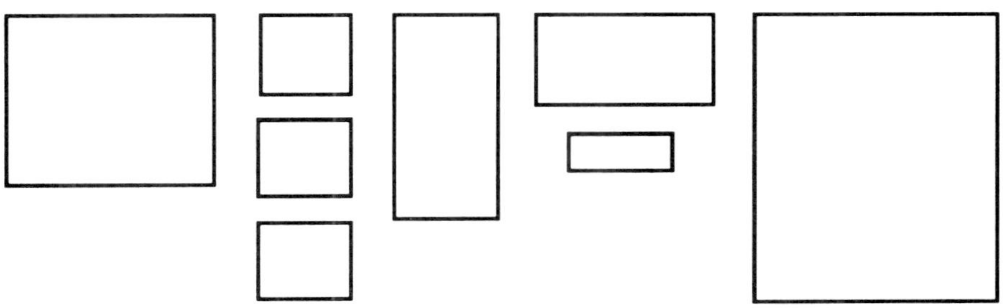

The ragged bottom never spoils the effect. So on the wall you mention you could either have a single line (quite closely hung), keeping the tops level; or you could have *Autumn* above your bureau and a group to the right as you suggest – but keeping the height the same as *Autumn*, so:

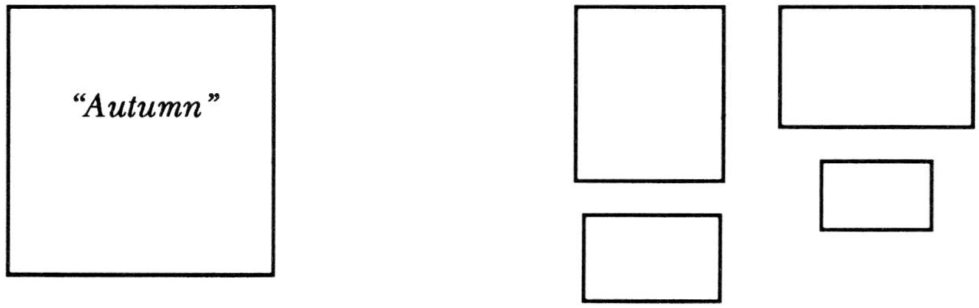

If the tops of the frames are at varying heights the result is invariably restless and unpleasing.

Last week I brought to birth two new etchings, called *November* and *February*, which will be shown in the March exhibition at the R.P.-E.

I'm enclosing some spare catalogues of 'After Many a Summer', which you may find useful. Too many were printed. . . .

LETTER 113

To Cecil Crouch.

[24th September, 1975]

. . . begun 24.IX.'75, on what must be one of the most perfect September days ever. After four successive nights of rain there have been three of perfect moonlight, followed by days of Keatsian mellowness that have been marvellous. Heather and I have been gathering our Coxes, Lord Lambournes and Bramleys – the first appreciable crop for quite fifteen years! It is most extraordinary. And not a single apple has any blemish, yet we never spray the trees. . . .

Heather has made apple-ginger, apple jelly, apple chutney, apple bread and apple cake! and every day (in my wonderful Braun juice extractor) I produce about three pints of clear and perfect apple juice. As I am said already to look like an apple I suppose I can't become more so! . . .

It makes me *very* happy that my prints continue to give you pleasure, because my only purpose in etching has been to try to communicate my feeling for 'my' England to anyone who might respond. None of the praise I get from reviewers means much to me, and when I read that in my plates I am fond of the womb shape, and that I return to my mother's womb in some of them, I hoot with laughter. My trees haven't yet been called phallic, but I'm sure that is to come! The world of art is as comic and as silly as it ever was. . . .

Estrangements that happen when we are not so young as we were seem to me to be the saddest of all. I suppose we get more like ourselves as we grow older, and our oddities, prejudices, foibles and eccentricities become more unpredictable and more exaggerated: in short, we become more and more 'difficult'. Why do so many people, when they become elderly, stiffen in their views, become Tory when once they were sensibly Left, and even go all formal over religion? I have a notion that a give-and-take attitude becomes less easy to maintain as we grow older, too, and we are certainly less forgiving. . . .

I don't really think we at Old Chapel Field can be as amazing (your word for it) as all that because we're on kissing terms with many people whom we love. I don't think we are really very exceptional. Do you know that many H.M.I. colleagues of mine, of both sexes, habitually embraced me on meeting and parting? and that many august headmasters and headmistresses and art teachers in Public and Independent Schools greeted me (once they knew me well) with a kiss? . . .

Heather has just said, 'Ask Cecil if he could do with 5–6 ozs (3 fifty-gram balls) of sock wool,' and perhaps the unfinished socks (one is done and the other is being re-footed) she was knitting for her sister's husband, when he died. I attach a sample – No: on second thoughts, I'll send it with your books, and if you hate it you can give it to an Oxfam shop, where it will be appreciated. . . .

LETTER 114

[16th March, 1976]

Dear Margaret [Pedley],

I'm glad the etching[1] reached you safely and that it doesn't disappoint you. Actually, I drew the large pepperpot tomb at Asthall – a few miles further along the Windrush valley from Burford, though they are similar. (There's a bad piece of English for you!) and the gable end is Asthall, too. The three near headstones I drew at Langley Burrell and Hullavington near here; and the large pointed one on the right is at Kington St Michael, a couple of miles away. The figure in its niche I drew pretty faithfully at Stanton St Quintin, three miles from here. It is a splendid one, contemporary with those in the south porch at Malmesbury, and is exposed – as I've drawn it. The signpost with an oil lamp used to stand at Castle Combe, but is no more. The lane and trees, of course, are Kington Langley.

Your reading of this print is so exactly what I was struggling to communicate that it makes me very happy. So few people seemed to 'get' it that Heather wrote down her own feelings about it, and I'll copy out her piece for you because in the main I think you'll agree with her.

No more prints will be made now: there are 52 in private collections and four, I think, in public galleries, including the Ashmolean. . . .

Love from all three.

Robin.

P.S. As you'll see in the catalogue enclosed, I dedicated this plate – with his widow's warm acceptance – to the memory of the great etcher, Griggs, whose centenary exhibition is now on show at the Ashmolean. When I was in my twenties Griggs was very encouraging to me.

---

1. The etching referred to is *Easter*, mentioned on pages 173 and 174 of *Double Harness*.

LETTER 115

[17th April, 1976]

Dear Denis [Thomas],
How good that meeting was! though we were sad that it had to be so brief. It would have been specially interesting to hear more about your etching class; I wish there had been time to talk to the thoughtful Stephen about the Ruskin College History Workshop, having just read Raphael Samuel's absorbing compilation, *Village Life and Labour*; and I wish I could have talked with the magnificently vital David about American poetry. (I wonder who are his great loves?) And I forgot to give Joyce particulars of those lusty, lettuce-like plants she saw in our vegetable garden, so let me repair that omission now:

CHICORY, 'Pain de Sucre'.
Sutton's seed. Catalogue No. 6520.
25 pence per pkt.

You treat the seed exactly like lettuce, but you must not sow it before mid July. Each plant ultimately needs 9″. The only enemies are slugs, wood pigeons and collared doves. Sugar Loaf Chicory is incredibly hardy; it is self-blanching; and it is easily possible to have a supply from December to May. The outer leaves have a slight but pleasant bitterness, which always reminds us of unforgettable salads we have enjoyed in little country hotels in France.

Your print, Denis, has given us all three a lot of pleasure. It is *far* more accomplished than you led us to believe: the pattern of black and grey and white is extremely telling, and I specially love the line treatment of the hair – making yet another tone – and of the figures. It was cunning of you to contrive that curved black triangle between the calf and thigh, making it a significant element in the design! (I can see old Pablo giving an approving wink about the whole conception of the plate!) How did you achieve those rounded corners? Or was the (zinc?) plate already cut like that? I think the design is a triumph: the foreground black and the background black, and all the white incident wedged between them. Do go on etching, and go your own way.

Although my way is different, I hope you and Joyce will find some interest in *The Old Thorn* which I'm sending. It comes with loving greetings.

We hope Pembrokeshire is welcoming and marvellous.

Our love to you all.
Heather, Dietrich and Robin.

LETTER 116

[18th October, 1977]

My dear Cecil,
. . . I'm glad The Book[1] is with you at last. The five copies I've bought have come too. I certainly don't think there's 'too much chat'; the introductory chapters could really have been longer, with advantage, and some of the biographies are disappointingly brief. 75 pages of illustrations is a pretty

generous dose, and it's good that they match the alphabetical order of the biographies. Yes, there is the usual crop of minor errors, in spite of double-editing. (Robin Tanner is R.E. not A.R.E. for example! But does it matter? Actually I'm one of the small band of *Senior* Fellows!) But as a total production, in 1977 of all years, I think the book is a triumph. I've finished signing impressions for the edition to be published by Prior in Portland, Oregon.

Now Robin Garton is all agog to reprint *Wiltshire Village*, and is in contact with Collins at the moment. Oh, the energy and the confidence of the young!

The Bath Bach Festival (3-yearly) is 'on', and Heather's sister is staying here for five days so that she and Heather and Dietrich can attend most of the concerts. Not for me. After two hours of Bach I go about ticking like a clock! I love the VIth *Brandenburg* greatly, and much else; but on the whole Bach fails to wound, batter, annihilate me sufficiently! Music *must* break my heart. That is why Schubert, Beethoven (late quartets), Sibelius and my beloved English composers speak to my condition. Heart means far more to me than head. As I sit needling I could enjoy hearing, say, Finzi's *Dies Natalis*, but Bach would force me to needle to his rhythm! . . .

---

1. *British Etchers: 1850–1940* by Kenneth Guichard (publ. Robin Garton).

LETTER 117

[13th November, 1977]

Dear Sam [Black],

Your characteristically warm and generous letter made me very happy.

I sent your cheque to Robin Garton immediately; he will be writing to you to say that your copy of The Book will be sent to you by George Prior of Portland, Oregon, who is publishing the American edition. (Not surprisingly, the English edition is already nearly exhausted.) The editions are absolutely identical. The Oxford University Press are the binders, and there has been some delay because of 'industrial action' – which of course means industrial *in*action! So be patient! I signed the three etchings for the U.S. edition long ago.

No: Heather and I found that vast printing job too much, so we sought help from Editions Alecto (the printers for Moore, Hockney, etc). They have a small offshoot called 'Tisiphone', composed of six good young artist-etchers who have learnt to print professionally . . .

I'm biting two new plates at last – after months of frustrating interruptions.

Now *do* tell me what *you* are up to! What and where is your gallery? When are you to be set free from the University? What are your plans for the future? How are Betty and your daughters? . . .

We all three send our love and Happy Thoughts to you Both.

Robin.

LETTER 118

To Cecil Crouch.

[1st December, 1977]

. . . The two new plates are slowly maturing. I can bring *The Wicket Gate* to its final state by the end of the year if all goes well, but the large and complicated *Cheese Room* will probably take much longer. John (and Elizabeth, who was here on Tuesday) greatly like the first crude state. John says it looks as though some pagan ceremony is about to take place, and the participants have just gone up the stairs to the loft to robe themselves! Elizabeth says it's mysterious and reminds her of Ali Baba and the forty thieves! True, there are eleven barrel-like cheeses sitting about! It is sad that neat cheese passes you by. My lunch is often a raw apple and raw cheese! At the moment we have in our pantry no less than six English cheeses, two Italian and four French! We haven't bought a joint of meat for many years, though occasionally – out of consideration for our friends – we buy Wiltshire gammon. . . .

Heather and I have pulled a proof of *The Wicket Gate* which I think I can declare FINAL. That is a relief. Now I can get on with the very extensive work needed on *The Cheese Room*. I hope by early January to be able to take them to be steel-faced, and then print some impressions for the R.P.-E. Did I tell you I have restored *Alington in Wiltshire*? The sky and the distance had faded, so I re-needled and re-bit them – successfully as it happened. It felt very strange to be working on a plate I etched 50 years ago! . . .

We send warm love and happy thoughts.

Robin.

LETTER 119

[9th December, 1977]

Dear Denis [Thomas],
At last I've been able to print *The Gamekeeper's Cottage* for you. I hope it will give you and Joyce and your handsome sons some pleasure. We send loving greetings to you all for Christmas; and may 1978 be a satisfying one for you all. . . . I've nearly finished a small etching called *The Wicket Gate*, and I'm working at a large one called *The Cheese Room*. For this I am using studies Heather and I made 50 years ago (three years before we were married) in a farm under the Wiltshire Downs, for illustrations for her book, *Wiltshire Village*, which Collins published in 1939. Have you a copy of this book, I wonder? . . .

With love from Robin.

LETTER 120

[begun 1st April, 1979]

My dear Cecil,
. . . Thank you very much for your letter. Remembering your discomfort at not being able to focus easily at the R.P.-E. show last year, I was sure you would be happier to keep away. Except that the eight impressions of *December* that were sold will bring in a nice cheque for the C.S.C.,[1] I can't feel happy. Etching in the real, traditional sense is practised by so few now. Paul D. wrote to me about my print, and begged me to continue to show in London, but I have doubts. I'm glad the plate gave you some pleasure. When a consignment of strawboard and packing paper arrives I will send you a proof. I've never poured so much feeling into any etching, except perhaps into *Easter* (which I consider a far maturer and better work than *Autumn*, by the way. The latter has some poor passages of which I am rather ashamed.) But I have decided to work at manageably *small* plates only now: the manual labour alone is quite tremendous in a plate like *December*. Etching is a strange experience for me. You see, I can never tell whether what I am trying to say will come across to others. Now Robin Garton quietly wept over *December*, because he said it filled him with 'an English sadness, a winter country twilight of nostalgia'. I could

have hugged him, for I wanted more than anything to convey that old, deep, sagging, late afternoon feeling that pervades the country just before Christmas. But maybe fewer and fewer people every year experience this. Last week I lingered, ruminating and drawing, in Langley Burrell churchyard among many thousands of snowdrops and aconites, thinking of my next plate. I found the atmosphere of that ancient rook haunted place most moving, but whether I shall ever convey *that* feeling I can't tell. In *December* I worked out a quite complicated composition – ovals within ovals; and I played a lot with acutely different textures – water, steel, stone, filigree of branches, blown grass, tilled earth and darkening sky; but I doubt whether many people looking at the etching sense *this* at all! In a way, I suppose etching is as intensely personal as a diary, and as such it is a rather private art. A painting declares itself at once, but a print conceals much that is only revealed with long acquaintance and close inspection.

Yes, I'm fortunate still to have good sight, though I now needle and draw under a magnifying lens. I've just finished the last drawing for *Woodland Plants*; it has greater detail than the first ones I did (in 1940), but then I only relied on my reading spectacles. . . .

---

1. The Crafts Study Centre.

LETTER 121

[2nd May, 1981]

Our very dear friends, Marilyn and Robert [Hapgood]: I was deeply touched that Robert 'phoned to California to report the safe arrival of *The Etcher's Craft* and then that you let us know. (Two copies I sent to friends in California have arrived, but two others to Seattle and Cambridge, Mass., still seem to be on their way.) . . .

What you say about that strange book greatly cheers me. When the City of Bristol Art Gallery curators asked me to do it I said I felt it would be altogether too specialised and personal, and too strong in its views, moreover! to have much public appeal. However, they persuaded me to write it, and they have been proved right. It sold immediately. Because there was no type-setting (the entire book was produced photographically) there was a great saving of money, so it was possible to have good paper, sections stitched in the traditional way, and decent binding. I'm so glad you are not disappointed.

Woodland Plants is being planned at the moment by the publisher. I don't know whether we have told you that we have just published, privately, the first part of a daily diary (written in shorthand, originally, by Heather's father, from the age of twelve till his death in his eighties)? A local printer has produced it very nicely. It is called *A Corsham Boyhood: the Diary of Herbert Spackman: 1877–1891*. We shall soon be sending you a copy by surface mail. Heather's sister transcribed the diary from shorthand, and they edited it jointly. You will enjoy it. My father-in-law was quite the happiest and most resourceful man I have ever known. . . .

LETTER 122

[23rd December, 1981]

Dear Denise and Frank [Brown],

Your extremely convincing and beautiful *Grevel's House* has arrived just as I was about to write to you. . . . A month or so ago I printed some very nice impressions of my etching, *The Old Road*, and I should like to give you one. But as it is large I don't care to risk posting it; we've had some unfortunate P.O. happenings lately. I will find some way of getting it to you by hand, probably via a friend in Moreton-in-Marsh whom we hope to visit in mid January.

We are delighted with your immaculate German script, which Dietrich assures us is idiomatic in a way that no 'English' person could achieve! Surely, a story must lie behind it?

We send loving Christmas Greetings to you both,
with warmest wishes for 1982.
Heather, Dietrich and Robin.

Campden under snow must look like Griggs's memorable drawing – later engraved on wood by C. Housman!

LETTER 123

[27th March, 1985]

My dear Cecil,

. . . I hope these two very different etchings will please you. It is very strange to me that each one finds its own mood or personality, though this is something I never consciously induce. They all look like my offspring, I hope, yet they are, I think, themselves.

I've just finished the Midsummer Day drawing for our new book,[1] and my hand aches and my fingers are numb.

Did I tell you I've resurrected and greatly improved a design for *July* – the last of the months? I'm afraid it's 12″ × 9″. 108 square inches is a vast area to needle, but I mustn't flinch. I can't remember whether I've already described it to you? You are inside a wood filled with Nettleleaved Bellflower, Honeysuckle, Creeping Jenny, seedheads of Bird's Nest Orchids, and flowers and fruit of Deadly Nightshade. Outside, in bright sunshine, stand huge and heavy elms in an idyllic landscape. . . .

1. *A Country Book of Days* (publ. The Old Stile Press).

LETTER 124

[10th June, 1985]

Dear Win,

What memories of long ago Madge's[1] visit brought back! Heather drove her and Paul back to Chippenham (via Langley Burrell), crawling very slowly through the village so that Madge could see her old haunts. She loved The Common, which is all gold and silver with buttercups and daisies; and Paul particularly enjoyed the flowering horse chestnuts, as a dreadful disease has killed them all in America. Meeting Paul was not at all like meeting someone for the first time; we felt we had always known him. It is splendid that he and Madge enjoy life together.

Last evening, when I was etching at my work table the telephone at my elbow rang and it was Madge! It seemed impossible that the voice came from Pawling, N.Y. She might have been in the room, it was so clear. Paul talked too. In fact it was such an expensively long call that I felt a bit worried, but they didn't! I had sent them five of my etchings (which they chose when they were with us) by air, and, miraculously, they had already arrived, so they wanted me to know.

They talked about their very happy meeting with you and your family. 'Win was just the same,' said Madge. 'Her voice was the same soft, warm, loving voice that I loved when I was a girl,' she added. And that is just what I thought when you telephoned me recently!

We all three send our love.

Robin.

---

1. Cousin of Robin Tanner.

LETTER 125

[4th October, 1985]

My dear Cecil,

. . . About my new etchings: I have a precious square foot of copper, which I must get someone to cut for three plates: *'The farms of home'* (A.E. Housman's poem) will be postcard shape, 5¾″ × 8¼″; *The Hazel Copse* will be approximately 7″ × 5½″, and *Weeds* will be about 6¼″ × 5″. *The Hazel Copse* I've long wanted to do; it will be our own, at catkin and green hellebore time. Oh, how I itch to begin! I have 'seen' it complete, many times. *Weeds* really will be garden weeds, like speedwell, bindweed, chickweed, shepherd's purse, etc, in a little cup (with a transfer engraving on it) by an open window. As you see, it will be small, but I want it to look rare and surprising, detailed and beautiful. I shall work at all three designs, I hope, in the coming months, and shall lay all three grounds at the same time.

Gordon (Cooke) comes to lunch on Monday to collect perfect impressions of *March* and *September*, printed at Thos. Ross's. . . .

[3rd–4th January, 1986]

My dear Cecil,

. . . [Samuel] Palmer was a pompous, class-conscious Tory and a high Anglican and a firm advocate of corporal punishment. I have no admiration for him as a man. He had no understanding at all of children, and it seems certain that his beloved older son really died of over-work. It is a pitiable story. . . .

Later.

The *Weeds* design is complete, and now I am 'going into contemplation' over *The Hazel Copse*. The copper for it measures 7″ × 6¼″, and the design will have something in common with the drawing on page 25 in *Woodland Plants* called 'The Woodland in Spring'. It will be lovely to do – but extremely tricky.

Weeds, too, will be difficult. In a white cup I have packed bindweed, speedwell, fumitory, shepherd's purse, creeping buttercup, heartsease, marestail, chickweed, pearlwort and dandelion. It stands at an open window with a faint, summery landscape beyond, and little fleecy clouds in the sky. The mixture of forms and textures presents subtle problems, and of course the distance will be difficult.

In *The Hazel Copse* I shall light up a hazel clump in the *middle* distance: both foreground and deep woodland will be dark: all the glory will be centred on this great clump. There will be a vaguely defined pathway and perfect stillness and peace and dewy, nascent freshness. That is the feeling I long to express. . . .

Love from us all.

Robin.

[13th June, 1987]

Dear Roy [Bateman],

You are extremely kind, and I am most grateful. The sight of this pristine sheet of copper[1] makes me itch to begin, though laying an acid-resisting ground and smoking it ready for the needling will be a tough job.

If I ever finish this etching you shall have the first proof.

Love from

Robin.

---

1. Roy Bateman lived in Kington Langley and cut copper plates to the size required. This plate was for the *July* etching.

Calligraphy

LETTER 128

This and the next letter are written to Jim Fairbairn.

[4th November, 1959]

Dear Jim,
The quite good cheap black ink I saw being used in a school in the New Forest recently was supplied by LYONS' Ink Ltd, WALKDEN, Lancashire. They make several colours, of which *black* is the best; I'm sure they would send you a sample. . . .

Love from
Robin.

LETTER 129

[22nd October, 1960]

My dear nephew!
Thank you for a very good letter, which we all three relished. (How nice, too, to find your penhold benefiting from our handwriting sessions! Get into the habit, Jim, of prefacing every piece of writing you do with a  exercise, until you hold your pen calligraphically without thinking. There's a piece of avuncular didacticism for you !) . . .

LETTER 130

[26th June, 1966]

My dear Edith,
I've just sorted out materials for Tuesday's handwriting lesson, and I find I can lend 24 wide felt brushes and a dozen black 'Free Art' crayons and 18 thick

black 'Infants' ' pencils. If you could possibly supplement this I should be most grateful. The need is for:

2 doz. 'Free Art' black (or other colours) Crayons
1½ doz. soft thick pencils
Any black ink you may have available
Some poor quality paper, e.g. sugar, newsprint, baker's wrapping – any old stuff will do. I will bring some also.
1 doz. wide felt brushes

I wish I could have got down to this earlier, but I find myself totally submerged! How to get myself laundered and pressed, sorted out and packed, and my mind free for next week's inspection is today's problem! . . .

LETTER 131

[31st January, 1973]

Dear Raymond,
You make such gentle and such generous onslaughts on my ignorance. True, I had heard of Albert Cousins, though I have never heard of his quite exceptional allroundness: I am always a little sad to find the scribe unable to cope with his own laying of gold and his own illuminating. In the rather precious, snobbish world of High Calligraphy I have heard slighting references to 'this amateur'. Now your beautiful tribute to him, which Heather and I shall cherish and are most grateful to have, shows clearly how wide of the mark the inner circle of scribes has been. I love the man's adoration for the craft, and I marvel at his unsullied vision. How happy you must have made him through your understanding and encouragement!

I am no scribe, but I have always enjoyed the physical act of writing. I am left-handed; and one day our 'greatest exponent of the italic hand' said to me sorrowfully when he watched me writing, 'A pity: there's no hope for you; give it up; you'll never write decently. Anyhow, only a few of us can!' (So in my 30 years as an H.M.I. I strove to prove him wrong in asserting that good handwriting is not for all. I still possess hundreds of beautiful examples by

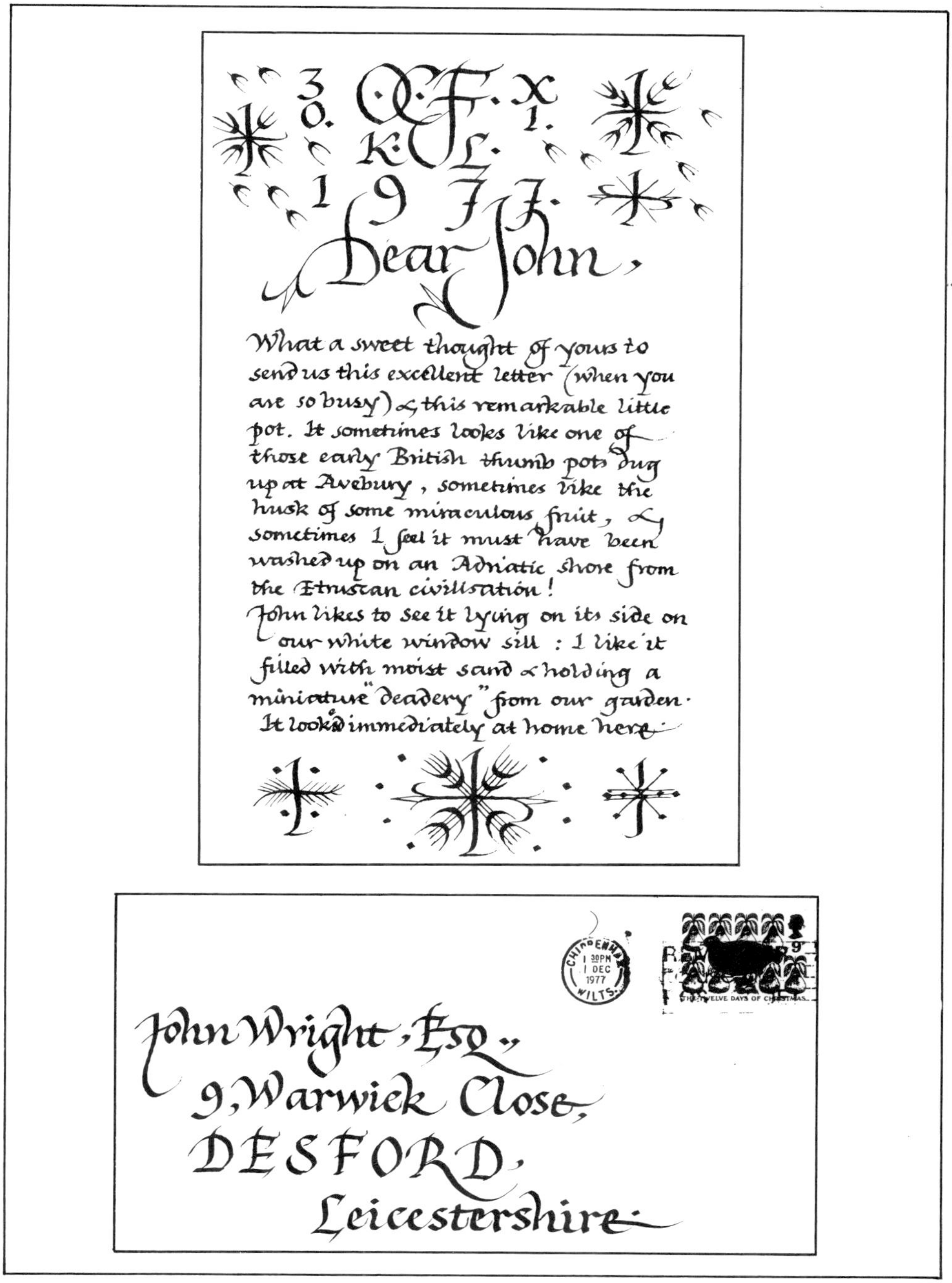

30. F. X 1. K. L. 1977

Dear John,

What a sweet thought of yours to send us this excellent letter (when you are so busy) & this remarkable little pot. It sometimes looks like one of those early British thumb pots dug up at Avebury, sometimes like the husk of some miraculous fruit, & sometimes I feel it must have been washed up on an Adriatic shore from the Etruscan civilisation!
John likes to see it lying on its side on our white window sill : I like it filled with moist sand & holding a miniature "deadery" from our garden. It looks immediately at home here.

John Wright, Esq.,
9, Warwick Close,
DESFORD.
Leicestershire.

John Wright is a potter and teaches in Leicestershire.

children and their teachers.) Thank you most warmly, Raymond, for a lovely thought. . . .

P.S. Thinking of Albert Cousins made me choose a scrap of honest paper to write upon – a piece left over from our last printing!

LETTER 132

Sunday [30th January, 1977]

My dear Les [Bennett],
Bless you! You've worked wonders with my dear old pen. Did I tell you that I've had it since I was a VIth form boy in love, and I wrote all my passionate notes to Heather with it? You have brought it back to life, and although it no longer founts I find I need to dip it in the ink very little. All this is being written with a single dip. How very thoughtful of you to enclose some crocus cloth, which I will use on one of my Osmiroids. My most grateful thanks, dear Les.

What a lot your new pen has done for your handwriting! The sharp contrast between the hair line and the full width is particularly beautiful. This morning I can hardly hold a pen at all: yesterday Heather and I printed 26 impressions of my large Elms plate – a physical feat that was unkind to my left hand and arm and shoulder. However, it is satisfying to have that job behind us. Prints are drying all over the house! . . .

LETTER 133

Although not possible to reproduce the original manuscript, as was planned, it will be clear to readers that Robin Tanner used several pens during the course of this letter.

[21st April, 1979]

Dear Fay Cori,
I find your 'new' handwriting very handsome. A broad pen such as you use slows the writing down, of course. This is a 'Medium' Italic (Perry's Osmiroid, for lefthanders – of which I am one), and I find it quite wide enough.

Im playing with new pens made by Perry. The LETTERING fountain pen is surprisingly sharp & clean, & will be invaluable, especially as there is a set cut 'left oblique' for lefthanded people. H. & D. tease me about my lust for pens; I can't resist them. Heather's prime lust is for wool, wool, & yet more wool! Dieti's is for little gadgets: he adores pencil-sharpeners, egg piercers (before boiling them!), tin openers, devices for separating the whites & yolks of eggs, & so on.

·2·

This really is a nice pen · I can't leave it alone · x

This is a 'Fine' version of Perry's Osmiroid Italic pen, and on the whole I like it better, though it gives less contrast between thick and thin strokes. All these cheap fountain pens are poor: I find Platignum ones no better. Yet when I went to Bush House itself to try to induce Parker's to find me a really sharply chisel-edged pen (regardless of price!) I failed. It is a sad business.

As to models: I think Irene Wellington's three copy books are quite the best. (This third pen is also 'fine', but broader than the second one!) You probably know them. She calls them 'The Irene Wellington Copy Books': Parts 1, 2, and 3, and I believe they are now published by Heinemann. They are beautiful. I often turn to them for refreshment.

My first sheet of paper is 'Three Candlesticks' (made by John Dickinson, and far too expensive!). I am more fond of this paper, which is Basildon Air Mail – Lightweight, not Featherweight. The latter is awkwardly thin. (This naughty nib has a habit of dropping blots without warning!) For general use I find this quite excellent: the pen moves over it so freely. I'm afraid I can't remember what paper I used when I wrote to you before; I often write on the scraps of precious handmade papers on which I print my etchings. And I always buy a supply of the amusing squared paper you wrote on when I visit France!

I'm afraid my lust for pens leads me to collect more than I really need. This is quite an old favourite. And this is one I keep for large work! I think you will soon find what suits you best.

With good wishes,
Robin Tanner.

LETTER 134

[3rd December, 1986]

Dear Tobias [Sir T. Weaver],
It was very good to hear from you. Yes, indeed: the Irene Wellington exhibition is a great triumph, and the book is marvellous. But you must get E.J.'s [Edward Johnson] *Lessons in Formal Writing* too. (We owe a lot to Justin Howes, who is working on the mass of E.J.'s papers left to us.)

I'm so glad you met Barley: she is a perfect curator, and much more besides. Did you not admire her standard of display throughout the Centre? She is extraordinarily versatile; she quarrels with no one; her efficiency is astonishing, and she is always looking ahead. . . .

But to return to Irene W.: I think it will emerge that – inasmuch as she carried E.J.'s teaching forward and in addition was a distinguished artist, and developed what one might call 'a late C20 Calligraphy' – she is the greater influence. Little did she realise that!

Yes: I vividly remember our discussions on inks half a century ago. Your No. 733 Sepia ink is lovely. I must try to find some in Bath. I am still searching for a decent left-hander's pen. This quite perfect paper is from W. H. Smith, of all people! – 'Quality Bond White Air Mail'. The block of 50 sheets costs £1.59. A similar paper is produced by Basildon Bond. It is quite a mystery that such good paper is available just for air mail letters. . . .

Our new book, *A Country Book of Days*, is about to be published by our friends at The Old Stile Press, which has moved from Blackheath to Llandogo, Monmouthshire. *A Country Alphabet*, of last year, has sold out. . . .

We send happy thoughts and much love to you and Marjorie and all the family.

Heather, Dieti and Robin.

Thank you for your beautiful edelweiss card.

LETTER 135

[4th April, 1987]

Our very dear friends [Tony and Hilary Heald],
You could not have known that yesterday, when your exciting package arrived, was the 48th anniversary of Dietrich's escape from the Nazis to us, and that today is our 56th Wedding Anniversary!! I cannot tell you what pleasure your exquisite, rare, immaculate, unique and entirely perfect present is giving us. Not one tiny detail of its lovely, sensitive craftsmanship passes us by; every detail, and the choice selection of paper, ribbon and ink thrills us. The entire conception and execution are quite marvellous; how Edward Johnson would

have loved it! We three will cherish it, and we shall also share it with our countless friends. Bless you for making us so happy. I just sit and stare at 'Quotation'[1] and I feel the subtly different textures with my fingers, and I read and re-read those memorable words about the 'spirit of love'. Oh, how true they are! . . .

---

1. The name of the piece of calligraphy by Brian Walker.

LETTER 136

[28th April, 1988]

Dear Ken [Pritchard],
. . . Now let me see what the new Osmiroid can do: I've been in correspondence with Osmiroid, because not one of my many pens is fit to use. As you see, this one is blunt and woolly; it has entirely lost its italic crispness. I've just ordered their new fine, left-hand oblique italic pen, and I'm hoping it will help me to restore some quality again to my handwriting. . . .

Yes: when it has 'run in' I think it will be good. At any rate, it is better than the pens I am abandoning. Some twenty years ago it was possible to buy pens that were more sharply chisel-edged. A zig zag line showed a great difference in the thickness of the left and right strokes . . . so essential for an italic hand.

I think your own handwriting is very strong and handsome, Ken, with a good rhythmic flow: I shouldn't tamper with it. Moreover, it is wonderfully legible. Heather and I suffer much from appallingly illegible letters. They waste so much of our precious time, and they are so ugly. . . .

We all three send loving thoughts and wishes.

Always your friend,

Robin.

My dearest Charlie. K.L. Tues. p.m.

Splendid! — And there's little time for more words if I am to catch the post with this "document" for the Staff of Walton Hall. We three are delighted. We send our very special love to **Freda**, and to our fine, wayward (his name for himself!) and greatly loved **Charlie**

we send all the wishes that could ever be wished for any young father; and to

David Scot

we send most loving greetings, bless him. This silver spoon for him was made 120 years ago (See the young Victoria still

·C·F·
·K·L·

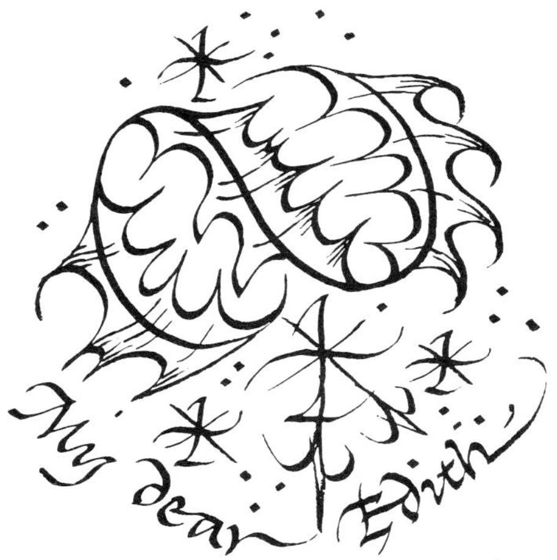

24.12·
1967.

Time was when we let Christmas rule us. Now we go our own unpunctual way. In any case, there is little beyond the pagan festival that can have any meaning today: to attempt to make merry when so many are underfed, and when our country virtually condones the war in Vietnam we find nauseating. Quite the most inspiring & heartening & stirring event for us this season has been Edmund Leach's courageous, audacious outspokenness in the Reith Lectures. What a man! And how reviled against by the smug & the conventional! If, in your busy life, you missed hearing these

Old Chapel Field, Kington Langley. 7th. July, 1970. My dear Olive, Posts nowadays are so erratic that we are sending these greetings early, in the hope that they will arrive in good time for your birthday. How vividly I remember sixty years ago! We had been sent to play in a hayfield behind Sowden School; it was hot, July weather; and when we came home Granny showed us with great pride our fair-haired, blue-eyed sister, about whom Dad, I remember, was very excited. We send our love and these sixty "candles" for your "birthday cake". We hope you'll give yourself an easy day for once. I wonder whether, now, you might be able to undertake less upholstery work & enjoy some hard-earned leisure at last? One can go on and on, wearing oneself out — and to what purpose? We set out for Provence on the 16th. & return on Aug. 7th. I hope we shall have some good transparencies to show you. With love from all 3, Robin.

60

Christmas 1971.

Dearest Charlie, Freda, & all,

We send you loving greetings, happy & warm thoughts, & all good wishes for 1972, with the earnest hope that all is well with you, & that life is much pleasanter

28 · 12 · 1977 ·

My dear CECIL

Your voice on Christmas morning was quite uncannily clear, & you sounded happy & relaxed. I hope the luncheon party was exactly to your liking. We were left blessedly alone (except for a visit by 3 nice neighbours, which was brief.) We four sat round a bubbling fondu of Heather's making, which we forked out on cubes of her good bread & devoured with a variety of vegetables cooked in butter. We drank a litre of sparkling dry wine, & we ate Heather's old fashioned Xmas pudding. (Yes: our spoilt pet robin had a feast of pudding crumbs in the greenhouse. He takes great liberties.)

We have listened to Dieti's new records — V.W.'s settings to Blake & Housman: Vivaldi Concerti (with Neville Marriner cond.): Dvořák's Symph. No. 7 in D. Minor & César Franck's in D Minor also! Then 3 Telemann Overtures (cond. by N. Marriner): & Haydn's Symphonies Nos. 44 & 49. I've read aloud Ivy Compton Burnett's witty, outrageous, absurd, unique novel, "Mother & Son", in which Plautus, the cat, is an important character!

Kington Langley.
14th May, 1986.
Dear Peter,

PETER

How very kind of you to encourage my lust for pens! I dared to cut the Berol Italic more obliquely, & this is the result. It is lovely to handle. Thankyou so much. I find it nice to use it on its edge, like this,

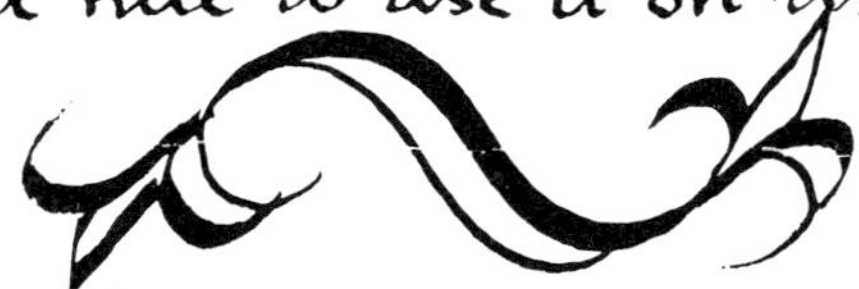

& it makes me want to play like this –

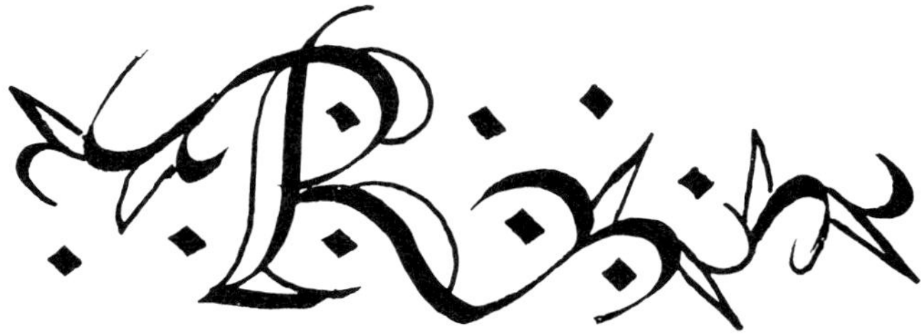

"Pertelote" hasn't turned up yet, but I've found a tiny book called "The Contributors", which

80
With our loving congratulations on this great achievement, and to wish you a very happy day: with love from Heather, Dieti, & Robin.

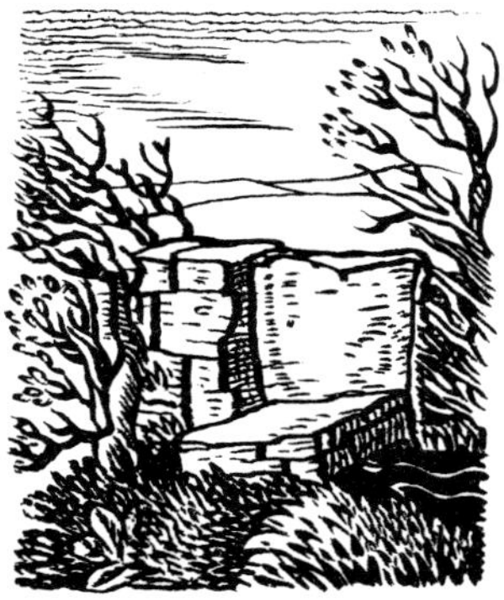

Primary education

This group of letters includes observations on courses and advice to teachers.

One correspondent writes: 'One of the pleasures of receiving a letter from Robin Tanner was the great burst of appreciation at the start of it. . . . One read the rest in a golden glow of enhanced self-esteem. That opening makes many of the letters unsuitable for publication.' To overcome this, several letters in this section have been reproduced in extract form.

LETTER 137

[27th June, 1967]

My dear Edith,

As Friday will be so full let me write a word now about your plans for a Primary Course. I haven't a single free weekend in September, I'm afraid; but, after having had searching talks with Heather and Dietrich lately – when so many requests for help at courses have come along – I've decided that the time has come for me to stop. The reasons are manifold, not the least being that I'm already two and a half years away from the schools.

But what I think would be right and wonderful would be for you to run a course at Sandywell, quite near the time you decide to retire, on the broad philosophy you've striven to live out in Oxfordshire; and let Ruth and me help you; and let me set up the most glorious exhibition ever; and let us have Traherne and Morris and Tessimond and Macneice and Cavafy; and let it be a grand reunion and a re-affirmation! Now I really would break my resolve for that, Edith!

I know you won't think me churlish or ungenerous – as I'm afraid a number of people do when I insist that my Course days are over. It's not just the time of the Course itself, but the long preparation and physical labour before and after that eat into one's time so deeply. And, conceited as it may sound, I fear, I want so much to pursue the painting and etching I've so long abandoned: for that, a fallow field is essential.

But your great final Course – that is an exception! I should love to serve you there.

Till Friday.

My love to you.
Robin.

LETTER 138

[8th October, 1968]

My dear Edith,

. . . My thoughts will be with you often and often during the next month or two, dear Edith. You will have many rich and full experiences; you will be able to set the seal on the continued happiness and goodness of Oxfordshire education; you will have countless long-standing friendships confirmed; *and you will lose nothing that is essentially permanent.* You know these people trust, honour and love you; and I believe you will *never* have any sort of feeling that they have displaced or discarded you. That you have chosen to depart while you are at the height of your powers shows a wisdom and unpossessiveness that absolutely ensure a good future for you and also leave a splendid residue. I spent only eight years with you all, but I can nevertheless understand how strange and sometimes baffling it must be for you who have spent so many struggling, selfless years in building up what those who are really far-seeing know to be something most rare and splendid.

My love as always.
Robin.

This letter includes the episode recorded on page 7 of *Double Harness*, and goes on to outline the 'Cradle and Chisel' story.

[15th May, 1969]

My dearest Charlie,
I was sad and concerned that you had that long journey for nothing on Sunday. But the room was full to overflowing with people directly involved in the Course, and so Bill had to refuse a number outside it, I'm afraid. . . .

I thought you might like to have my talk [at the Course]) all on your own, in the privacy of your own home. So I'm sending you my scribbled notes to read. I must ask you to return them, I'm afraid, as an old colleague begged me to give them to him. I'm sorry to put you to that bother.

Perhaps I ought to outline the 'Cradle and Chisel' story, which I told to demonstrate the force of the environment. It's a rather rude story:

I was a horribly perfect little Edwardian, made much of in my Infant School, where I got all my sums right, and my teachers patted my curly head and said I was wonderful – all of which I smugly accepted. But one day I committed a crime. The boys' lavatory was a tarred wall, at which we stood in a line. When the surface was dry it was a dull dark gray colour. By cunning manipulation I could produce marvellous swirling wet patterns on it. I was six, and I had a six-year-old sweetheart. I arranged to take her and give her a performance. After all, this was something she couldn't do! She stood by and watched delightedly, and then she went and split on me. My teacher was horrified, and called me a disgusting little boy. She gave me a note to take to my parents.

I found them both working with planks of oak in their little workroom. My mother read the note and handed it with a smile to my father, while to me she said, 'Well: you've never performed that trick for me!' – And I felt secure and happy again. I asked what they were making. 'We're having another baby,' said my mother, 'and this is a new cradle.' My father was jointing its parts, and I watched him closely. 'What d'you call those funny joints?' I asked. He playfully slapped my bottom and asked me what I thought they looked like. 'Pigeons' tails,' I said, rather cheekily. 'Good. You're right. We call them dove-tails. Make one!' And he handed me a razor-sharp chisel. We all three worked in silence: I don't know for how long: I don't remember what help I was given. I certainly didn't cut myself, and I was certainly in bliss.

A little while ago one of my relatives said he had found our old cradle. I had a look at it. There was one cooked-up dovetail joint – mine, which my father had accepted and rendered workable.

You can imagine what a lot of 'lessons' I drew from this story!

Now I must superintend the laying of a telephone cable to this cottage. Dietrich needs a telephone badly in his job, so Heather and I have 'given in', at last.

This note brings my warm love as always.

Perhaps we shall meet at Woolley in June?

Robin.

LETTER 140

[6th January, 1971]

My dear Edith,

Not only your splendid New Year's Eve letter has brought you into the centre of our thoughts; Les Bennett was here at the weekend, and we played him the tape of that fine, unique talk you gave at your Special Sandywell 'course' in 1967, and we three exclaimed again, 'Edith MUST write this remarkable story down, and expand it at those points where she tells her audience she wishes she had time to tell a lot more.' Les was completely bowled over by it. He says he views Oxfordshire quite differently now, and is itching to start work there. He is filled with admiration, and he, too, longs to see this strong, direct, human story of real educational growth put in print for all to read and profit by.

. . . D. says it would be perfectly easy for you to play and stop the tape, just as you desire, to help you with your writing. The whole design of that talk is so good. True, it is only the skeleton, so to speak, of what you would write, but it is so well defined and so beautifully shaped that you would encounter no difficulties of composition.

Heather and Dietrich and I urge you, with great eagerness and a deep sense of its importance, to embark on this long, delightful and satisfying piece of work, Edith. Only make a start, and it will carry you away and absorb you! . . .

We send warm love . . .

Robin.

LETTER 141

[28th June, 1973]

Dear Rosemary [Devonald],

A visit to you is always a great delight to us, and last Sunday was wonderful. Thank you very much indeed for it – for all the good conversation, your perfect food, meeting your mother and dear Thomas and Clare again, and for sharing with us that fine and very moving work of your students.

I honour you greatly for discovering so abundantly all these hidden gifts and graces in what people call 'ordinary women'. Clearly, you have doubled their stature and changed their lives; in my view, you have done an astonishing, very human and tremendously far-reaching piece of work. I hope you feel a glow of pleasure and a sense of fulfilment because of it. We three came home feeling singularly refreshed and stimulated – and full of admiration.

Our love and thanks to you all.

Heather, Dietrich and Robin.

LETTER 142

[20th February, 1975]

My dear Edith,

. . . When I had a day or so of mild lumbago, I made myself continue writing 'Teacher and Etcher' instead of trying to be physically active. I certainly won back my interest, and have now reached 1952, which was a momentous one for me. A great international conference of potters and weavers was held at Dartington, and I was sent by the Ministry of Education to speak on 'Children'. That was my very first visit to Dartington – my first meeting with

Dorothy and Leonard, Hans and Lucie, and Hamada and Yanagi from Japan. How long, long ago that hot July in that fabulous place now seems! And what a harvest it brought forth! . . .

LETTER 143

[16th February, 1976]

My dear David [Evans],
I wonder if you could help me? I think I may have told you that one of my retirement amusements is writing my autobiography – not for publication but (I hope) to give some pleasure to my friends.

I've reached 1956, which for me was the beginning of The Golden Age, and can get no further. In my memory those eight years are one long series of happy visits to schools, evenings in kindly hostelries with teachers, conferences and courses – national, regional and local; and I can't give any chronological form to it all. Can you set me going by jotting down some dates, (the full inspection of Langford, for instance) and the themes or topics of courses, and the places where they were held? Can you remember the Dartington Courses individually? Then, I made a number of little anthologies for special occasions, e.g. our Christmas poetry readings. Can you give me their titles? It is facts like these that I so sorely lack, and you – more than anyone else, I'm sure – could supply them.

There is absolutely no hurry at all, David. And if you feel I'm asking for too much research, and you would rather not attempt it, I shall of course understand. The earlier years – in Leeds, Gloucestershire and Bristol – which were far less good, I can remember in quite stereoscopic detail, but my last eight 'working years' are too much of a happy blur.

You will have heard, I expect, that Christian Schiller died last week. Mercifully he was spared a long illness, and he had lost none of his amazing powers. No man taught me as much as he did, and I find it hard to accept his departure. England has lost a very great prophet, alas. . . .

We send you both our warm love and happy thoughts.

Robin.

The extracts from letters 144 and 145 to Cecil Crouch of 31st May 1976 and 17th July 1976 are about Christian Schiller.

LETTER 144

. . . On July 10, in the Great Hall at Goldsmiths' there is to be a very large gathering of people for a Celebration of the life of Christian Schiller. (He was a Humanist, and this 'service' will be like a Quaker or Humanist one.) The speakers are to be Lady Plowden, Sir Alec Clegg and plain Robin Tanner. I little dreamed when I took part in *The Rivals* and *Arms and the Man* in that hall that I should have to face this ordeal. But it will at least give me the opportunity to spill yet more beans and to condemn further the Establishment! I worked with Christian, in double harness, so to speak, for many years, and I was constantly aware of his greatness. One day England will wake up to it. He has had a far greater influence than, say, Heath or Wilson or the archbishop of Canterbury! . . .

LETTER 145

. . . Actually it was a very moving occasion at Goldsmiths'. (I suppose you know that Richard Hoggart is the new distinguished Principal?) I don't know who but Christian Schiller would have drawn that great concourse of wonderful men and women together. His wife and family told me how comforted and happy the celebration had made them. Somehow it felt almost natural to be standing on that stage and addressing the multitude, though I must confess it took a lot out of me. We had tea up in the Art School – but apart from the red brick front façade – now cleaned and much smartened – you would not know Goldsmiths'. Its new buildings stand where there were streets of artisans' houses in 1921, and because of a one-way system that starts at the Marquis of Granby, less traffic actually passes the College. My head was full of strange memories: I saw young C. W. Crouch . . . and lanky A. P. Friend pass down that main corridor – no longer a corridor, but a wide thoroughfare (tiled in black and white) with a lounge and bar and bookshop on the right, and rebuilt lavatories. My far past rushed back to me. I found it by no means unpleasant, either. . . .

New Year's Day [1978]

My dear Les,
Your truly memorable letter about India and your experiences there has greatly moved us, all three. It was most generous of you to write it: I've read it aloud several times (this morning to Jim Fairbairn, who is staying with us for a few days), and I can assure you that no tiny detail of that gripping and oh, so sensitive account has passed us by. It must have been very satisfying to share everything with Richard: it would have been a great strain to have to bottle everything up within yourself. And what a unique experience for him! We naturally felt anxious about you when news of that terrible cyclone reached us. How little we in England realise our good fortune! We make a fuss about a modest flood or fall of snow, and rarely suffer from really violent weather.

It is hard to see how any substantial educational progress in India is possible, where physical standards are so meagre and where attitudes are fixed and criteria so falsely based. I suppose the British in their day merely ignored the problem. It must be heartbreaking to you to know that teachers who have now become inspired by you will be frustrated in their efforts: my heart aches for them. Oxfordshire teachers know they have you behind them (and in front of them, too!), so they feel secure. I keep thinking of that girl who, with you, did wonderful things about the Papaya tree, and has gone back to that squalid school with its wretched headmaster. How she must honour you! yet how she must now despair! The alarming inequality in the world weighs more heavily upon me than anything else.

Now I read that pollution from factories to be built near Agra will virtually destroy the Taj Mahal. Surely these stupid plans will be abandoned? Your visit to the workshop where the craft of inlay is practised must have been both moving and harrowing. I am haunted by the picture of that little family wearing themselves out before their time in the practice of their craft.

It would interest us tremendously to read your Indian diaries/journals when you can part with them for a while. When I spent a day with John he told me he was about to go to Saudi Arabia to advise on Primary Education; money would not be lacking, but I imagine he would find awful unenlightenment and the worship of false gods!

I ponder much on the situation in Oxfordshire and earnestly hope 1978 will see the turning of the tide. But a county that presumes to be administered by a body of excessively Tory administrators who do not believe in the state system they are administrating, and who, indeed, want it to fail, is in a perilous position. The answer is clear: dedicated and supremely thoughtful teaching in every school. Insults and material economies must not be allowed in any way to diminish the teachers' sense of devotion to children. If Oxfordshire teachers keep faith and hold on with quiet authority and dignity to their beliefs, they will win, and the autocratic, ignorant 'overlords' will lose utterly. Your influence is a powerful force for good, Les. May this year bring you rich fulfilment, and deep happiness.

Our warm love to you all.
Robin.

LETTER 147

[29th January, 1979]

My dear Edith,
. . . I'm sure Stephen knows he can learn a lot about children from you. The beliefs and convictions of so many educationists seem to fall to bits when religion is considered. Being eager for any fresh experience, and being biddable, children will respond to whatever adults provide; and I suppose it may be thought that the influence of this goes deep and is lasting. I have doubts. As you know, we three seriously wonder whether religious experience as we adults understand it can possibly be a part of childhood. Of course children could plan their own service, and they would do it as well as they would pursue any project and make a visual success of it. But if the aim behind it is to draw young children into the church, I think it is doomed. We can take advantage of childhood too easily, don't you think? We three have always felt that religious conceptions are no part of childhood, and so we would have no religious education as such; rather, believing that all we do throughout each day should have a sacramental element about it, and we see no reason for

isolating 'religion' from it. Nor do we feel that that minority religion called Christianity (which, alas, has brought wars and divisions in its train) is the only true one; by accident of birth we belong to a so-called Christian country. (It is one that spends its millions on preparing for a nuclear war which it knows full well would destroy the whole world. And Jesus himself was a pacifist! That is why I say 'so-called'.) Reverence for all life, love of our fellows, love of the beauty and wonder of the natural world, these things, it seems to me, must be the overwhelming concern of us all; and these are things, moreover, which children *can* grasp. But all theological notions – such as those contained in the Anglican Apostles' Creed, for instance – are, I believe, positively harmful to young children. If, as I hope, they are aware of another dimension, of something beyond us, then let us leave it there to develop with time. In short, let us apply to 'Religion' the standards and values we apply in all other aspects of children's growth. I would positively protect them from the horror stories in the bible, and from the anti-Semitism of Easter. But many of the beautiful myths and the incomparable literature of the authorised version I would want to share with children as part of their heritage. Dogma and theology and sectarianism have caused many to fail to see the wood for the trees. If, instead, we lived out the truth that God is Love (and Love is God!) all would be well. So we are very glad that Stephen has access to your long, long experience with children and to your great wisdom concerning them. . . .

LETTER 148

[4th May, 1979]

My dearest Charlie,

. . . I've searched for a nice copy of Memorable Speech, but I seem to have given them all away. I'm so sorry. The one I'm sending is, I believe, complete, except for Cavafy's important poem, 'Ithaca', which is missing. But perhaps you have that poem elsewhere? If not, I'll write it out for you. I send these loose sheets with all my love. David bound one or two nicely for me, but they have all gone. I hope you can somehow manage with this.

I'm also sending my Autobiography, 'Teacher and Etcher', as far as it has gone – that is, up to 1956, when I began work in Oxfordshire. I call it

'Selective' because I have chosen to concentrate on my two great passions – teaching and art. I wrote it primarily because so many friends begged me to; and I enjoyed doing it. Actually, the happiest years of my life have been these since 1956, yet they seem too near to fall into perspective, and I'm finding it much harder to write about them. Needless to say, I've not written for publication at all, but for friends like you – and Jim. He has already read it, so you can talk freely to him about it. Jim kept it for months, and was loth to yield it up! Keep it as long as you like, Charlie, but there is still a queue waiting for it. Maybe Freda will like to read it too. It's a plain, simple, ordinary story, but it does happen to span six interesting decades of human and educational and art history.

I'm also sending, just for your interest (please keep this copy) an Anthology Heather and I compiled for a recent Oxfordshire Day here. Les Bennett – one of Oxfordshire's advisers, who is a dear friend – asked if we would meet twelve young Heads (nine men and three women), all of whom had heard a lot about 'the Golden Age in Oxfordshire', and wanted to meet us. So they were all strangers, so to speak. They arrived at 10.30 a.m. in a minibus, and after coffee we sat round the blazing logs till lunch time. They had prepared questions to ask us three, but we only covered one, as it raised so much good discussion! It was put to me: 'Robin, as both an artist and an educator you must have experienced a great conflict. How have you attempted to resolve it? And if you *had* to put one before the other which would it be?' The answer, of course, was simply this: 'No, there has been no conflict: the one has somehow complemented the other. And I should undoubtedly put educator before artist.'

Then came lunch, using both rooms. People ate heartily, and wine flowed freely. After coffee, the anthology was read – almost everyone taking part – round the fire. It was really very moving. All except Tessimond's (which *is* now published of course!) are poems by our friends and us. Dietrich read the German most movingly. We had thought that the party might then like music, but they wanted to explore the house, handle pots and textiles, talk about paintings and etchings, ask for recipes, and so on. Then we had tea. And in the twilight, by which time we had fallen in love with every one, they left for home. It was a day you would have loved, Charlie – 'a miniature Dartington', Dietrich called it. . . .

LETTER 149

[11th June, 1979]

My dearest Charlie: I bought this comic students' notepaper on our last holiday in France – in Angoulême. I don't know why I like it, but I do; I think perhaps it's because it isn't squared. I've always preferred oblongs to squares!

Those miraculous recoveries from 'waste paper' – both the book of early postcards and that poignant record by wounded soldiers in the First World War – excited us. We do hope you can ensure their safety. At this destructive time such records are more vital and important than ever before. I should like to think these two will come into *your* care. Jim spent Saturday and yesterday here. He had been caused to address a group of Wiltshire teachers, which he says he much enjoyed; then he went to our Crafts Study Centre in Bath to see 'Pots of Inspiration' (a remarkable collection of old Korean, Japanese, Persian, British and Chinese pots which Bernard Leach collected, loved and learnt from, together with pots of his own – all of which Bernard gave us just before he died); and then he came on to us. . . .

I expect you've had your copy of *Christian Schiller – in his own words*. I think Christopher Griffin-Beale has done the editing very well, and I'm sure Christian would approve of the clean typography and discreet binding. I read the book once, and found it singularly telling. Whether a stranger would find it so, I can't say. As I read I was of course full of recollections; I could hear that sometimes rather frightening, passionate voice, and I remembered some of the occasions when the talks were given. What a man! What a prophet! What utter simplicity of vision and of language! . . .

LETTER 150

[20th August, 1979]

My dearest Charlie,

. . . I'm glad you and Freda have found interest in my very simple autobiography. I feel encouraged to finish it – at least, I mean, to bring it up to the present. But, as I may have told you, I find it extremely difficult to describe the years since 1956, yet these have been quite the happiest few decades of my life. I will try. But regarding publication: I can't think that anyone who didn't know me personally would ever want to read such a book. My life (to me) has been very good, but uneventful and undramatic. As a period piece, a social document, a sort of commentary on educational growth, I suppose it might interest *a few*; but I think it's best left in typescript. If I am ever able to get a few copies made, however, I should like you and Freda to have one. . . .

The Autograph Album has brought back sad and terrible memories of those dreadful years of the First World War. It is a tragic document. I think it ought to be preserved in the Keighley archives – in a local museum, perhaps? I'll send it back to you later on. The contributions show all the false glamour of the time, the yearning to get back to normality, the thin veneer of patriotism, the extraordinary taste (visually!) of those years, and a moving, touching impulse to create something out of boredom and misery. I'm so glad you saved it. Sometimes I wonder if we've learnt much since that time. The appalling facts about nuclear energy and nuclear arms stare at us, and yet we go blindly on, pursuing a mad and immoral course, unheeding, selfish, with not a thought for the future your sons will have to live through – if, indeed, there *is* any future.

On September 22, at Merton College, Oxford, there is to be a great Oxfordshire Occasion on The International Year of the Child, (with music, and with poetry about, for and by children). I've been asked to give the opening address, and I'm sure you can guess the burden of my talk! Our nuclear policy makes a travesty of The Year of the Child. I felt proud to be English when Thatcher's longing to bring back capital punishment failed: I feel ashamed to be English when I contemplate her wicked determination to press ahead with nuclear developments. I wrote her a letter last week! . . .

LETTER 151

[31st May, 1980]

My dearest Charlie,
No one can write a letter like you. We often vow not to hoard any more – and then comes this wonderful outpouring of your very lifeblood on paper, which can never be destroyed. Like me, you recognise that, in spite of what many

people assert, letters are still vital as a means of communicating thoughts 'recollected in tranquillity', of underlining, so to speak, and of giving pleasure. Yours gave (and continues to give) all three of us immense pleasure. You must have known that when I prepared that talk on Morris and the one on etching I kept you in mind, and was constantly estimating your response to this or that; so it was good and gratifying to know that I evidently did not disappoint you. . . .

How right you are to make your own special contribution! Memories and stories of the past are no part of you: the passionately held convictions of one who is still young, who is tolerant, questioning and unassailable . . . have a singularly vital contribution to make to Woolley. Simple, thoughtful, first-hand sharing of experience is what you can give in masterly fashion, as I believe no one else can. But you mustn't be hurried. If I were you I should slowly carve out the shape of what you want to say, and jot down your ideas over quite a long period, and then assemble them in an assimilable (is there such a word?) and telling form. The Course on Imagination and Inventiveness sounds a vital one.

Yes: we have said we will help at a Course in July, 1981. Then Heather will give one of her own very personal sessions. . . . She will be 78 by then, but she goes on thinking.

We thought Jim's summing up at Woolley was superb. He had so little time in which to prepare it, yet it was shapely and deep. He's a wonderful influence. We're so glad about his new house. Living near his beloved Minster will be most satisfying. . . .

Bless you all.
Heather, Dietrich and Robin.

LETTER 152

[5th January, 1982]

My dearest Charlie,
. . . I suppose it should have been explained that 'A Personal View' was a hastily scribbled first rough draft. As I was pressed for time I failed to make a readable copy. It was made for myself only. I hope it was legible enough for

others to read. I don't mind at all that such a hurried scrawl has been distributed, however: people should know what goes to the making of a talk. Those pages were written straight off the cuff, and with passion and a sense of urgency. If that doesn't emerge, then I failed completely.

I think these meetings of Woolley tutors with Jim are vital. You are, together, achieving the most necessary of all things today – a sense of purpose and commitment. Even among my dear Oxonians there is a good deal of disillusionment and near despair, and it is terribly important to support the downcast and disappointed. What is clear is that Thatcher is determined to maim state education irrevocably, and she must be fought to the death. Mercifully she has no access to children. Teachers still have it in their hands to defeat this immoral woman. Sometimes, when I contemplate the wanton, callous destruction of all I and many others gave our entire working lives to achieve, I wish I had etched and drawn and painted instead. Then I try to comfort myself with thoughts of your splendid generation still holding the torch high. . . .

The only really interesting event during the London exhibitions of the 82 original drawings for *Woodland Plants* is on Wednesday, 12th May, at Goldsmiths' College Art Gallery (New Cross). My dear old friend, the etcher Paul Drury, is to chair a public Seminar, at which Heather and I are to speak. Then Margaret Benton (the B.B.C. TV producer at Bristol) is to show the 30–40-minute documentary – seen up to that date on West Region only. Then follows a Buffet Supper. That should be a nice evening. I think Robin G. has reserved some 1st edition books for sale then, and of course, the 2nd edition (@ £21) will be available.

We shall do no more books. Heather has a few (philosophical) essays in mind, and she and her sister want to assemble family documents (not for publication). I want to complete my autobiography (not for publication), and there are at least four designs in my mind, waiting to be etched. Also I want to resume egg tempera and watercolour painting. . . .

[27th August, 1982]

Dear Tony [Heald]: Your deeply questioning, brutally honest, thoughtful (and, incidentally, beautifully written) letter has not made me want to blow you sky high: rather, it fills me with admiration. I'm not well equipped, however, to give it the reply it deserves. If I now tell you more about myself I think you'll see why:

I was born with some pronounced 'deficiencies'. I have absolutely *no* competitive urge: I've never wanted to *win* anything. I saw as a boy that my obsession with drawing and painting, and with elements of the beautiful untroubled landscape in which I grew up, separated me, in many ways, from my fellows, but this didn't really please me. I had no use at all for games of any sort; I found gadgetry and machinery positively repellent; I remember first seeing a motor car, in 1908, and I shrank from the invader! I was by no means a solitary, however; I had many friends, and I bossed them a good deal. I don't think I wanted to show off, yet I loved an audience. I would recite and tell stories and draw for my hapless band of followers! I was always teacher's pet – this good, 'clever', curly-headed, smug little Edwardian boy! For 78 years, Tony, I've been 'spoilt', and I've always liked 'spoiling' others. Then, too, I was born with too selective a vision. What is ugly has often made me physically sick, so for as long as I can remember I have inhabited my Ideal World and striven for it. I don't mean I haven't faced ugliness, for I seem to have been born with a social consciousness and conscience. I relished teaching in the slum of Deptford, and my pacifism has, of course, led me into uncomfortable experiences. Then there is my perhaps over-strong belief in the power of love. . . . This outgoing love does not blind me: it makes me want to share much of the good I know with my fellows. I have another huge 'deficiency' – a complete lack of ambition and no wish whatever to be well-known or win fame. I simply wanted to teach and etch, and I've been fortunate to do and enjoy both. I never asked to be an H.M.I. I was invited to be one; and, moreover, I was encouraged . . . to work in my own way, which many called 'unconventional'! This total failure to be ambitious has led me to share all I have, know, think and believe with as many people as possible. 'Squandering your gifts,' many people have called it, but they are wrong. You may like to read the enclosed address, in which I tried to express my belief in the creative powers of *every* human being. The 'great' artist is much less my concern than 'that of art' in everyone. What is, I suggest, extraordinary is that Heather was born with most of these leanings, too, and that Dietrich (who only came to us from Nazi Germany in 1939) shares most of them. Heather's aim in writing, and mine in etching, has been primarily to share our own deep pleasure. Financial gain has never entered into it. We give away all our royalties and fees to causes we care deeply about, preferring to live very simply. If we have become 'well-known' that has never been of our own seeking. . . . No, Tony: I never want to be famous. Before I die I hope to leave, through my etchings and book illustrations, and a few paintings, a record of or sort of tribute to my love of a small piece of England as I knew and loved it. That is all. And now let me try to meet your questions: You're an artist because you can't help being one, and whether you ultimately achieve fame or not I believe the glorious 'obsession' that goads you on will always be with you. It is clear for all to see that your work is distinguished. I entirely agree with you about this disgraceful charlatanism in contemporary art, which often obscures the genuine. But ultimately the still small voice *is* heard. Do not worry; pursue your determination to achieve the very best that is in you, and all will be well. Let what you call 'fame' look after itself: there's no need to seek it. The children you teach and your family and friends are all fortunate to have in you that extra something we call an artist. We who are so made, Tony, (and I sometimes feel that in a sense we are all related – we are all of one artist-family) are doubly fortunate; we inherit a precious gift, and we have to pass on what we have been privileged to feel and see. But whether, in our lifetime, we become 'famous' or not doesn't really matter. What matters is that we fulfil ourselves. That is my great hope for you. You are young, with a happy family and a happy school; and you have unusual artistic power and a passionate desire to use and perfect it; and I think it's perfectly natural for you to desire proper recognition. It is far wiser to keep one's art independent of earning one's living than trying to live by it. Those who attempt the latter either fail or become servants of demanding agents – having to produce what 'sells', what is the fashion of the moment. You are free. *Keep* free, Tony. Regarding Art as an investment is, I agree, a most pernicious practice. People do it with my etchings; they strive to get a rare impression – perhaps of an etching in an early state, before it is 'final' – because of its potential money value. That is disgusting. You are *not* 'foolishly idealistic' (your phrase) to refuse to play that game. As you say, your prime aim is to satisfy a personal need, and, I'm sure, at the same time, to give pleasure. If you call exhibiting your work 'promoting' yourself then of course you are absolutely right to do so. It is an artist's main way of communicating. (I shall show two new etchings at the Royal West of England Academy (Bristol) in the autumn, and again in London in the spring at the Royal Society of Painter-Etchers annual show.) When I was your age I used to exhibit paintings and etchings at the Royal Academy every year, but few people took much notice of my work. Not until I retired from the inspectorate eighteen years ago, and I resumed etching, was I 'acclaimed', as they say, and now I can do no wrong! There has never been a struggle, and I can't say I've ever suffered disappointment. Maybe this is because I have no great opinion of my own work; it is essentially minor, and its range is deliberately narrow; its idiom is traditional rather than what we are pleased to call 'modern'; and its appeal must be limited to those tuned in to the English pastoral tradition. Financial gain would be jolly useful to you and your wife at this time of bringing up a family, and if it comes your way you must of course accept it gladly.

Continued later.

I've scribbled these thoughts at such a rate that I've just realised they're in one huge, confusing paragraph! Please forgive it. What I want most to say is that I'm absolutely certain that you have your priorities right. You put the struggle towards perfection in your art first. And that, of course, will be a lifelong struggle. (I've just finished a plate called *September*, and although it is my 34th etching I've found it more exacting than any other. I find that nothing becomes easier with experience, but I cope with the inevitable problems more easily: that is all.) You wouldn't be human if you had no wish for your work to be seen and enjoyed; and since a labourer is worthy of his hire it is surely right for you to expect a reasonable return. Unlike, say, Van Gogh, you paint/draw from the safety of a fixed income. I wouldn't say that Van Gogh should have done so, though I believe he would have sacrificed very little if he had had some regularly paid work. As you know, hardly any artists today can contrive to rely solely on their art for a living.

I wonder if you watched Iain Bain's wonderful TV half-hour on Thomas Bewick? Easily England's greatest wood-engraver, yet even now known only to a few. In his life he never became rich, though he knew the joy of fulfilment. Do read his Memoir, if you don't already know it. (This will amuse you. I haven't yet met Iain Bain. I wrote to thank him for his marvellous evocation of Bewick, and he replied that he would like to come to see us. I happen to know that he likes my *Wren and Primroses*, so I've just sent him an impression.)

To return to the artist's position. It is true that a lot of appreciation – glowing reviews, etc. – has been bestowed on Heather and me, but apart from the satisfaction of being able to give away [to charities], quite the nicest result has been the great host of letters – many of them from total strangers – that have descended on us. To have given pleasure has been our reward: we could wish for nothing better. Many of those letters have touched us deeply, and have reinforced and heartened us; and truly they have meant more to us than the very generous reviews by celebrated critics. I doubt whether 'fame', of itself, could make an artist/writer/musician happy. I've just read the disturbing biography of Graham Sutherland, whom I knew as a young etcher at Goldsmiths'. He strove zealously for international fame, which eluded him; he was anxious, touchy, unsatisfied, and rarely completely happy. Had he been content to remain the superb English romantic he once was all would have been well.

I realise, Tony, that I must be a good deal more than twice your age, and although I don't *feel* old I must seem ancient to you. Now I have never subscribed to the notion that the aged are full of wisdom, so don't take my rambling thoughts very seriously. Your own are just as valid. But if what I've written has cheered and reinforced you I shall be happy. You'll come back after your strenuous time at Blackwaterfoot full of ideas for paintings and drawings, and I hope they will take you a big stride forward through the autumn and winter. I doubt whether you will have contrived to draw, but I'm sure you will have absorbed much. I find that when it isn't possible for me actually to sit down and draw I can look and see so intensely that – in my mind, so to speak – I have executed an elaborate drawing! I expect you do the same. It's a good way of learning.

It isn't possible for us to take a holiday this year as so many friends, especially Americans, want to visit us. Quite a number of strangers call, too. I must say that so far they have all been lovely people. Dietrich leaves for a month in America on September 15. We shall be glad when the holiday season is over and we can begin some of our own work again. I've designed an etching called *The Fritillary Fields*; the copper is cut, and I itch to begin.

Heather and Dietrich and I send our love and
warmest wishes to you all.
Robin.

LETTER 154

[5th May, 1983]

My dear Tony,
We have shrieked with laughter over your marvellous exposition of Heather's grandmother's 'warning'! We must somehow share it with Patricia and Jim and Charlie and other friends. That grandmother was an amazing human being. She was a musician, who still played the piano well into her nineties. She bore nine remarkable children. She said to us once, 'They have something called an anaesthete today: I always found it very natural.' Her father made an Infant Prodigy of her; she sang and played publicly from the age of seven, and (cruelly) without words or score. We still have the playbills and programmes.

You couldn't have given us greater pleasure, Tony. Yes, indeed: that Saturday night at Woolley was heaven-sent. It sometimes comes over me that we may not have many more hours together; if I live till I'm 90, even, shall we meet only ten more times? But for the most part I put the horrid thought away and rejoice in the present. If I were 40 years younger what things we would do together! On the other hand, how fortunate that our paths have converged, even at this late hour! I gain special pleasure from the knowledge that among Jim's special allies there is an artist – for you have a vital part to play, Tony. Together, Jim and you and Charlie and Margaret and Dorothy are spreading a fine and deep influence; and because of your great gifts as an artist your contribution is unique. It makes me so happy that you are all working valiantly to preserve and develop what many of us gave our entire professional lives to create and build up.

We are very glad that you enjoyed our Saturday night session, for we put many weeks of work into it. At one stage we thought we would make it a duet – Heather and I conversing, so to speak; but in the end we decided that one voice only should speak the text.

We all three send love to you four. . . .

Robin.

LETTER 155

[28th November, 1984]

Dear Janet [Poynton],

How very kind of you to write to me and to send me that amazing 'November'[1] – which could only have been written in 1984! Do please thank the writer of it for me; it is quite wonderful.

I was ashamed at first that I hardly recognised you at Ivy Lane, but I couldn't believe it could be you, since Abridge is so far away. It was most heroic of you to undertake such a journey. I only hope you found it worthwhile.

I must confess that to be suddenly surrounded by 'boys' and 'girls' I had not seen since I taught them half a century ago was singularly moving. I was glad I could remember all their names. Some who couldn't get into the meeting have visited me this week to talk about those far off days.

Dedicated people like you, Janet, will be all the more needed to resist the latest retrograde proposal, which is virtually Payment by Results!

We three send warm greetings. We hope you will enjoy a good long rest at Christmas.

Every Good Wish
from Robin.

---

1. The reference is to a piece of writing done by an eight-year-old boy in Janet Poynton's class when he suddenly noticed on a dull November day that a ray of sunshine was split into a spectrum when it passed through his plastic ruler: 'The sun in winter makes lovely colours and you can make your own rainbow and you need some dark so you can have a bright lamp and some oil and water and a little bit of time.'

[17th January, 1985]

My very dear Tony,

. . . I've been needling away at a second ground on my large 'Aldhelmsburgh' plate all the morning. We have a light sprinkling of snow, and it is very cold; but the over-population of birds in our garden is well provided for. . . .

My fingers are tired, so I'm having a rest and watching the birds. . . .

It was very good to hear from you, and to know that all is well with you all, and that school is as satisfying as ever. I do, though, understand and sympathise with your occasional yearning for change. A larger school would entail much dreary administration and less direct contact with children. Lecturing in or advising on Primary Education you would do extremely well, but both have their snags, and such work is perilously invasive of one's time. Only you can decide. An Oxfordshire Head came to see me recently, who gave up teaching for commercial art – mainly book illustration. He earned a high salary, but felt so homesick for children and teaching that he applied for a headship again, and is happy once more! Perhaps he will break out again one day! You are singularly well endowed, Tony; to be as distinguished an artist as you are, and also to be a fine educationist, will always saddle you with the problem of how to live two lives in one. I have lived happily with that dualism and have been thankful for it. And so will you. We who – for want of a better word – are called artists are all children of the same mother, so to speak: I mean, we share the same privilege – or mad streak, if you like! We can never be bored, anyhow, and we are so made that we love humanity and never totally despair of it.

In these hard and bitter times I imagine your gallery is not very active; but if people can regard it as a haven to come to where they can be sure they will always see 'things men have made with wakened hands and put soft life into' you are making a vital contribution to life. It is our wretched government's callous erosion of the arts, education, the social services and every civilising activity that saddens me most today. . . .

Fortunately I am so made that not even the present disastrous situation can destroy my 'inner happiness' nor rob me of my optimism. I'm sure there are more good people in the world today than there have ever been, but alas! they are still a minority. If only we could turn it into a majority! . . .

We send warm thoughts to you all, with our love.

Heather, Dietrich and Robin.

LETTER 157

[10th May, 1985]

My dear Les,

You and Margaret have been very much in our thoughts throughout this period of celebration and farewell. . . . Like me you found your best years in Oxfordshire, where your influence will live on. And not only there; you have conquered Oregon, India, Botswana, Mauritius and elsewhere; I am a parochial, limited, stay-at-home in comparison. I glory in the breadth and depth of what you have done, Les. Even in these frustrating latter years you've forged ahead. . . .

Yours was a wonderful letter, and it touched and moved me deeply. I suppose we shall never understand why 'fatal' meetings (like ours at Alderney) happen, but, as you say, they make our lives. Why were Heather Spackman and Robin Tanner put to share a dual desk as VIth Formers? It is all very strange and very wonderful. How much we have to be grateful for! . . .

Yes: they told me about the book production apparatus they were buying for you; that seemed to us three to be a perfect way of demonstrating their affection and understanding. You will produce some memorably handsome work. Were I your age I should pursue both bookbinding and typography really seriously; they are civilised and civilising crafts.

Your three weeks in Mombasa in August will have about it a specially vital quality, because you will feel so utterly free. To cast off day-to-day responsibilities lightens life in a quite amazing way. I'm so glad you are going to Santa Cruz. Do please give that dear family our love. . . .

We send warmest thoughts and wishes.

With our love,

Robin.

[30th June, 1985]

Dear Janet [Webb],
It was so good to have your happy, spirited letter, and to know that all is well with you three. Dietrich usually has hay fever at this time, but the constant wet weather has almost kept it at bay this year. Another bonus is vegetables: lettuces, etc., have never been so lush, and we began digging Maris Bard potatoes three weeks ago. But weeds grow head-high in a week! *Birds* love wet weather, of course. A pheasant laid her twelve eggs under the filbert on the lawn, in full view. Her camouflage was complete. She looked like a mottled pebble. We weeded close to her, but she never moved. When three chicks hatched she went off with them, and squirrels or magpies cleared the nest. Our wrens usually nest in the log store, but this Spring they built in the coal house! It was a comic sight to watch the fledglings emerge over the coal, miraculously clean. Dietrich photographed them. There are now baby goldcrests, longtailed tits, bullfinches and blackcaps about the garden.

About Franz Cizek: He was certainly one of the first to recognise that children are artists: few teachers before him had reached that conclusion. True, he deliberately chose to teach selected gifted children. Their work often had a fairy-tale, decorative, art nouveau character, which must have come largely through his influence. Even so, there was a childlike innocence about the work that few teachers before him had revealed. That is what I admired. He directed his pupils, as you know, when drawing the human figure to make it absolutely stretch from top to bottom. But that was not wicked!

Then there was always in the children's work a direct reference to the natural world they knew well. And Cizek exploited that *sense of design* which so impressed me in the Deptford children I taught from 1924 to 1928. One might say that Cizek *pointed the way*. It was fortunate that Dr Viola deified him. My own London children were not impressed at all by the Austrian children's work. It must be remembered that to break away from tradition in the twenties was a brave, bold thing to do.

It isn't easy to suggest an old Ivy Lane pupil for you to talk to. Have you heard the tape of my talk on that December meeting at the school? Several old pupils were briefly questioned by the teacher who made it. We could play it to you, if you like, next time you come.

There is . . . *Reggie Baker*; he runs a grocery shop at 12, London Road, Chippenham. I'm sure that if you contacted him, he would co-operate with you. . . .

With our love,
Robin.

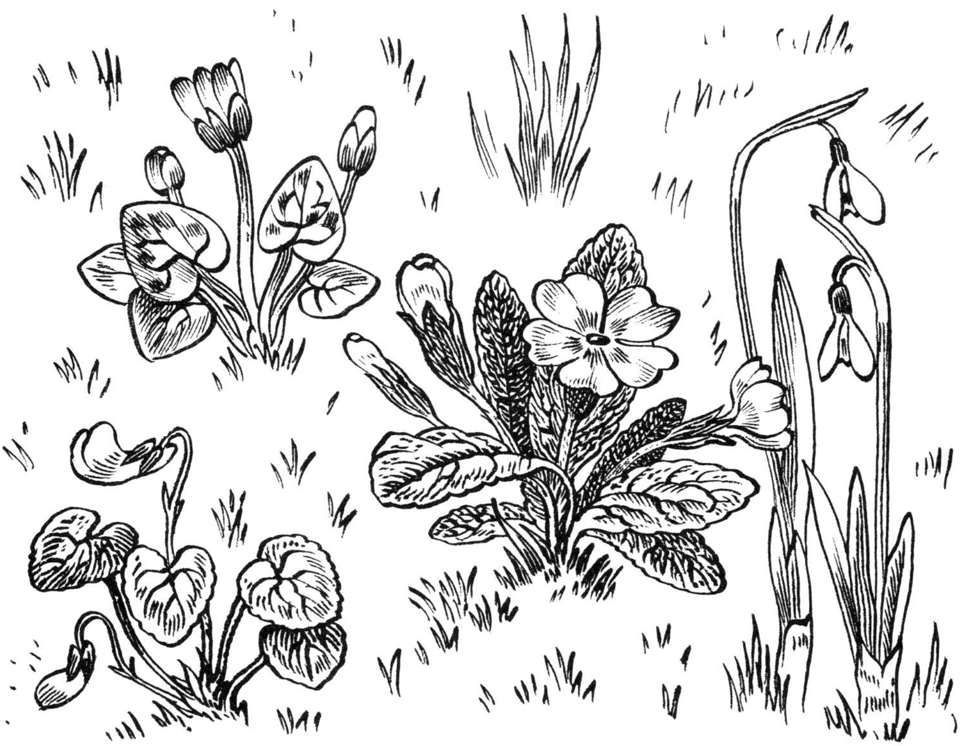

Natural history

This sub-section opens with a selection of letters written to the Taylor family. The son, Peter, and his schoolfriend Matt Jones (both about ten years old) first wrote to the Tanners: 'We are admirers of your work and proud owners of a copy of *Woodland Plants*. [We] edit *Eye on Local Nature*, copies enclosed. It would be a great honour and a real scoop for us if you would please answer a few questions for us about your work.' These letters, and those to other correspondents, include observations on plants and animals (mainly birds) at Old Chapel Field and in the countryside.

LETTER 159

[26th January, 1983]

Dear Peter and Matt,
It was very kind of you to write to us, and we are very glad to know that *Woodland Plants* gives you pleasure. We think *Eye on Local Nature* is a splendid venture, and we have greatly enjoyed reading the four numbers of your admirable magazine. They are so good that, if we may, we should like to keep them. (I enclose 48p in stamps to cover the cost.)

I enclose your questionnaire, and you may also like to have my drawing of Winter Aconite buds.

We send you all our warm congratulations and good wishes.

Yours sincerely,
Heather and Robin Tanner.

P.S. You may like to know that during the last war and until 1955 I was an H.M.I. (Inspector of Schools) in Bristol.

1 *Have you ever tried Winter Heliotrope? (See my picture Issue 13, page 3.) It is hard to make it look beautiful!*
Yes: I have drawn it in black and white, and also in colour. Your description is quite perfect. We love this plant. We have a patch in a wild part of our garden. It is very invasive, we find.

2 *Are there any plants you find particularly hard to draw?*

Yes: mainly umbelliferous ones – such as Hogweed, Pignut, Hedge Parsley and Hemlock – because of the difficulty of showing each individual tiny flower and at the same time conveying the true portrait of the plant as a whole.

3 *Is there any plant left you would like to draw?*

Yes: Lady's Slipper Orchid (*Cypripedium calceolus*), which we have never seen growing in the wild. As you will know, there are only a few plants left in England, and it is right that they should be carefully guarded.

4 *Which are your favourite seasons of the year?*

I enjoy them all, but especially early Spring (or late Winter). Heather (my wife) dislikes Winter because she hates the cold; I, on the other hand, dislike the heat of summer! Winter is full of life, if you look for it.

5 *Is there anything else you would like to tell us, please?*

We had no intention of writing a book about woodland plants. When the stocks of our book, *Wiltshire Village*, and blocks for the illustrations were destroyed in a raid in 1940, our publishers (Collins) asked us to write another book, but woodland plants did not interest them. We have always been specially fond of them, and from 1940 to 1980 I made pen drawings of the plants as they appeared, and Heather wrote about them. This was for our own interest only. When the print dealer and publisher, Robin Garton, saw the drawings and the manuscript, he begged to be allowed to publish them as a book. We tried to dissuade him because we felt sure that very few people would buy such a book. He thought otherwise, and he was right. The first edition sold out within twelve days.

You may like to know that we accept no payment at all for our work. Instead we arrange for cheques to be paid direct to causes about which we feel deeply – The World Disarmament Campaign, The Woodland Trust, The Crafts Study Centre in Bath, which we helped to found, The Campaign for Nuclear Disarmament, and Friends of the Earth.

[8th March, 1983]

Dear Geraldine and Keith,
What a full and fascinating agenda will face us when we meet at the end of April! The wonders of Leigh Woods; the writings of John Clare, Edward Thomas, Thomas Hardy and Andrew Young; and that giant of a man – William Morris. I was delighted that you found the reference to the watch in Paul Thompson's excellent book. I like Philip Henderson's, too, and best of all, I think (though it makes tough reading) is E.P.Thompson's *William Morris: Romantic to Revolutionary*. As a young man I read Mackail's *Life of Morris*, not realising then, of course, that it concealed the sad facts of W.M.'s personal life, and underplayed his Socialism as being hardly respectable! Only E.P. Thompson faces up to the real man. In July Heather and I have to address an American audience on William Morris (at Gonville and Caius College, Cambridge) at which she will wear a dress printed in W.M.'s lovely design 'Powdered Flowers', in the original Merton Abbey printing. You must see it when you visit us.

To me, Geraldine, Hardy's 'Neutral Tones' is one of the saddest and most moving poems in our language. It speaks volumes, of course. Although I love his lighter, easier poems (such as 'Weathers', 'On a Fine Morning', 'The Oxen' and 'The House of Hospitalities') it is his deeply penetrating, heartbreaking poems that to me are the greatest – 'Wessex Heights', 'Afterwards', 'Thoughts of Phena', 'In Tenebris', 'I Look into my Glass', 'The Darkling Thrush', all those remorseful poems written after the death of his first wife, and many more.

As you know, Hardy liked *The Woodlanders* best of all his novels. We love it, though perhaps I should put *Tess* first of all. The final lines of *The Woodlanders* are engraved on my mind, as are the opening ones you quoted from *Under the Greenwood Tree*, and the first paragraph of *The Return of the Native*, describing Egdon Heath:

> 'A Saturday afternoon in November was approaching the time of twilight, and the vast tract of unenclosed wild embrowned itself moment by moment. Overhead the hollow stretch of whitish cload shutting out the sky was as a tent which had the whole heath for its floor.'

. . . Perhaps I told you that in November pheasants unearthed and devoured quite a thousand crocus corms. What is extraordinary is that they selected only the white, cream and yellow ones: they did not touch the purple ones. Those they stole were precious species which we had cherished for years. We must now start again!

We all three send happy thoughts and our love.

Heather, Dietrich and Robin.

Dear Peter,

We're glad we were just in time to stop you from buying *Wiltshire Village*! We're glad, too, that you are enjoying it. Every word in it was true: only the names – for obvious reasons – were changed. England in the twenties and thirties was very different from England today. The book has had a strange history. We finished it at the end of 1938, when we were struggling to get a permit to rescue Dietrich from Nazi Germany. . . . We rescued Dietrich in April, 1939 – the day he was due to be sent to a concentration camp. (Alas! we were too late to rescue the rest of his family, who were all murdered in the gas chambers.) As soon as the book was published, in November, 1939, it became a best seller, but in 1940, in a raid on Glasgow where Collins' store was, the entire stock and the blocks for the illustrations were destroyed. We thought that was the end of *Wiltshire Village*! But in 1978 Robin Garton begged to be allowed to republish it in facsimile. The etchings are poorly reproduced, but the rest is good. Now, I'm afraid, there are few copies left.

It is wonderful that you have photographed Green Hellebore – with its strikingly white stamens. And what a compensation it is that you can indulge in some private bird watching in the Hawthorn tree while in school! *HOW* Gilbert White and Richard Jefferies would approve!!

. . . I will close this shared letter with love from us all three.

Robin.

LETTER 161

[7th June, 1983]

Dear Peter and Matt,
How extremely kind of you to send us this precious seed of the rare white Herb Robert! We are most grateful, and we send our very warm thanks. And do please thank Mark Smith of the Botanical Gardens for us.

As the ordinary pink form of Herb Robert revels in our acid sand we propose to sow some seed heads direct into the soil, carefully marking the spot. But we are also going to sow some in a peat-based compost in a pan, so that we can keep it under close observation. It will be exciting to see what happens.

The variety you describe – with white petals, but which has pink-red stamens and stems and seed cases – must be very striking. You two are doing really valuable pioneering work on plant variations!

Many years ago we were given a plant of the uncommon Dusky Cranesbill (*Geranium phaeum*). Now we have quite a colony of it and have caused a number of friends to introduce it into their gardens. We love the strange, almost black colour of the petals, and we find that bullfinches love the seed.

We hope your camping went well. Greetings and thanks.

Heather and Robin.

LETTER 162

[24th June, 1983]

Dear Peter and Matt,
Would you like to visit us? If so, I wonder if next Friday, 1st July, or Saturday, 2nd July, might suit you? If Friday, I would write to the Head of your school (or telephone), to ask if you might make this visit in connection with *Eye on Local Nature*. We have shown copies of it to a friend of ours. . . . She says she would be delighted to drop you here on her way to school and pick you up on her way home. She would call for you at Apsley Road.

Alternatively, you might prefer to come on Saturday, the 2nd, by train from Temple Meads to Chippenham, where we would meet you with our car.

(There is a 10 a.m. train, reaching Chippenham at 10.24; and there are return trains at 15.50 and 17.14.)

If neither of these dates seem convenient we will think again.

All good wishes
from Robin and Heather.

LETTER 163

[6th July, 1983]

Dear Peter,

It was most kind of you to write to us; I'm sure we enjoyed last Friday as much as you and Matt did. Would you be so kind as to post the enclosed letter to him? When he wrote he gave no address; if what I found in the telephone directory is incorrect, will you kindly put it right for me? I'm glad *Wren and Primroses* gives you pleasure. It is the smallest of my etchings, yet it is the favourite of many people. There is an impression of it – which I printed on 'your' 1825 paper – in the permanent collection at Bristol City Art Gallery. All the tall white Campanulas here have suddenly come into bloom, and they are very handsome; the best have almost black hearts. We have never been able to decide which variety they are, and we do not know how they came here. Certainly we did not introduce them.

We have told the story of the two albino forms of Herb Robert, and have shown your remarkable photographs to a number of our friends, and all have been lost in admiration.

We all three send greetings and good wishes and warm thanks.
Heather, Dietrich and Robin.

LETTER 164

[10th September, 1983)

Dear Geraldine and Keith – if I may so address you,

Your very kind and beautiful letter touched Heather and Dietrich and me deeply. The happy relationship between you and us, let it be admitted, is all due to Peter, who had the courage and confidence, in the first place, to write to two complete strangers and seek their co-operation!

In all my years as an H.M.I. and in Dietrich's as a College of Education lecturer we never met work of the quality of *Eye on Local Nature*. True, Peter and Matt have been most fortunate to be supported by you, but their sustained and searching scientific and aesthetic interest is quite remarkable. How we wish Gilbert White could peruse any number of the journal! How he would rejoice!

Fortunately, Peter will be able to take the academic demands of Bristol Grammar School in his stride, and although he may have less time at first for natural history it is clear to us that none of this first hand interest and experience will be lost. Few boys of his age are possessed of such knowledge and such a sense of wonder as he is. As you say, even in this difficult and uncertain age, magic and wonder do exist, and a boyhood like Peter's is the best possible start in life: he will never be bored or idle!

With our Greetings and warmest Wishes,

Robin.

LETTER 165

[27th December, 1983]

Dear Geraldine and Keith and Peter,
I find myself writing those names as to old friends, until I realise that we have only met Peter! I think it is because of our common interest in and love of living and growing things, and because of that remarkable journal, *Eye on Local Nature*, of course.

Of all the . . . greeting cards . . . this Christmas – from far and wide – none have given us quite such acute pleasure as your extraordinarily fine and telling photographs. We have shown them to a number of our friends already, and they are amazed at your skill and what I can only call your sympathetic, sensitive understanding of that solitary violet and those remarkable orchids. We are filled with admiration. We shall keep these precious records carefully, for they are most valuable. . . .

We hope you have enjoyed the first Christmas in your new home. As I write, a missel thrush is singing its wild song from our tall white poplar, and the air is warm. We have seen fieldfares, but, so far, no redwings; and surprisingly our big yellow-berried holly and a thickly berried stransvaesia have been left unmolested.

I expect you would welcome snow, Peter; I must confess that we three love a mild winter! Although our robins have plenty of wild food, they ask to come into the greenhouse for their favourite luxury, grated cheese!

We send loving greetings to you all, and our dearest wishes for 1984.

Heather, Dietrich and Robin.

LETTER 166

New Year's Day [1984]

It was lovely to have your very kind letter, Geraldine, with the meaty and altogether fascinating January issue of *Eye on Local Nature*. First, I read the entire number aloud to Heather and Dietrich. *How* we agree with you about the winter leaves of goosegrass! And of course you are right about the scent of violet leaves. Maybe my sense of smell is strong, for I am always teased when I insist that glass, china and wooden things all have their own peculiar smell. A friend who called yesterday said, 'Oh, it's good to come back to this wood-scented house!' He insisted that it wasn't the smell of the logs we burn, but what he called 'its essential woodiness'!

It is probably wrong of us to give our robins and their two special blackbird companions (who know us well) cheese, but they do relish it. The ripest Stilton – mainly rind – is a great favourite with them. We haven't begun to supply the tits and nuthatches and greenfinches with peanuts yet because they find all the food they need in this mild weather. Goldcrests are flitting about the garden, and a missel thrush is singing, loudly and passionately, at the top of the white poplar.

We are glad you have seen your first winter heliotrope (*Petasites fragrans*), Peter. A rather invasive mass of this strangely beautiful plant with a heavenly scent grows near our garage, and the first flowers are just opening.

Your Celandine Survey will be revealing, I expect. You may remember my page of drawings of variations in *Woodland Plants*, perhaps. In France we have met the form known as Grandiflora, which is quite a foot high and extremely handsome.

We are glad the early C19 print pleased you. We are delighted to have the drawing of Berkeley Road in Edwardian times. I'm sure 'Kindred'[1] will soon attract birds. Fortunately we rarely see a cat. Magpies and squirrels are our birds' worst enemies. We have a lovely cock pheasant and six docile hens here; they are singularly at home, and I expect they will lodge here until the breeding season. They wisely leave the woods when the disgusting practice of beating and shooting begins. Although they can do a lot of harm in our garden we are glad to give them sanctuary. (And I must say they are a splendid sight!)

Your link with Bristol Museum is splendid. The sight of badgers crossing the Suspension Bridge would be amazing! . . .

Warmest thanks from
Heather, Dietrich and Robin.

---

1. The name of the Taylors' house.

LETTER 167

[24th February, 1984]

Our dear Trio,

Spring is earlier with you than with us, for we have no celandines yet. Our Lenten hellebores – white, pink, deep plum, and lovely spotted sorts – are our best flowers at the moment, and our little copse is thick with snowdrops. Moschatel has strange ways; sometimes it is here in plenty, sometimes not, but as it entirely vanishes at the end of its season I fear we may sometimes – inadvertently – destroy it. This year we will keep a more careful watch in our garden. . . .

I am delighted, Keith, that my great hero, William Morris, means so much to you. I owe more to that 'super-man' than to any other, and his philosophy and all he stood for are immensely appropriate for today. We have several examples of his original Merton Abbey printed papers and chintzes, and when you visit us I must show you one of my most precious possessions. This is

William Morris' own beloved gold watch, which he wore throughout his life! When he died he bequeathed it to his close friend and typographical adviser, Emery Walker. When Emery died he left it to his only child, Dorothy. She advertised for a companion, to share her life at 7, Hammersmith Terrace, and Elizabeth de Haas was chosen, and the two lived together in great harmony until Dorothy died some 30 years ago. She left everything to Elizabeth, who is a dear friend of ours. The house and all its amazing contents are just as they were in Emery Walker's and Morris' day. A few years ago, Elizabeth, who teasingly calls me 'a second Morris'! forced me to accept this famous watch. I often finger it, and think how that giant of a man used to. His initials are engraved inside the back; possessing it is a great responsibility. I wish I knew where to place it. The British Museum or the V. & A. would put it away for safety, and at Kelmscott Manor it would not be easy to display it safely. And somehow, I'm afraid to wear it.

Your stall at the May Day Fair, Peter, is a splendid idea. We are sowing six varieties of wild flower seed in our open glade this Spring – including the albino form of Ragged Robin (*Lychnis flos-cuculi alba*). Yes: the *April* etching and *October*, which I've just finished designing, will leave only *July* to complete the twelve months. Actually, I have made a design for *July*, which Dietrich likes very much but which doesn't satisfy me. I must try again! Every day sees some new sign of Spring, and we cannot find time to watch and examine as much as we should like.

We send happy thoughts and our love.
Heather, Dietrich and Robin.

LETTER 168

[22nd March, 1984]

Our dear Kindred friends,

First, let us thank you most warmly for the really superb portraits of the Green Hellebore. I say *portraits* because (unlike so many flower photographs) they catch the peculiar, essential characteristics of the plant. We feel honoured to have them; they will be cherished in our precious 'Eye On' file – the first item of which is your very first letter to us, Peter! Do you realise that it was that plucky request to two complete strangers that started this fruitful and happy friendship? We owe it all to you!

What a paradise for you Leigh Woods must be! I haven't seen them since my teens. One day we mean to return. Bristol is indeed fortunate, especially as the kind climate of the Gorge is so favourable to all forms of wild life.

You asked about Yellowhammers. Here, on the ridge, we never see one, but down the hill (on the stiff stony limestone soil, totally unlike our own) there are Yellowhammers in plenty. Similarly with larks; we seldom hear them, but there are many over the flat arable fields a mile away. On the other hand, our beloved blackcap, garden warbler, tree-creeper and nuthatch keep to our bosky haven.

I should have told you that we managed to get permits for Dietrich's parents – but too late. Stettin, where they lived, was the first city to be 'liquidated', and they – with Dietrich's brother and wife and baby, and Dietrich's grandmother (who was much loved and well known for her great humanity) – all perished together. Even in England Dietrich suffered humiliation. Although declared an 'innocent alien' he was interned and treated badly at the time of the invasion scare. We felt very ashamed of our own country.

Yes: we will show you the Morris dress, and also an indigo blouse, designed, made, embroidered and worn by May Morris. Heather sometimes wears it. . . .

We send happy thoughts and our love.
Heather, Dietrich and Robin.

LETTER 169

[3rd May, 1984]

Dear friends,
Yes, indeed: that was a good day we spent together. Thank you for your extremely kind letters. We enjoyed the story of Peter's arrival home after his first visit to us![1] The new Wood Spurge photographs are splendid, and we are most grateful to have them. It was truly noble of you, Keith, to make that long

and arduous journey on behalf of the White Herb Robert. We are nurturing it carefully in the greenhouse until it is well established; then it shall have an honoured place in the garden. . . .

The blackbirds near the greenhouse have young, you'll be glad to know. The garden was wonderfully refreshed by some rain yesterday, and I am greedily hoping for more. Forgive this brief, hurried note, which nevertheless brings our love and thanks.

Robin.

---

1. That visit, mentioned in letter 162, was described to Peter's parents when Peter and Matt got home. The description lasted half an hour, non-stop!

LETTER 170

[3rd July, 1984]

Our dear 'Eye On' Trio,

Your July number is stimulating and delightful, original and varied, enthusiastic and dedicated. How I wish millions more people shared your concern! The four drawings are all convincing and true. I specially admire the beautifully veined Columbine leaf and the rendering of Yellow Pimpernel and Quaking Grass. Every page is full of interest. How the founder of *The Countryman* – J. Robertson-Scott, long dead – would have enjoyed it! Heather's sister, Faith, became his private secretary in 1937 (at Idbury, high up on the Cotswolds); and when he died, Sir Stafford Cripps' son John became editor, and he, with Faith as assistant editor, ran the journal for many years. The present editor is a splendid fighter for the countryside – Christopher Hall. He is fearless and devoted and forthright: *The Countryman* is in good hands.

The Columbine photograph is exquisite, Peter. Grateful thanks for it. It is a real portrait of that astonishing flower.

I'm sorry to say that the rabbit is stricken with disease. He is nearly blind, and his head is strangely swollen, with nearly bald patches. He eats freely, and does not seem to be in pain, but he doesn't move far from the fruit cage, and he sleeps a great deal. We seem powerless to help him. At least he is safe and unmolested, but it is terrible to witness his rapid deterioration. It was so stupid to introduce myxomatosis. Man is often a thoughtless, shortsighted creature. This little rabbit cannot be more than about three or four months old, and we hope, for its sake, that it won't live much longer. The garden looks lovely – until we realise that this helpless victim is languishing there. He doesn't seem to fear us at all. We give him/it water, but I doubt whether he/it drinks any.

Do you know the beautiful blue Meadow Sage (*Salvia pratensis*)? We used to have many plants, but now have only one – probably because it is a lime lover. I will try to save seed. You might like to grow it. It must be the finest pure blue wild flower, I think.

How sweet of you to send an envelope for Heather! As she has not seen it, it shall remain a secret until the 14th. Dietrich's birthday is 16th May. When are your birthdays? Love to all three from us three.

Robin.

LETTER 171

[30th September, 1984]

. . . The arrival of *Eye on Local Nature* is always a very special occasion, and the October number – with its wider and wider appeal and the variety of its contents – is most heartening and satisfying to read. Thank you very much for it. You undoubtedly go from strength to strength. We are particularly delighted that Peter's old primary school has invited him and Matt to advise on establishing a conservation area. That is the kind of influence we greatly admire: it is a tribute both to the school and to Matt and Peter. Your excellent photograph of autumn Lady's Tresses shows the unique arrangement of the flowers perfectly. What a splendid variety of fungi you and Matt's family found in Leigh Woods! Yesterday, in Kilvert's Field – our meadow just across the lane – I found a giant Puffball weighing more than a pound. Fried in butter it made a delicious supper dish. It is our favourite 'mushroom', and its fragrance is unforgettable. Westonbirt Arboretum, being quite near, is one of our favourite haunts. Better than the formal Arboretum, we think, is the ancient piece of adjacent forest called Silk Wood. You reach it by walking from the car park straight ahead (instead of bearing right), and the path makes a circular tour. We have never seen more Toothwort, Wood Sorrel and Primroses than there. The Arboretum in autumn is of course spectacular; Acers, Liquidambers, Tulip Trees and the like are quite amazing. *Our* loveliest feature at the moment is a drift of about 300 very large, pure white, tulip-like 'Autumn Crocuses' growing in the grass (the now extremely rare *Colchicum speciosum album*). We started many years ago with a few dozen corms which I bought for twopence each from a keen gardener called Miss Brown of Longformacus in the Lammermuirs. We corresponded but never met. Now a single corm of this nearly extinct variety costs £2.50! It is all very sad. I mark plants that become too crowded, and dig these up in July, when I usually find four or five nice corms where originally there was one. I've often given specimens to friends, most of whom have, sadly, been unsuccessful with them. Our light acid sand seems to be their favourite soil. . . .

Heather, Dietrich and Robin.

LETTER 172

[27th–28th February, 1985]

. . . Your splendid letter, Peter, and the March number of 'Eye On . . . ' arrived just as I came in from gardening. I had watched Dietrich's bees going out on cleansing flights, and some bringing in pollen. For the first time it has been warm and sunny enough for the crocuses to open really flat. Many of them are self-sown natural hybrids of *Crocus tomasinianus* – white, grey, deep purple, many pale pinky mauves, and best of all, deep warm ruby red-purple flowers with no hint of blue. We planted only 100 many years ago: now they have invaded the vegetable plots, and they are so thick on the paths that it is almost impossible not to walk on them. I wish all bulbs would multiply as quickly.

As always, 'Eye On' is a delight both to read and to look at. Keith's splendid paragraphs are most heartening. We shall be with you in spirit on March 3rd. That is Edward Thomas's birthday. I know how angry he would be if the badgers were disturbed. His poem, 'The Combe', ends with these lines:

But far more ancient and dark
The Combe looks since they killed the badger there,
Dug him out and gave him to the hounds,
That most ancient Briton of English beasts.

Heather was of course particularly fascinated by your 'Language of Flowers', Peter, with your charming drawings. And I particularly like your Wardening Journal,[1] Geraldine, with its hint at another dimension. . . . Many thanks, dear Peter, for sending us this very well realised Hedgehog. It is wonderful that The Woodland Trust is winning more and more support, since at last people are beginning to realise the urgency to halt the appalling destruction of our woodlands. Over the need for 'a nuclear freeze', and ultimately total nuclear disarmament, people are slower to face facts rather than to absorb propaganda. Heather will write out the crucial truths in a few sentences. These cannot be disputed. We three spend a lot of time confronting pro-nuclear people with them. We find it takes a very long time for them to be believed, because of the conditioning that the Government has done for so long.

I expect you and Matt enjoyed the television programme on a Cotswold Wall? We thought it excellent.

Strangely, we have seen fewer redwings and fieldfares than usual, yet friends who have suburban gardens have had great flocks. My sister, who lives on the edge of Chippenham, has fed large numbers in her garden on surplus Newton Wonder apples. The berries here have not yet been stripped.

What excellent advice Dr Ernest Neal has given 'Eye On' about badgers! And what a delightful description Matt has written about his unique compost heap!

I'm just going to plant out a number of hellebores which I grew from seed in pots; they have lived in the greenhouse till now, but I think they can stand whatever weather is in store for us in March.

We send our love to you all.
Heather, Dietrich and Robin.

---

1. The Taylors are voluntary Wardens of Leigh Woods, Bristol.

[29th April, 1985]

Dear Taylor family,

. . . When we came here 54 years ago, this windy, treeless, hilltop field had hardly any birds at all. Making the hazel copse, planting trees and shrubs (far too close together, some people think) and clothing the walls with Irish ivy have turned this virtually into a bird sanctuary. All the following have nested here: Tree Creeper, Nuthatch, Greenfinch, Chaffinch, Bullfinch, Wren, Goldcrest, Thrush, Missel Thrush, Blackbird, Blackcap, Garden Warbler, Willow Warbler, Robin, Dunnock, Wood Pigeon, Turtle Dove, Collared Dove, Blue, Great, Coal and Longtailed Tits, Chiffchaff, Whitethroat and Starling. Probably the Green and Spotted Woodpeckers, too, have nested here. Their holes are evident. There's nothing at all remarkable in this list, but it is comforting to know that in little more than an acre there are both space and food for this typical range of birds – not to mention bats, hedgehogs and squirrels! True, we sometimes realise that they – not we – are the rightful owners of Old Chapel Field! And it's nice of them to let us live here too!!

Four cock blackbirds (whose nests are on our walls) hop about the lawn about a yard apart. It looks rather comic! They don't fight, but nor do they mix; I suppose each is guarding his territory.

Robins are feeding their young just outside the kitchen window. Wrens have, as usual, chosen our log store. I think we've told you that the missel thrushes' nest is placed conspicuously at the top of an apple tree. The hen's tail shows up plainly, sticking out beyond the nest. The male thrush attacks magpies when they come near. If only they would choose a secret spot to build in!

These scraps of paper are 150 years old. They are waste cut-offs from a book I have just made. I think this must have been common writing paper in the 1830s. It is delicious to write on. I wish I had more of it. . . .

On Saturday night we suffered three degrees of frost. It browned a few magnolia blossoms, but harmed nothing else. We have been ravaged by bullfinches. Every apple tree and most of the cherries have been stripped of their flower buds. What is so strange is that the birds don't appear to *eat* the buds; I've watched them nip them off and throw them down. If I clap my hands in an effort to deter them, they evidently think I am applauding them, for they continue their destruction vigorously, heeding me not at all!

Last year I obtained seed of the rare Elizabethan gold-laced and silver-laced polyanthus, and the plants are now flowering. They are small and so dark as to be almost black, and the gold or silver edge to each petal gives it a strange, formal appearance. Their scent is delicious. I shall try to propagate from them. Because some of our camellias set seed I thought I would sow some, and already I have four little plants! I wonder what their flowers will be like? As you see, I am delirious with Spring!

We send our love to you all.
Heather, Dietrich and Robin.

LETTER 174

[20th June, 1985]

Dear Peter,
What a memorable photograph that is of you noble three painting out the slogans on the rock face of the Avon Gorge! Let us hope it will never again be necessary. Your photograph will go into the rapidly swelling Taylor archive. Very many thanks for it. . . .

Heather (who is more musical than I am) will add something about the difference between the song of the blackcap and the nightingale. To me, the blackcap's song is as pure and melodious as any bird's, but it is happy and not passionate. Nor is it prolonged, nor full of variety like the nightingale's.

Continued later.
The wrens slowly emerged from the coal, not looking at all soiled! And their mother led them into the copse, where they are now having their first view of the great wide world! Dietrich attempted to photograph them, but they moved so swiftly that he wasn't sure whether he caught them.

We haven't found the long-tailed tits' nest yet, but the large family is very happy. If only we could spend more time, just watching, we should see many wonders that pass us by.

A young rabbit scampered through the garden yesterday; I hope it will not decide to adopt us – just when our lettuce and kohl-rabi and spinach are in their prime.

Our love to you all.
Heather, Dietrich and Robin.

LETTER 175

[18th January, 1986]

. . . What an interesting study that tiny minority, Quakers, will be for you, Peter! Their early history, with appalling persecution, and their development from being people who rejected the arts to becoming champions of them, you will find extremely interesting. The Society of Friends will never grow large: the responsibilities of every member are too great. There are no priests, and there is no hierarchy. We conceive of 'God' as that of good in everyone, and in our lives we must recognise this and seek to answer that of good in everybody. (That's not easy for me when I think of, say, Mrs Thatcher or Keith Joseph!)

Central, of course, to Quakerism, is the Peace Testimony that Friends presented to Charles II in 1660 or thereabouts. It was our whole agreement with this that led Heather and me to join the Society more than half a century ago. (Previously she was a confirmed member of the Church of England. I had always been a pacifist, but had never joined any church.) For a number of years Quaker Meeting for this area was held here – in our living room. Now the nearest Meeting is in Malmesbury. The work of reconciliation plays an important part in the Society of Friends: they have always been identified with the Peace Movement, so they often find themselves in direct opposition to their Government. . . .

I'm sure Bristol Friends will be helpful to you, Peter. *Do* visit the early Meeting House, with its old stables, at *Frenchay*. Those well-preserved buildings will give you an excellent picture of the early years of Quakerism.

To sit for an hour, often in complete silence, in what is called Meeting, is too much for most people. There is no 'service', nor music, and there are no hymns. Anyone can speak if they have a thought they want to share. Ask

Bristol Quakers about their *business* meetings, Peter. These are conducted quite brilliantly. There is no voting, not even a showing of hands. Instead, the Clerk 'takes the sense of the Meeting', and that always seems to work.

Every year there is a great gathering of the Society, usually at Friends House in the Euston Road, which lasts for several days. It is called Yearly Meeting. At the end it issues an 'Epistle' – that is, a statement of the main issues and thoughts which arose throughout this great conference.

I hope you'll enjoy your study, Peter.

As always, we send our love to you all.
Heather, Dietrich and Robin.

LETTER 176

[26th January, 1986]

Dear Peter,

It was brave of you to sit through that long silence in a Friends' Meeting. Was it at Redland, I wonder? Most people prefer an ordered 'service', with music and prayers; they feel the strain of a long silence. In this noisy world I should have thought silence would be a welcome relief. When I wrote to you about Quakerism I should have said that Quakers believe that they should try to obey their conscience, or 'the inner light', to use the historic phrase. It is more important to act according to your conscience than to the laws of the State. I also forgot to give you the exact wording of the Peace Testimony which 'the harmless religious Society of Friends' boldly presented to Charles II in 1660. It might be useful for you to quote in your essay. Here it is:

> 'We utterly deny all outward wars and strife, and fightings with outward weapons, for any end, or under any pretence whatsoever. This is our testimony to the whole world. The Spirit of Christ by which we are guided is not changeable, so as once to command us from a thing as evil, and again to move unto it. And we certainly know, and testify to the world, that the Spirit of Jesus, which leads us unto all truth, will never move us to fight and war against any man with outward weapons, neither for the kingdom of Christ, nor for the kingdoms of the world.'

I think I forgot to mention that a Quaker wedding is a very informal, simple affair. Some years ago we had one here in this room. (I'm glad to say it has proved to be a very happy marriage!)

I expect that you know that the Society of Friends issues a weekly journal called *The Friend*. It is in most public libraries. We could send you a copy if you needed one.

We are relieved that the badgers were not disturbed by the Orienteers.

We send our trio of love to the Kindred trio!

Robin.

LETTER 177

[28th May, 1986]

Dear friends,

It was very good to see you in your own home; and it was a nice surprise to meet Jean-Luc, and we were very glad at last to visit the main source of *Eye on Local Nature*. When we took Matt home he begged us to come and see his garden – and particularly his frogs! So having after much difficulty found a space in which to park the car, we paid a very happy ten-minute call. What a choice and varied collection of plants thrive in that small space! It was very kind of you to prepare a picnic, and generous of Nature to provide most of us with a seat. Sunday was a day to remember.

I gave my Bath Festival talk yesterday. Unfortunately twice as many people wanted seats as there was room for, so there was much disappointment, but the University recorded the talk, which people can obtain from the museum.

We send our thanks and our love to you all.

Heather, Dietrich and Robin.

LETTER 178

[6th March, 1987]

Our very dear friends, (I'm trying to cope with a recalcitrant pen!)

It was extremely kind of you to write about *A Vision of Wiltshire*. . . . The most general comment is that it was refreshing to watch a quiet, gentle, visually beautiful and non-violent film, in contrast to the noisy, ugly, violent programmes so often broadcast. Clive North's photography is of course superb, and James Hogg's commentary is quite perfect; but the creative genius behind it all was the producer, Margaret Benton. It was she who conceived and shaped it over many months, with immense skill and tact, and with an uncanny understanding of us three. . . .

What a superb job Jean-Luc has made of *Wiltshire Village*![1] The cover reproduction of *Christmas* is by far the best there has ever been, and the deliciously black type and bright white paper are a rare joy. Small wonder (as Jean-Luc tells us) that it is selling quickly, for it is a bargain. Jean-Luc's promptness and unfussy efficiency and sensitive understanding continue to amaze us. He really is a fine and rare human being. You must have found him a great pleasure to work with. . . .

How good it is to hear blackbirds in full song again! And the cooing of wood pigeons and the unmusical call of collared doves in our copse also give us pleasure. I fear that many people would call the thousands of invasive crocuses in our garden weeds – for they bloom in every path, in the vegetable beds, in the lawn and even out in the village Common. They are white, cream, ruby red, a rather sickly mauve and deep purple. We love them all.

Our warmest wishes and our love to you.

Heather, Dietrich and Robin.

---

1. The paperback edition, published by Impact Books.

LETTER 179

[8th May, 1967]

My dear Bill [Asbridge],
It was good to have your and Marie's wishes. Rather more than three weeks ago I 'caught' (I believe, on a visit to London) that disgustingly humiliating malady, shingles; and it still grips my left thigh and back. At first, sleeping was impossible; but, although the pain never goes, that is better now, and the actual rash is healing. It is the neuritis accompanying it that makes walking difficult.

However, the blackcap sings all day and the swifts scream, and cuckoos both call and bubble; and species rhododendrons and azaleas and camellias are wonderful. So – bad as I am at this unwonted rôle of patient – I count my blessings . . .

Your vital, vivid letter from Africa delighted us. One day we should love to hear more about that surely quite unique experience. We hope all is well with you four, and that you are enjoying marvellous Spring happenings along your riverside.

With love, as always, and with grateful thanks for your very sweet thought.

Robin.

LETTER 180

[31st May, 1976]

My dear Cecil,
. . . This year I am growing female hops – for beauty and for Dietrich's beer-making. Ami put me on to the renowned Mr Fuggle of East Grinstead, but because of a virus disease Kent and Sussex are not allowed to sell hops outside that area. Mr Fuggle suggested Selbourne, but Hampshire also is forbidden to 'export' hops! Then Cyril found an advertisement from Herefordshire in *The Observer*, and I bought five excellent plants, which are now doing well. Do tell me the normal height of hops, Cecil. One of mine has reached the bedroom window already! . . .

LETTER 181

Also to Cecil Crouch, later in the year.

. . . All round our guestroom window are hops. I bought female plants from Herefordshire so that Dieti could have hops for the excellent beer he keeps us supplied with. I never expected them to reach the roof! I must say they are a splendid sight. Do you wait till they are dry and papery before you pick them? Is that usually in late September or early October? Does the bine die then? And does one cut the plant down to the earth in late Autumn?

I suppose hop growing still flourishes in Kent? If so, is the gathering still done by swarms of Londoners? Or is it now done by machine? I should like to see the remoter parts of rural Kent and Sussex again. Do the old country ways persist there at all, I wonder?

LETTER 182

[22nd October, 1978]

My dear Edith,
. . . Did I tell you about Percy and the bats? For many years they have roosted in our porch, but we did not know that they also favoured a hole under a coping tile until Percy found them sleeping there when he came to remove the tile. 'But we let 'em bide,' he said, 'an' 'ave their sleep out, and wake up natural.' That was typical of his and Philip's sensitivity. . . .

LETTER 183

[11th May 1979]

My dear Edith,
. . . We have had a great 'to-do' with squirrels! One morning I watched four young with their parents basking in the sun, on our bedroom window sill!! They devoured everything within reach! Dieti was flattered that they had so honoured us! And of course the babies *do* look enchanting. The dray was behind the elm boarding, and in the wall cavity. The scampering noises were

awful: we felt really invaded. John came to breakfast, and he agreed that the situation was fast becoming intolerable. He said he would get us a can of Fox Oils and that this would do the trick. We soaked hessian in this strange liquid (smelling like unclean humanity), and Dieti climbed our tall ladder and pushed it into the larger of the two holes. The squirrels were quite unmoved, so John urged us to plunge a *second* piece into the smaller hole, shutting the creatures, only temporarily of course, inside the wall! They reacted at once by scratching to find a way out, and making a great scampering. So after two hours, almost, we pulled out the second piece of sack cloth. We did not see the exodus, but all six squirrels have disappeared. They are certainly not in our garden nor in Kilvert's Meadow. They obviously could not bear having Fox Oils near them! John says it will unfailingly stop a fox from invading sheep folds and hen houses. The peace and the silence in the garden, without the squirrels, are marvellous! . . .

LETTER 184

[25th September, 1979]

My dear Edith,

. . . Have I told you how a young squirrel vandalised our bedroom a month or two ago? He knocked over our precious Hamada, Leach, Cardew and Lucie Rie pots, and he wetted everywhere. Miraculously, nothing was broken. We heard the rumpus just in time. It wasn't easy to persuade him to leave, and he cursed us vehemently. I do hope we're safe from invasion at last! Living among wildlife is all very well: townspeople have no idea what it is really like! Every morning we have to sweep our front doorstep and porch, because for many years bats have roosted there. They roost above the logs in the garden house, too. We're pleased to share our space with them, but oh, the droppings! Moles are everywhere. They lift up plants sometimes that die, and they do real damage, yet we love them all. Bullfinches strip all our fruit trees: we can't love them, I'm afraid. . . .

We all three send love and warm thanks for a wonderful letter.

Robin.

LETTER 185

[18th September, 1979]

My dear Jim [Fairbairn],
I had just finished the dreaded, tricky and quite exhausting job of laying and smoking the grounds on my two new plates, and was longing for some respite, when Peter-the-Postman brought your beautifully packed box. What a delicious surprise! What a wonderful present! What a breath from hot, sunny, rocky places! The scents, as I slowly unwrapped each one on the just-scrubbed kitchen table, immediately permeated the room, and as I sit writing in the big room I can smell that wild, small-leaved Rosemary, the Oregano (a wild Marjoram far more pungent than our native one), the long sprays of some kind of Mint which I cannot identify, and the other warm, spicy ones which are unknown to me; one smells like old violins, one a bit Juniperish, and the other has rather a thyme-like fragrance. But what a sweet thought of yours, Jim, to send them to us! When Heather returns from her 4–5-day stay at Charney Manor I know she will straightaway make a bouquet garni, put it in a muslin bag, and devise a wonderful casserole in which to plunge it. But we shall put *a portion* of each sort into a pot pourri which we keep in our bedroom in an early Winchcombe covered jar: we cannot let *all* of it be expended. . . .

Love from Robin.

LETTER 186

[19th May, 1982]

My dear Cecil,
We do have some strange visitors. Yesterday a very splendid peacock arrived, strutting about the garden as though he owned it. In the evening he flew into our very tall and spreading White Poplar, now in delicate filigree leaf. It was like a bit of C18 Chinoiserie or a piece of Chinese painted wallpaper. He roosted there. At 4 a.m., just before the dawn chorus, he woke me with his piercing yell – four times over, then a pause, and four times again. I went into

the garden at six, and looked up at him and said I would be glad if he would go. He fidgeted but stood his ground, until he realised that his presence wasn't wholly welcome. And he flew away, high above the aspens and over and beyond Kilvert's Field, his enormously long tail swaying behind him. Now tree creepers are active, and the missel thrushes have their young, and chaffinches are feeding theirs. Except for a few corpses from winter the garden now looks right: apple blossom, six 'wedding cake' viburnums at their best, our entrance massed with hawthorn, and The Common all gold and silver with buttercups and hedge parsley. What a moment it is! . . .

Much love from us three,
Robin.

LETTER 187

[3rd June, 1983]

My dear Cecil,
A warm drizzle has sent me indoors just as I was enjoying using my non-bending technique for weeding a patch of soil before planting out Hubbard Squashes grown in peat pots in the greenhouse. I use a very long-handled fork to prise weeds out of the earth and lift them on the fork and hurl them into my waiting wheelbarrow; on this light sand this is easy. Even large dandelions can be prised up, shaken (on the fork) free of soil, and cast into the barrow to be burnt. 'Upright gardening' is a great help to me!

It is a day full of bird activity. For some unknown reason the dunnocks have deserted their four young, and have started to build a new nest. I have a feeling that a marauding magpie took one of the original five fledglings, and this was enought to cause the sad desertion. Two young robins, at the speckled brown stage, have come close up to my fingers, in quest of worms, as I have planted out Polyanthus seedlings. Their fearlessness is very touching. When, I wonder, do they start to mistrust us? Certainly, here, where every bird is safe, it comes as a shock when some fly off at our approach. I feel rebuffed when that happens! I bless one Collingwood Ingram, a gardener who became famous for cherries, who lives at Benenden, near Cranbrook in Kent, for a splendid hybrid he produced, called 'Tridel'. It becomes a huge, mounded bush, thick with large white flowers like roses. It really is a marvellous shrub. Ours kindly layers itself, so that we are often able to give away vigorous young plants. Technically, the plant is, of course, a raspberry. We have another sort, called *Rubus parviflora*, also with large clean white flowers, and with striking vine-like leaves. This was given to me 45 years ago in Yorkshire, at a college I was inspecting. Now it takes over a large area, and we bless it. The warm air is fragrant with the scent of Azaleas, and the curious smell of May blossom is everywhere. May (hawthorn) is very late this year.

Continued 4th June.

Devoted fans from Great Waltham . . . visited us yesterday, bringing us plants from their garden and getting us to sign books. They stayed for a tea party . . . They took a large box of plants for their garden, including ferns, but as their soil is stiff limy clay I doubt whether these plants that thrive in our acid sand will survive the change.

Their visit was followed by one from two dear ex-students of Dieti's, called Sarah and Richard, who both teach in Oxfordshire. Richard is a good potter and Sarah embroiders. Richard has such long, curled lashes that they look unreal! . . .

We've actually had a dry, hot day at last – 'flaming June' in fact. I encountered a handsome slow-worm this morning. A spotted flycatcher came into our bedroom, happily exploring. It was nice to see it at close quarters.

Continued 5th June: 5 a.m.

The cuckoos woke me half an hour ago, calling 'cuck-cuck-cuckoo'. I expect your Girton ones have changed their tune, too. I am so glad you have them. They are wickedly immoral birds, but Spring would not be Spring without their peaceful call. But as England rips up hedgerows and many species lose their habitats, the cuckoo will soon find life here almost impossible. Already we notice an increase in hedge-nesting birds – obviously driven West. The people from Great Waltham told us that where they live there is nothing but vast fields of rape and barley and sugar beet; and the farmers are fantastically rich. And the unwanted grain mountain continues to swell – while we leave many thousands of people to starve. Of all the parties fighting this election, only Ecology is compassionate and sane about this. . . .

Continued 9.30 p.m.

We've had an interesting day – first, lunch with old Quaker friends in their wonderful old house at Steeple Aston in North Oxfordshire; and then a rather remarkable gathering of Oxfordshire and Warwickshire Friends in the ancient, disused Quaker Meeting House at Adderbury. Just once a year they occupy it. Perhaps I told you earlier that Heather and I were asked to speak on 'Two of our many lives'. We did it as a sort of duet. The gathering was so warm and easy and of one accord that we said all we wanted to say. . . . Afterwards, on the sunny greensward we had a delightful tea party. I forgot to say that we were introduced by a teacher from the Friends' Boarding School at Sibford Gower nearby – . . . whom we have known since she was ten, and used to come to Meeting with her parents at Old Chapel Field. She was married here in our living room!

All the 60-mile journey to Adderbury was like a bridal way, with hawthorn and cow parsley lining the roads! The roads out of Kington Langley look like processional ways! No queen ever had anything so beautiful, surely. . . .

LETTER 188

[2nd July, 1983]

My dear Jim,

. . . Yesterday two Primary School boys from . . . Clifton – Peter Taylor and Matthew Jones – spent the day with us. Peter's and Matt's botanical knowledge and absorbed observation astonished us. Gilbert White would have been thrilled. They photographed Cornus Kousa; they recorded; they took home plants for their garden of wild flowers; and they were delightful guests. (I gave each an inscribed impression of *Wren and Primroses*, and they brought us extraordinary photographs they had taken.) They have recently been studying Herb Robert, which, as you know, has bright pink flowers. But they discovered an albino form of it, with white stamens, and another albino form with normal stamens. They could find no record of this occurrence in any book and most people doubted them. . . . Meanwhile they searched in Bristol Library, and were lent the very early records of a Bristol botanist; and they found not only his notes and description of white Herb Robert but its exact site – and that is where, after all these years, it is still growing! and where Peter and Matt *re-discovered* it!! Their full-size photographs of it are perfect. . . .

We all three send warmest thoughts and our love.

Robin.

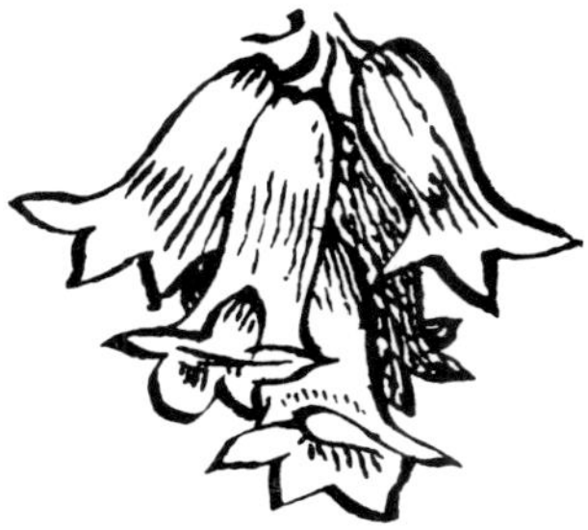

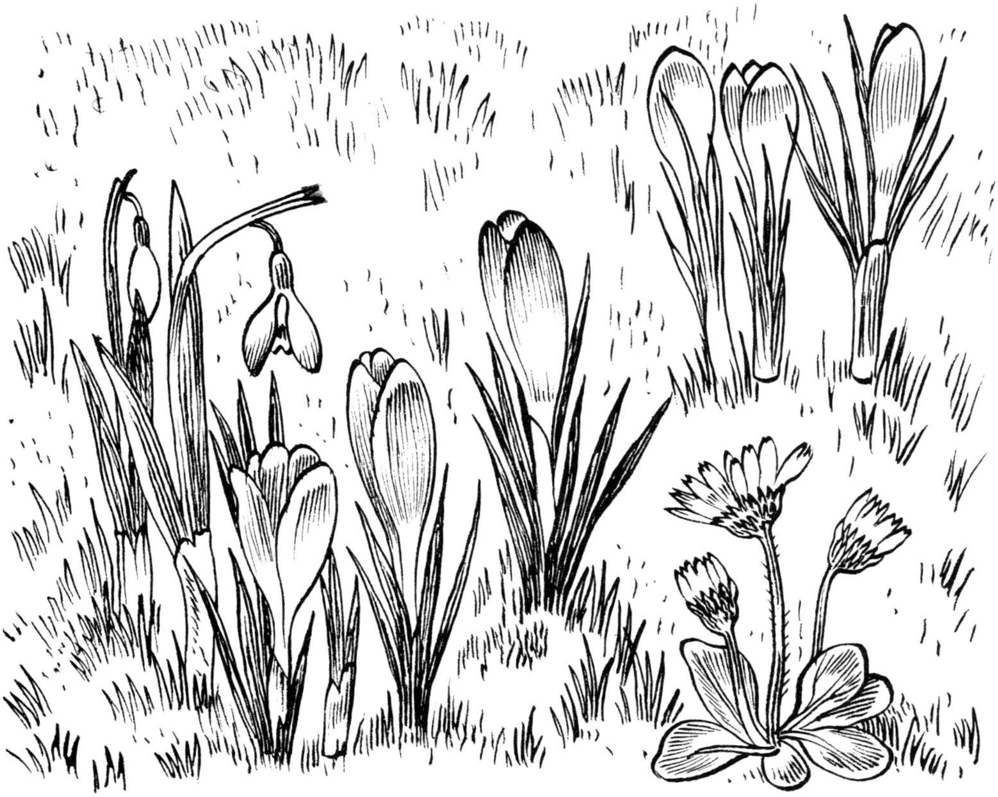

Exhibitions and art galleries

These letters include some observations on films and books.

LETTER 189

[25th May, 1966]

My dear Edith,

Among the great host of letters we have had about the Barron and Larcher Exhibition,[1] truly none has been more marvellously understanding and perceptive than yours; it was positively inspired. How wonderfully sensible of you, too, to take your colleagues with you! Yes: it WAS an immense labour of love. We are thankful to have accomplished it at last. Never can it happen again like that, and one cannot but feel sad that so many people missed seeing it just because they put other (quite minor, personal and fleeting) priorities first. Unhappily there were two thefts. Can you believe it? I'm afraid I dare not risk another show where anything can actually be touched. It is very sad. Many people want to see the collection beautifully and permanently housed. But where? and how? And what about the care and maintenance of perishable textiles? Well-meaning people urge me to do this or that, but that is as far as they go! I should like to talk to you about the whole problem when we meet. What is abundantly clear – and this is something *you* perceive intensely – is that Barron's work has tremendous significance for us all today. Just how to ensure that it is cherished and used is my conundrum. . . .

But let us talk of EVERYTHING when we meet! We all three send warm love and our very special thanks for your most memorable letter.

Robin.

1. At the Royal West of England Academy, Bristol.

[begun 31st July, 1974]

My dear Cecil,

. . . But to answer your last letter: The cuttings you send are always an entertainment as they come from sources we don't habitually use. Do continue, please! . . . Yes, indeed, Cecil: we *have* to be organised: life forces it upon us! Take this etching publication enterprise, for example. Joe is marvellously businesslike, so we have to keep up with him. Even the label for the handmade portfolios to contain the 50 sets of twelve etchings I have to design and letter. For the show in Bath from 6th November to 6th December Heather and I are working at a display to make clear The Craft of Etching. Work, work, work!! Perhaps you'll be able to see the exhibition when it comes to the National Book League for the middle two weeks of January? The first of five exhibitions will be at Abbots Hall Gallery, Kendal, from 22nd September to 22nd October. Joe has written a good catalogue, which I hope you'll like. Raymond Lister has written a long, chatty essay, which I think we shall use later on, not for the exhibitions.

On July 4th I spent a most fascinating day at Goldsmiths'. I had to address the post-graduate group on their last day at College. I read them a piece from my own diary, written on July 4th, 1924 – *my* last day at College, exactly 50 years ago! You would hardly recognise the place. The main building is so clean that it looks new. The dirty laurels are no more. That long entrance corridor (now tiled in white and black) has been widened to take in a book shop, bar and other 'amenities'. But I lectured in that theatre old Bobby White used to use, and that was *exactly* the same. The streets to the left and right of the college are now just blocks of Goldsmiths'! – New, comfortable, enormous towers! The unfamiliar London skyline seen from the top floor (with a little, dwarfed St Paul's) was strange to see. But, oddly, I feel at home at Goldsmiths' and still love the place – the Art School rather less than the Education Department. I taxied to and from Paddington (£3 each way, but not paid by me!) and that, too, was an entertainment! – the old '48' and '53' bus routes! I thought of you a great deal. A beautiful young Cypriot (with a mini-cab) drove me back to Paddington, and asked 100 questions: why had I visited Goldsmiths'? Had I been a student there? But *when*? When I said 1922, we nearly had an accident! . . .

Your white campanula – three great trailing pots full – is glorious. . . . We speak of you often – not only at breakfast in the greenhouse when we marvel at it! We all three send our love as always. Forgive a rushed letter. People are walking down the garden path. . . .

Robin.

LETTER 191

[10th March, 1976]

My dear Cecil,

Your letter came at breakfast time, so I read it aloud. The more testy and irritable and scathing it became, the more we hooted with laughter! 'Well: he's certainly *well* and himself again!' exclaimed Dieti. And as I read more and more of your sharp and sarcastic dismissals of my solicitous suggestions and queries I positively shrieked with mirth! Though we did agree that such an outburst might well put off some people from ever replying to it.

But I was wrong to worry about your domestic and social arrangements (or, rather, the lack of them); we must all be allowed to kill ourselves at our own rate and in our own way; so in future I will make no enquiries, and will assume that your life is as you want it to be, and that all is well with you. . . .

After taking my two new etchings to the Painter-Etchers' show on Monday, I took a taxi to The Tate, queued for one and a half hours, and joined the great throng to see Constable. It wasn't comfortable, but even so it bowled me over. This great, warm, humane and marvellous man comes out of it magnificently. Not even those over-popular large works seemed stale. In fact, I loved the well-known huge paintings almost best of all, though the incomparable drawings ravished me. I'm taking Heather tomorrow, when we hope to arrive by 10 a.m.

We want to see the R.P.-E. exhibition in the afternoon. The Constable catalogue, by the way, is superb. . . .

No: I agree that you can't insert sensitivity into people, but I have yet to find one who can't be helped to discover his own, even where none was apparent. I do not believe that anyone is born without the capacity; I say that only because of my own direct experience of people. . . .

Nor can I say I have 'lost the ability to trust', as you put it. People continue to disappoint us and even let us down, but Heather and Dietrich and I can point to far, far more instances of the reverse. So we shall go on trusting. . . .

On Saturday we go to The Ashmolean for the private view and a little celebration-luncheon-party on the occasion of the Griggs Centenary Exhibition. His old American friend, Francis Comstock – a great benefactor of the museum – will be there, and we are entertaining him and his family and the Griggses here on Sunday. (Francis Comstock wrote the great book on Griggs, and it was he who first introduced my work to New York and Boston.) I hear that The Fitzwilliam, too, is to put on a Griggs exhibition. Can you discover whether this is so? Hitchin, where Griggs was born (just a century after Constable), is staging one. . . .

This comes with love and happy thoughts from all three.

Robin.

LETTER 192

[1st September 1977]

My dear Cecil,

. . . Yesterday we three braved it [London], first to see the Graham Sutherland portraits in those glorious galleries at Carlton House Terrace (the 'extension' of the National Portrait Gallery) and then out to Walthamstow to the William Morris Gallery in his boyhood home. The Sutherlands really are an astonishing achievement, and they are beautifully backed up by countless searching studies and photographs and an excellent catalogue. I'm still haunted by the moving and sad portrait of Edward Sackville-West, and it was good to see Somerset Maugham and the outrageous Helena Rubenstein again: a really wonderful exhibition. The underground journey to Walthamstow (WHAT a dreary, depressing place!) was quite easy, and the museum wonderful. We were received like old friends, and had a nostalgic, refreshing, really invigorating afternoon there. I hadn't realised what a fine C18 house the museum is. What would William Morris say about the surroundings now? . . .

Gordon and brother and friend are bringing my exhibition back tomorrow, when we shall have a festive lunch party. Our bare walls will look strange, being clothed again. *The Listener* had a review of my work that was exactly the review one dreams of but knows one doesn't deserve, so I feel greatly humbled by it, yet also much encouraged. I find it quite astonishing that the reviewer (Denis Thomas, that very good writer) should be able to get right inside me, so to speak, and understand so exactly what it is that I long to express on copper. He has done it with quite rare understanding, I think. . . .

I hope you'll enjoy the Bruckner and Mozart Concert on the 9th. Would you agree the Schubert *Quintet (Op. 163)* – that he himself never heard – with that marvellous and heartbreaking slow movement – is one of the most beautiful works ever written? We have a fine record (Weller), which I can hardly bear to hear, it wounds me so. . . .

Our warm love to you.
Heather, Dietrich and Robin.

LETTER 193

[25th March, 1978]

Dear Denis [Thomas],

. . . I must thank you for your reviews of the Green Man book and of Blake at The Tate. You are by far the most understanding, illuminating and warm reviewer writing now, Denis. (I made my first drawing of the C14 Green Man in Sutton Benger church, two miles from here, when I was seventeen.) We have not yet had our day with Blake, but hope to soon. This has been a terribly busy period. Our exhibition of the marvellous block-printed textiles of Phyllis Barron and Dorothy Larcher (of the twenties and thirties), which opened yesterday, is one you really must not miss, and although I say it as shouldn't, it is very beautiful. This is our first major show at the Crafts Study Centre. We are just launching our Appeal, and I will enclose a form in case you may be interested.

Then the Painter-Etchers' exhibition has kept me busy – cutting mounts for sixteen of my prints that were sold. I managed to finish *The Cheese Room* and *The*

Wicket Gate just in time. Heather and I thought this year's work – especially in wood engraving – above average. . . .

We send our love to you all.

Robin.

LETTER 194

[21st April, 1978]

My dear Edith,

. . . We spent my birthday in our beloved Bradford-on-Avon, and next day I went to The Tate, and came home completely bowled over by that great, visionary, brave, outrageous, prophetic, sometimes quite mad, excessively inventive, brilliant, iconoclastic, ruthless, innocent, holy, alarmingly versatile, misunderstood and under-valued BLAKE! Of course the engravings, the curiously printed books, and the glowing late tempera paintings moved me most of all. The Catalogue (incredibly cheap at £1.80) is a work of scholarship and an excellent guide. Oh, what a day that was! . . .

This brief sign-of-life bears happy thoughts of you and our warm love.

Heather, Dietrich and Robin.

LETTER 195

[27th December, 1980]

Dear Joe [Graffy],

It was wonderful to have your warm, vivid, positive, generous, Joeful letter! We have enjoyed it tremendously. I'm glad *The Etcher's Craft* pleases you, for let it always be remembered that it was you who more than anyone brought about a renewed interest in my work, and you are still regarded as one of the patron saints of The Crafts Study Centre – now flourishing and always extremely beautiful.

The book was not of my own seeking. Nor was the exhibition. Both were conceived by the dear, perceptive, scholarly, sensitive Bristol curators, Francis

Greenacre and Kate Eustace. I think The Scholar Press has served us well, don't you?

The exhibition – as an exhibition – is really distinguished. Francis and Kate worked at it for four months. . . . With the aid of unobtrusive screens, it was possible to make a nice whole out of a heterogeneous collection. It would be lovely to see you at the private view (2 – 4 p.m.) on January 16. Invitations will go out soon. . . .

We send warm love and dearest wishes to you all.

Heather, Dietrich and Robin.

LETTER 196

[8th January, 1981]

My dear friends, Francis and Kate,
As the days of the exhibition are numbered you are in my thoughts a very great deal. Every day, still, people write to me about it. 'The atmosphere of serenity and order and peace in that gallery' one wrote, 'is something I have rarely experienced. An artist in display must have been responsible for creating such harmony.' 'The labels in themselves are an education,' wrote another, 'and it was a brilliant notion to lead people from zone to zone, gently and with reason.' Many such comments must have been made to you, I'm sure. I find them gratifying because they prove that none of your care and thought and invention were wasted.

I've grown to know and to feel so completely at home in that exhibition space that already I begin to feel homesick for it – I'm childishly glad that I shall have a last look on Sunday when Dietrich takes photographs! Oxford will be very different. I'm not apprehensive about it, though. . . .

I sometimes feel that words are an inadequate vehicle for expressing thought and feeling. Several times I've tried to tell you what a totally, unreservedly splendid experience we have found it to work and play with you over the past months, but I never feel I've been able quite to convey how satisfying and stimulating it has been. Even if in 1981 we have to invent reasons for meeting from time to time do let us invent them!

We all three send warmest wishes for the exhibitions you're about to devise and arrange. . . .

. . . heartfelt thanks and our love.

Robin.

LETTER 197

[January 1981]

To all my friends at the City of Bristol Museum and Art Gallery – to Francis and Kate, who were the inspiration behind the exhibition and who designed it in its entirety; to those fine craftsmen who (at an awkward, busy time when the Natural History Gallery was about to be opened) coped so generously with mounting drawings, sanding down frames and making new ones, restoring paintings, erecting screens, adapting show cases, and much besides; to the busy but always helpful office staff; and to the attendants who did so much to create a warm, welcoming, friendly atmosphere in the exhibition – I offer you all my grateful thanks.

Many letters have reached me, from old and new friends, from pupils I taught fifty years ago, from men and women who were students with me, from teachers and artists, and from many complete strangers. The letters have been very kind and heartfelt, and they have touched me deeply. It is very heartening to me that so many of them speak not only of the pleasure the actual paintings, drawings and etchings have given them but of the superb way in which my very mixed collection was welded into a beautifully complete whole. There has been great appreciation of the actual display – the way in which visitors were led easily from one zone to another, with everything clearly shown and labelled; the careful grouping and placing of etchings and paintings, the beautifully arranged smaller pieces in the cases, the humanising effect of the whole contributing to create what to me will be an unforgettable unity.

I cannot truly feel that my work merited such masterly and loving treatment.

I feel honoured that it received it. And I know that countless visitors to the exhibition would like to thank you. And I should like to offer you all my deep gratitude and admiration.

Robin Tanner.

LETTER 198

[12th January, 1981]

Dear Beth and Tony and All [Winterton],

What a wonderful letter! It must go into the Tanner archives. It left us all three heartened, stimulated, deeply touched and very happy – and positively exhilarated too. Thank you so much for it. How noble and sweet of you all to travel to Bristol! I'm so glad that the heterogeneous collection of my work gave you pleasure. . . . Those two fine curators, Francis Greenacre and Kate Eustace did all the subtle selection and arrangement. . . . I've been much encouraged by heartfelt letters from complete strangers; I long to be needling again! I'm delighted that Adam is being initiated into the craft of etching; we must talk about it next time we meet.

There is little about us that was not revealed in Francis Greenacre's catalogue; and the rest was freely spilled over half a page in *The Guardian* of 2nd January! But we find that in what is called our 'old age' nothing need be hidden: we have nothing to lose. It would be lovely to come to your SILVER celebration, and we will have a small GOLDEN one here, to which you must all come.

I'm afraid we have to co-operate with the making of a B.B.C. television documentary in April. What a month of events it is going to be!

Let us talk about egg tempera painting when we meet. As you know, the fresh, luminous, jewel-like quality of the work of Fra Angelico, Fra Lippo Lippi, Botticelli and the rest is the result of using earth colours tempered with yolk of egg. As this is an emulsion it holds the colours in suspension only; there is no chemical change, as there is with oil, so there is no darkening at all. The paintings of those great Italians are as brilliant now as when they were painted. I'm glad you liked *Portrait in April*.

We all three send warm thoughts and wishes to you all (including the girls!) with our love, and vigorously well Heather sends special gratitude to Tony for all his wonderful help.

Robin.

LETTER 199

[27th February, 1981]

Dear Kim Taplin,

We had been talking about you just before your letter arrived: your review in the *Times Literary Supplement* of *The Simple Life* was so much more perceptive and understanding than Patricia Beer's quite good one in *The Listener*, and it came as a splendid antidote to the foolish and rather nasty non-review of the remarkable C. R. Ashbee exhibition at Cheltenham, also in *The Listener*.

Your letter has touched us very deeply. Nothing is more heartening in these dark days than to discover scattered pockets of friends who share common ideals and convictions. We can all help to encourage one another. It was a lovely thought of yours to send us this beautifully inscribed copy of *The English Path*, which we shall always cherish. Prompted by a review (could it perhaps have been by Ronald Blythe?) we bought it and greatly enjoyed it as soon as it was published, and we often return to it. It is so fresh and original, and the theme is one that has long cried out for the loving and scholarly dedication you've given it. Now we shall give that first copy to Heather's sister, who has already read it with great relish and will love to possess it. . . .

I am sending you one of my etchings, which I printed here on a gilded page from a book bound in 1823, of paper made by one T. Edmonds. I hope it will give you some pleasure. It comes with our warm greetings and good wishes, and with thanks for so generously understanding us.

Heather and Robin Tanner.

[22nd February, 1981]

Our very dear friends, Marilyn and Robert [Hapgood] and – by proxy, so to speak – Susannah and Miranda,

It was lovely to hear from you and to have those hauntingly beautiful photographs. . . .

Since last I wrote to you we have had few frosts, and not one flake of snow. 'Ah, but we shall have to pay for it!' say people in our village, gloomily, to which I reply, 'At least this year we have something to pay for! Snowdrops, crocuses, winter aconites and Lenten hellebores are all lovely, and our first warm pink rhododendron is in bloom.' . . .

But how tame all this is compared with your wild, natural, romantic coast! Your photographs delight us. We keep that marvellous one of the coast with birds (November 1980) on view before us all the time. It is magical. The colour, too, is amazing: it really is a very remarkable photograph. Dietrich . . . talks daily of his memorable American holiday, one of the highlights of which was the time he spent with you. We've all three gone dottily American! I'm reading (and re-reading) American poetry, and I'm re-reading Thoreau; and Dietrich has made Apple Butter and Carrot Cake, and we dress our salads with soured cream and lemon juice! America made a very deep impression on him. The countless Art collections (mostly far richer than England's); the unfailing, warm welcome he was given; the astonishingly beautiful countryside – he still feeds on them, and so do we.

Life with us is still frantically busy. Our next job is to co-operate with a nice, sensitive young B.B.C. television producer over a documentary. Heather has delivered the text of *Woodland Plants* to the publisher. *Gray's Elegy* will be published next month, punctually on time.

My exhibition at The Ashmolean finishes today. I heard a week ago that there had been . . . more than 4,000 visitors, to date, and that the book is selling well. (I hope your copy, which I sent in one of those convenient padded bags, will eventually reach Cove Road!) It will be nice to clothe our denuded walls again, and I long to begin etching again, too.

I've always loved the silver-point drawings of Leonardo and Raphael and

Botticelli, done on a specially prepared paper called Baryta Paper, and I've used silver-point a good deal myself, but unfortunately this paper is no longer made. A diligent friend, however, has just found the remains of the stock of a very old London firm – twelve sheets; and I'm revelling in drawing on it. I've just drawn our first celandines for you. Is the Lesser Celandine a flower of Maine? American wild flowers are so various and rich that I expect it is. Here, alas! it is stupidly persecuted as a weed by many people. It is utterly harmless, and we love it. Its golden petals and its leaves (spattered with dark patches) are a delight to find in the early months of the year.

We all three send warm thanks, happy thoughts, and much love.

Robin.

P.S. I forgot to say that as you draw with a silver point, the lines oxidise under your very eyes and achieve the inimitable warm grey tone. It is not possible to erase a line, nor to plan your drawing: you have to draw direct, and hope for the best!

LETTER 201

[1st March, 1981]

Dear David and Angel [Gould],

I was very touched that you should write to me about my 'old fashioned', heterogeneous collection, and I'm so glad the exhibition didn't disappoint you. I never wanted it to happen, and nor did I want to write *The Etcher's Craft*; I thought my work would be far too traditional to have any public appeal, and the book seemed altogether too specialised and personal and strong in its views to attract attention. So when those two dear, sensitive, perceptive, scholarly Bristol curators, Francis Greenacre and Kate Eustace, put their proposals to me I tried to dissuade them. But I gave in; and they spent days and days here, tactfully uncovering, gently probing, selecting and planning. I had no hand in the venture at all, for I quickly came to trust them entirely.

. . . The whole happening is a great surprise to me, and I'm very humbled by it. Now I long to start working again: three etching designs keep worrying me to be realised. But first we two have to face the ordeal of a B.B.C. television documentary. The older we grow the more leisure eludes us.

It will be nice to crowd into 9 Lancashire Court on the 17th. I think Nicolas [McDowell] has done his job beautifully.

Yes, indeed; we thought Barley[1] was quite masterly with Beano's[2] pots. It was an unforgettable show. One day I must show dear Barley your witty drawing. As I've said before, David, you are squandering a rare talent. If only *The Guardian* or *Vole* or some other enlightened journal would 'use' you! We're missing so much. It's an awful waste.

I expect you've enjoyed the C. R. Ashbee show and Fiona MacCarthy's brilliant *The Simple Life* as much as we have.

Dietrich was 60 last May, and in August he joyfully retired. He now wonders how he ever found time to cope with students.

We send our love to you both.

Robin.

---

1. Barley Roscoe, Curator, Holburne Museum.
2. Katharine Pleydell-Bouverie.

LETTER 202

[2nd January, 1982]

Dearest Elizabeth [de Haas],

There was something specially lovely about yesterday. Dorothy's[1] own youthful words returning to that beautiful room made nonsense of death; the grey river beyond those tall windows; your sweet, playful, ingenious and unique Christmas decorations; that perfect, sacramental lunch – of what Rupert Brooke called 'many-tasting food'; your beautiful presents to us; and all our talk – both light and serious, happy and sad; – all these things and much besides made a truly memorable day. Thank you so much for it.

We are so delighted that you will soon be in warm Morocco. That is a wonderful thought. . . . I wonder if any flowers will be in bloom?

I've just finished a first close reading of Dorothy's diary for 1900. It has some choice and important entries. It is quite extraordinary that December 31st,

1899 passes into January 1st, 1900 without any comment! I should have thought there would have been national celebrations at the dawn of a new century. . . .

We hope so much that 1982 will see an end to your financial worries, and that life will be much less demanding. When you return from Morocco you must visit Sapperton and come to us. I hope to read more of Dorothy's diary to you then.

We send warm love and thanks, with our dearest wishes.

Heather, Dieti and Robin.

---

1. Dorothy Walker – see E de Haas in list of correspondents.

LETTER 203

[1st May, 1982]

My dear Cecil,

. . . We greatly enjoyed the extraordinary exhibition yesterday morning, at Bristol City Art Gallery, of the work of that underrated sculptor, Michael Rysbrack (1694–1770), which Kate Eustace has spent many months preparing. The terracotta portrait heads were most moving. Now I'm reading the sumptuous catalogue. Margaret Benton (producer of our film) had asked us to lunch and then to a preview of the film on a very large screen. And we saw it again at home at 10.15! The telephone has been busy ever since, and I gather many letters have been sent to the B.B.C., asking for the film to have a wider showing. Olive says the *Western Daily Press* has a paragraph about it. I don't know how you'll react to it. I have to admit that we three think that *as a film* it really is very good. It makes a shapely whole, and there are no loose ends left dangling. The slow pace, the utter peace, the occasional background of birdsong and 'The Lark Ascending', the excellent standard of photography and the subtle colour together give it a quality which we hoped it might have. And, anyhow, it seems to have given pleasure to a lot of people. It's an extremely *English* film. The various stages of my *March* etching were well shown, I thought. And James Hogg's commentary was perfect. It is nice to have got that behind us. . . .

We hope to see you in twelve days' time! Take immense care.

We send warm love as always.

Robin.

LETTER 204

[28th August, 1983]

My dear Tony [Heald],
I constantly return to thoughts of your Art and Crafts Gallery dream, dear Tony; and I'm sure it will come true. There are far, far too many so-called Craft Galleries everywhere, purveying mostly spurious stuff which should never be offered for sale. You four will, I'm sure, vet everything before you decide to include it. Here, I think, you have to be quite fierce and uncompromising. Last week we attended the private view of the 50-year-old Guild of Gloucestershire Craftsmen annual exhibition and sale, at Painswick, and we were dismayed to find that even that august body had admitted some things that were trivial, gimmicky, useless and offensively ugly and ill-conceived. It will help you if you know you can rely on a few really good painters, engravers, spinners, dyers, weavers and knitters, a potter or two of repute, and perhaps a calligrapher, and certainly an able wood turner and a furniture maker. They would establish a standard, below which you would refuse to fall.

I'm sure you'll consider carefully the texture and colour of your walls, and the kind of basic equipment and furniture you require. I, personally, would keep the entire environment simple, neutral (mostly whites and greys), home-like, light and unostentatious. If you admit craftsmen actually at work you will very greatly increase your load of responsibility and you will also change the nature of the enterprise. Better, I think, to start, at any rate, as a place to receive, display and sell local work.

I've jotted down a few brief extracts from William Morris's lectures which might interest you and be of some use.

If the nice old stone building is still called Ardsley Lodge, why change it? 'Ardsley Lodge Gallery' sounds very euphonious and inviting to me. I hope that one day you may be able to visit the Crafts Study Centre at the Holburne Museum in Bath that Heather and I helped to found, and to which we gave the bulk of our treasures. You would feel at home there. . . .

LETTER 205

[6th June, 1984]

My dear Cecil,
We escaped to The Hayward yesterday, and spent the entire day enjoying the staggering exhibition of English Romanesque Art from 1066 to 1200. It far exceeded our expectations, and the brilliance and ingenuity of the actual display of such a vast and varied collection astonished us. Fonts and tombs and capitals and sculpture had been lent by many churches: whole tympanums, too! HOW the transport of all this heavy stone had been managed I just can't imagine. The manuscripts are breathtaking. The entire Winchester Bible is there. For the first two hours we had the galleries almost to ourselves, so we were able to pore over the fabulous illuminated manuscripts at leisure. Now we are slowly beginning to absorb the magnificent catalogue. Sadly, The Hayward has very few seats, which are most uncomfortable, moreover. My old legs quickly tire, and by the end of the day I was glad to fall into a taxi! But it was a most memorable day. The exhibition is a remarkable revelation.

Heather and Dietrich are joining the C.N.D. demonstration in London on Saturday, and we all hope to see Hans Coper's Retrospective at The Serpentine Gallery on 3rd July.

On this beautiful morning I must sow parsley, lettuce, spinach, french sorrel and basil: this is real 'growing weather'. We hope you're enjoying it.

Now I'm writing to brave Greenpeace about their magnificent *Commandos for Conservation.*

Love from all three.
Robin.

LETTER 206

[24th June, 1984]

Dear Francis [Greenacre],
That was a lovely and characteristically kind thought of yours to urge us to see 'English Romanesque Art: 1066–1200'. . . .

You and Kate, who know so much about the subtle art of display, must have found some parts of the exhibition breathtaking. That ungainly building was nevertheless a perfect setting, surely.

We are going to see the Hans Coper show with Lucie Rie on the 5th of July. I think Tony Birks' biography is remarkably understanding and just and true; Hans' wife agrees. We listened to the Radio Critics yesterday; not one of them, I felt, made any significant appraisal of Hans' work.

What an inspiring Isle of Purbeck visit you and Edward made! It is some years since we heard nightjars, alas! I hope Edward really enjoys Eton, now.

We send happy thoughts and our love to you, all five.

Heather, Dietrich and Robin.

LETTER 207

[25th June, 1984]

My dear Sam [Black],
This is a *marvellous* still life of 'Mushrooms with Knife'. What a one you are!! Each mushroom is exquisitely seen, and the loose but subtle and artful composition is most satisfying. I've examined each separate fungus under my strong etching lens; each is an individual in its own right, yet each contributes beautifully to the whole. It must be a rare and extraordinary painting.

What other still-life pictures have you made yourself do lately? Still life is, of course, the perfect discipline.

We have recently seen two television masterpieces: (1) *Journey into the Shadows* – the life of Gwen John. Anna Massey, who took the part of Gwen John, is exactly like her, and she was brilliant. Gwen was, of course, a greater artist than her brother, Augustus. But what a tragic life hers was! To have collapsed and died on Dieppe station (and buried anonymously as a pauper) was a sad end to a great artist. (2) *Commandos for Conservation.* This Greenpeace production was brave and very convincing. (As you know, it originated in Canada – though Canada didn't come out of the film unscathed.) The courage and dedication of Greenpeace, in the face of appalling official opposition, are amazing. Thatcher's latest crime is to order the Minister of Agriculture 'to draw up specific proposals to counter the rapid increase in popular support for the Conservation Movement'. . . .

June continues dry and blazing hot. Heather and Dietrich love it, but I take refuge in my cool studio, where I'm needling a big plate.

Oxfam will be most grateful for these exciting stamps, Sam. . . .

Our love to you both.

Robin.

LETTER 208

[13th December, 1984]

My dearest Charlie,

. . . The six-day holiday we spent with Jim was a perfect one; we stayed the first and last nights with him. The second night we stayed in Moffatt, and next day we visited the marvellous Burrell Collection at Glasgow. This was a thrilling and very moving experience, for this fabulous work – stained glass, ceramics, sculpture, paintings, tapestries, furniture – is housed in what must surely be the finest C20 building in the country. It is all glass, steel, wood and stone. It stands among great trees, and trees are growing inside the galleries – Rodin's bronzes stand under them! . . .

Now that holiday feels far off, for we have been absurdly busy ever since. An exhibition of my work is touring thirteen Wiltshire libraries, (this is a penalty for being 80), at some of which I have to speak. Then work for C.N.D. and the Conservation bodies has greatly increased; and there was the very pleasant, lighthearted Alphabet for The Old Stile Press: that was a pleasure – a delightful diversion. Now I'm in the throes of four new etchings: *January*, *April*, *October* and a very large one called *Aldhelmsburgh*, which is founded on the little town of Malmesbury, near here. . . .

Love from Robin.

The Crafts Study Centre

These letters include some comments on craftsmanship.

LETTER 209

[24th February, 1972]

My dear neglected and long-suffering Edith,
. . . The Bath enterprise has been non-stop. We had just returned from a University meeting when you telephoned last night. It was at that gathering that it was decided to postpone our Holburne exhibition till July 10 – August 5. This is because of unforeseen delays in preparing the great Appeal document . . . , etc. The autumn is full, and these are the best dates available.

After the extravagantly favourable 'report' on our C20 Crafts Collection by a V. & A.-Sotherby's expert we are being encouraged to produce a full, detailed, well-illustrated catalogue. Now just picture my nightmare job of having to *envisage* every tiny detail and every single item in the exhibition, and making a numbered catalogue of them, long before we ever start to mount the show!!! That is my present job. It ties me in knots. It's no use pleading 'I'm torn!' I can't allow myself to be torn, and I can't have any afterthoughts. . . .

Love from all three . . .
Robin.

LETTER 210

[3rd May, 1972]

My dear Edith,
. . . To our immense relief, we have handed the substance of our Exhibition Catalogue to the printer. (The time is July 11 – August 5, by the way.) This includes 45 biographies, 220 descriptive entries, a detailed bibliography, 12 photographs and an introduction. I have had the nightmare job of envisaging exactly where each of the 220 items is to be placed. This has meant making

scale plans, templates of wall cases, and using one's imagination as never before! I only hope it turns out all right. . . .

We send our love as always.

Robin.

LETTER 211

[13th July, 1972]

My dear Edith,

. . . It was VERY sweet of you to send good wishes for the Exhibition, Edith. We worked flat out for five solid days, on two of which Ewart and Christine helped; and on the sixth we did the lighting. So all was ready in good time. (Chrissie was very slow indeed. All she managed in two days was three small show cases.) As I had designed the show to the last detail, even to the placing of every separate item and all the numbering, everything went smoothly. It was very satisfying, I must confess, to see my dream come true. . . . How I wish you could have been at the Preview! . . . There was a vast crowd, all extremely appreciative. The Vice-Chancellor gave an excellent opening speech. Ian Lowe was grateful for the poster you so kindly delivered.

I know you will love the Catalogue. It costs £1.00, but is a bargain. The double cover (using Dietrich's photographs) is a triumph. With all the descriptions, the illustrations, the 44 biographies and the bibliography, it really amounts to a textbook - and the very first in this field. I really think John ought to place one in every school library. . . .

Much love from all three.

Robin.

LETTER 212

[17th November, 1975]

My dear Cecil,

. . . I spent last Thursday in London with Lucie Rie (in her house and pottery in Albion Mews of happy memory), to choose work from recent firings for our

Bath collection. I chose seven frail, airborne, swan-necked pieces of porcelain – some with copper lustre – that looked as though they were an advance showing from the 21st century: marvellous, audacious, elegant and accomplished beyond belief. Old Bernard L. and Hamada are surely right to assert that Lucie is the greatest potter working today in the whole world. We had a lovely day together. Lucie drove me to and from Paddington, which was a luxury. (And yes, she kissed my cheeks many times, saying they were like Cox's Orange Pippins!) My homeward journey was on Western Railway's new 125 m.p.h. train, to my surprise – I had vowed I would never travel on it. It was quite extraordinarily comfortable, with no sense of movement at all. That was most uncanny. We covered the 100 miles even quicker than was scheduled, and reached Chippenham far too soon. . . .

Yes: I do agree that some aspects of growing old are very irksome; three hours of raking up leaves is enough for one day; five hours of etching makes my eyes weary; a day's printing gives me a rheumatic shoulder; driving my faithful old Volvo for more than 100 miles tires me completely; listening to radio sends me to sleep; I forget everything – and so on! But there are compensations, such as becoming more tolerant, less hurried and anxious, and, on the whole, more sure that there *is* progress – and this in spite of all the awful things that happen. . . .

LETTER 213

[27th November, 1976]

My dear Cecil,

. . . Reconstruction at the Holburne Museum for the Crafts Study Centre is finished, and our . . . fittings and lighting are complete, and the place is really handsome and shipshape. On December 1st, Heather and I take our treasured pots to their final home, and the textiles will soon follow. We shall feel a bit bereft at first, but oh, the extra *space* we shall have! That is a lovely thought. Most of our Leach, Cardew, Coper, Rie, Pleydell-Bouverie and other pots will go. It is exciting to see the dream coming true after all these years of struggle. . . .

[4th December, 1976]

My dear Edith,

. . . I've finished the large etching, *The Old Road*, and that is a great relief. No plate comes out as well as I hope, but if this one gives my friends pleasure I shall be happy enough. The new moon came just when I wanted it (tangled up in bare elm tracery) for my *next* etching, *December*; so altogether this has been a fruitful week.

The last two days have been quite the most fascinating. I bought two old oak beer barrels from a Cornish brewery, each holding 45 gallons, to catch the rain we waste along the *front* of our cottage. Some friends thought the idea awful, and said it would spoil the look of Old Chapel Field, but I knew our dear village builder would cope nicely. One butt stands tucked in the ivy to the left of the smaller studio window, and the other nestles among rose and ivy and choisya and garrya at the south-west corner of the house. It was necessary, of course, to raise the tubs high enough to place a watering can under the tap, and each had to be connected by a drainpipe to the guttering. I left the problem with rough, ill-spoken Ron and his young mate, Les. Ron loves stone. He has done a lot of stone-walling and tiling for the National Trust at Lacock, so he was in his element. He built for each butt a solid cylindrical base of Cotswold stone! ''E 'ave got to bear 450lbs weight of water, see,' he explained. 'But how did you produce a perfect circle?' I asked him. 'Well, I dunno. Same as a thrush do, I s'pose, when 'e do build 'is nest. He 'aven't got nor a pair o' compasses, an' no more 'aven't I. Do it by me eye, like. It do come out all right that way.' And what Ron and Les have left behind is a genuine, rough piece of country craftsmanship. It will be a sad day when these village trades disappear and all is 'taken over' by big firms. Small is beautiful! They've trodden the grass badly and upset a few plants, but I think Nature will come to our aid. I must say Old Chapel Field looks even more romantic! . . .

It is amazing that you go straight to the heart of 'Teacher and Etcher', dear Edith. No one quite 'gets' it as you do. . . . You so clearly understand what I'm trying so hard to convey. It is most encouraging. There were dark and difficult times to describe, yet I saw no point in dwelling too much on them. But the core, of course – as you see so sensitively – is the love story. That my life and Heather's, from early teens, should flow as one is a miracle to be eternally amazed at and grateful for. With such an incredible blessing I ought to have given far more than I have. Not much credit is due to me. . . .

Much love and happy thoughts.

Robin.

LETTER 215

[28th February, 1977]

My dear Edith,

. . . I was greatly cheered, too, on reading the Programme of the Bath Festival (3–12 June), to see a sensible paragraph about the Opening of the Crafts Study Centre and Michael Cardew's lecture on Leach there on the 9th. That gives us a good start.

We have endless meetings at the Holburne. I've got out of actually doing* the opening exhibition, which will concentrate on *Pottery*: (only Leach, Cardew, Pleydell-Bouverie); *Furniture*: (only Gimson and the Barnsley brothers); *Calligraphy*: (only Johnston, Hewitt and Wellington); and *Textiles*: (only Barron and Larcher, Mairet and Marx). It is going to be a thoroughly didactic show, for which I have to letter/write many captions – large and small. This seems to us appropriate, for the educational function of the Centre must be stressed. . . .

Perhaps I told you about our offensive floors at the Crafts Study Centre. We've now earned the £580 needed for carpeting, and the carpet is on order!

Just as I had thought (and rather hoped) that interest in my work might now wane, a fresh project has appeared! Robin Garton (fine art dealer, New Bond Street) . . . has been three times to see me. He is going to publish a hugely expensive Dictionary of English Etchers from 1850 to 1940, with many biographies and illustrations. Also, following the C19 tradition of publishing original prints, as well as 'illustrations', *in the book* (some of Palmer's, as you know, were published in this way), he proposes to have three of mine: *Full*

* Neville Ward, who designed the Crafts Study Centre, is responsible, I'm glad to say.

Moon, Wren and Primroses and the new one, *The Old Road.* That is to say, three actual prints will be contained in each book. The first edition will be 500, and Robin Garton now has to find a printer who will make in all 1500 proofs! A tall order, but he's young and confident. I hoped there would be other prints than mine. Paul Drury hoped to have one of his included, but for some reason the idea was abandoned. I've promised to sign all 1500 proofs! How long will that take?? . . .

We all send our love.
Robin.

LETTER 216

[20th June, 1977]

Dear Marilyn [Hapgood] – and Robert, too, if he will allow it!
Happily married couples like you and like us are becoming all too rare; we are always spoken of and referred to as HeatherandRobin, and we always speak of you as MarilynandRobert! Do you know, your letter of March 30 arrived on April 4, our 46th wedding anniversary! So it seemed most appropriate that you should mention your 27th wedding anniversary next month. We send our loving greetings, happy thoughts and warmest wishes. . . .

Dietrich has just tutored six girl students on exchange from Illinois for six months. They have just returned, and the college at Bath misses them very much. They were fine ambassadors for America. We gave them a supper party here, and we loved all six. . . .

Did I tell you that our twelve-year dream of a Crafts Study Centre in Bath has at last come true? It was opened by the Vice-Chancellor of the University on June 1st. He addressed the multitude in the sunny museum garden, and although he is an eminent scientist he spoke like a poet, and with the sensitivity of an artist. We are fortunate to have as curator a wonderfully tactful, scholarly, enterprising and understanding girl of 25, whom everyone loves. She looks like a daughter of William Morris!

By the way, I bought that magnificent catalogue of the fabulous exhibition at the Pierpont Morgan Library! The Oxford Press reprinted it and bound it beautifully. It is a cherished treasure.

I'm sending, just for your interest, the Prospectus of a book on British Etchers: 1850–1940, which is a bold venture. The edition is 500, and in each volume three of my etchings are being enclosed. I am now in the middle of signing all 1500 prints!! A team of superb young printers (who are themselves etchers) have done the work under my direction: it has been a monumental job! *The Old Road*, which I finished only a few months ago, is an elegy on the great elms of Wiltshire, of which so few are left, owing to Dutch Elm disease.

How much Miranda [daughter] must enjoy Nancy! That great baroque Stanislas Square always thrills us, and the museum is marvellous too. At twenty, what a lot Miranda has accomplished! So tell us the title and publisher of her book, so that we may buy it when it is ready. . . .

And our love to you all.

Robin.

LETTER 217

This letter was written on Robin Tanner's 75th birthday, 17th April 1979. The Hapgoods were then in Japan.

Dear Marilyn – and, of course, Robert and Miranda and Susannah, none of whom feel strangers to us, . . . Bernard Leach has often described the Tea Ceremony to us. Dear Bernard, now 90 and blind, visited our Crafts Study Centre in Bath recently, and I described it in detail to him. He has given 100 of his pots, spanning his entire life; and next month we are putting on an exhibition called 'Pots of Inspiration'. These are the pots he has collected because he loves them and they have inspired him: old Korean, Japanese, Chinese, Persian and English. He is giving us the collection. He declares that we now have the best Leach collection in the world! Bernard revered Hamada above all others. Yes, I knew him. He used to bring his wife every spring to England to see the bluebell woods. I once watched him build a kiln at Dartington, and I bought one of the pots he fired there. We have two others, which we bought at a London exhibition. . . .

We're so glad our book[1] is giving you pleasure. (It has been extraordinarily well received, but we've had to endure much unwanted publicity, including radio and television. However, as we are giving the royalties to our Crafts

Study Centre we are glad it is selling well!) Yes, this new edition is an exact facsimile (produced photographically) of the original 1939 one, except that I re-lettered the title page and dust cover. In 1940 the stocks and blocks were destroyed in air raids, and the book therefore became both rare and costly. Except for the far too black etching reproductions, the new edition is, if anything, better than the original. . . .

How I envy you the sight of Mashiko! I wonder if you have visited a museum of Japanese craftsmanship founded by Hamada's friend (now dead), Dr Yanagi? He was a delightful, learned, humble man, passionately eager to save old Japan from total industrialisation.

Our warm thanks for giving us such a vivid idea of your life, and the hope that we may meet before you return to America.

Robin.

P.S. A few weeks ago one of the Oxfordshire Advisers asked if he could bring twelve young Primary School Heads (whom we had never met) to spend the day with us. So we provided two meals for sixteen of us, and we discussed and chatted and read poetry and enjoyed books and pots and garden, etc; and we answered countless questions. It was a lovely experience, and we fell in love with all twelve teachers – a splendid new generation!

---

1. *Wiltshire Village.*

Poetry

LETTER 218

[15th January, 1974]

My dearest Charlie (which of course includes Freda),

Well! The 'dying art of letter writing' is certainly vigorously alive with you. That was a marvellous, vivid, witty, full letter . . .

You mentioned Ruth; yes, she retired some years early because of deafness, which has now been successfully coped with. She loves her new house, and we see a lot of her. She is one of the saints – like Heather and Dietrich. Heather was 70 in July, and I shall be in April. Although we still work quite fourteen hours a day, we never achieve what we set out to do. (Last night Heather addressed a 'women's lib.' group – at its request – on the wrongness and stupidity of war, and the alternatives to it. She helps serve in an Oxfam shop, is still The Wise Woman of our village, and copes with a thousand jobs and numerous unpopular causes – like factory farming, civil liberties, anti blood sports, commons and footpaths, and so on.) How heartening that you still keep your discussion group going! That is splendid.

You have been much in my mind lately because of John Tessimond. We have recently made a new friend who knew him well and worked with him in advertising. But more than that, we have had talks with a woman who has collected all his known poems (I found two unpublished ones for her), and has written a brief biography and appraisal of his work. J.T.'s literary executor has lent her photographs, told her a very great deal about him, and has even lent her a bunch of his letters (which I've read) to one of the many dolly girls he fell for. He spent his all in search of the perfect one: he wanted non-intellectual, highly made-up, empty young things, but was never able to establish any satisfying relationships. Most of them fleeced him. It is the saddest, most sordid story . . . Yet he was greatly loved by a host of friends. Whether this work will be published isn't certain; but isn't it wonderful that it has at last been done? If we ever meet again there is a lot to tell you. . . .

[17th September, 1976]

My dear Jim [Turner],
This is a sheet from an 18th century parson's book of sermon notes. (Notice the gilt edges – still bright.) I use a page occasionally just for the sensuous pleasure its incomparable tone and texture give. Alas! it makes even our best handmade paper of today look sterile and brash.

We were delighted to hear of your visits to the Whittington Press. That is just how I imagined it would be. I find it so right, so inevitable, and so entirely satisfying that you should see your work really well printed – and on your own home ground, moreover. There could be no nicer nor more fitting happening during your retirement; and how happy it will make all your friends! Often when I'm gardening or etching I find myself saying:

Was there a shadow on the grass?
I do not, cannot know, alas!

or:

The clicking latch and the complaining door
Promise the warm seclusion of the house,

or, even more often:

Perhaps light airs will breathe awake
My sleeping spirit for your sake;
Crinkle the pool below the mill,
Trouble the barley on the hill,
Move in the valley . . . then be still.

The simple truth is, Jim, that *you are a poet.*

We like this subtle 'Child at a Festival' very much. You have caught – so delicately yet unsentimentally – that precious fleeting moment. In eighteen lines you've told a long story. Bless you for sending it to us. I do agree: the Muse can't be cajoled or rushed. It is quality, after all, not quantity that matters. (I am struggling so slowly with my large – and far too ambitious! –

etching in celebration of our doomed English Elm, yet I know that this must be: only my supreme best is good enough, and if I produce, therefore, only one plate in a year I must not protest.)

I must confess to being mightily relieved to have RAIN and clouds and a cool air again at last. We returned from comparatively green Yorkshire to a desert, but blessed steady rain has already worked miracles: the lawn is almost green: little cyclamen and autumn crocuses are good, and most of the sadly languishing shrubs have revived. Surface-rooting subjects, like rhododendrons, azaleas and magnolias have suffered, and we may even have lost a few. It is too early to tell. Vegetables are very good, because we've used our precious rainwater on them. Nature heals plants miraculously, and we shall be patient.

The abbeys at Rievaulx, Jervaulx, Easby and Egglestone were enchanting, and Wensleydale and Swaledale – although more tourist-catering than when we knew them in the mid-thirties – were immensely satisfying. York was glorious.

We think of you both very often, and we send our love and warm wishes, with special thanks for the poem,

Heather, Dietrich and Robin.

LETTER 220

[11th October, 1976]

My dear Jim,
What a boy you are! TWO POEMS in one week, and both of them first-rate too! Heather was away all last week, helping her sister give two seriously epileptic women a holiday. When I read 'The Ward' and 'What Seeks the Revenant' aloud to her and Dietrich they exclaimed, 'Unlike most of our friends who write verse, Jim is not a versifier but a true poet,' and I'm absolutely certain that that is a true judgment.

With her great love of form, and of the *spare* statement, and of an unhackneyed and personal choice of words, Heather responded to both poems immediately. We find 'The Ward' neither neurotic nor convoluted (your words!). It is strong and direct, and it probes far below the surface; and it reaches a great solemn crescendo with 'The long slow menace of the night'.

We think your first choice of 'solace' in the third verse is better than 'comfort'. The shape and economy of this poem seem quite perfect to us, and if someone forced us to judge I think we might rank it even higher than the happier, easier, wonderfully musical, equally deep and probing 'What Seeks the Revenant'. One day you must give me the pleasure of reading these two poems to you and recording them. How wise you are to take time, to consider long, to contemplate each idea before committing anything to paper! Heather and I share this attitude very closely with you. (Two new etching designs in my mind tend to wake me in the small hours, but until I can 'see' them, crystal-clear, I cannot attempt to give them shape.) You use 'the privilege of confinement' – as the staunch Jacqueline du Pré would call it – as a sort of tool, and a wonderfully sharp one it is; I mean, you use *time*, to shape, prune, consider, choose, reject, appraise – and this is why your work has an unhurried completeness and inevitability. You are unassailable, dear Jim!

It makes us three very happy to think of you in your creative travails, with that noble Effie at your side. All creation is in a sense painful; but how fortunate we are to have something to say and the passionate urge to say it!

Our love and warm thoughts to you both, with our grateful thanks for your two poems.

Heather, Dieti and Robin.

LETTER 221

[27th March, 1977]

Our dear Jim and Effie,

Perhaps it was cruel to inflict non-poetry on you (one single page of it makes me blush!), but such bad work does make doubly clear what our criteria should be. I wonder, if she read your work, she might see the vast, vast difference between art and counterfeit? Alas! I doubt whether she has the sensitivity and perceptiveness to discriminate. And that is very sad.

'Cotswold Parson' is flawless, and a vivid, true portrait. It places the man so neatly and completely, and dates him most charmingly and generously. And, as always, the craftsmanship is most cunningly and unobtrusively wrought.

I wish I could say with you, 'We still live quietly.' Anything but! Visits to

London (to the Royal Society of Painter-Etchers exhibition, where nine prints of *The Old Road* were sold, and to the Bernard Leach exhibition at the Victoria and Albert); Heather's preparations for showing two C.N.D. films in Chippenham soon; a supper party for Dietrich's six American students; having marvellous 'quad' stereo equipment installed at last (and what a glorious revelation it is!); countless visitors – most of them lovely, but a number unannounced and only wanting our help; constant work at the Crafts Study Centre; and much to do in the garden.

Spring is quite exceptionally early: some daffodils already 'over', and a camellia, a rhododendron and magnolia stellata are already at their best. The Abbey Grounds must be looking very beautiful.

As soon as a tardy friend returns the 1931–1956 part of 'Teacher and Etcher' I will let you have it. I'm afraid I've written very little more so far.

I've had a heartsearching time recently. The University of Bath wants to confer on me the honorary degree of Master of Arts in July. As you know, I dislike national honours, and am not interested in academic awards. So my first reaction was to decline. But after a long discussion with Heather and Dietrich I could see that it might seem pretty churlish to reject a scientific university's gesture to the arts. So I accepted – but letting the vice-chancellor know my reservations. (Ironically, the Chancellor, who will perform the ceremony, is Lord Hinton, who was at school with us as a boy, and whose father was the stern Head of Ivy Lane School where I taught! It is a small world!) The vice-chancellor has been most understanding.

You are often in our thoughts, and they are invariably happy ones. Our love to you both, and warm thanks for 'Country Parson'.

Robin.

LETTER 222

[22nd September, 1977]

My dear Jim,
This is absolutely splendid. The photograph is very good; the text of the piece is unusually sensible, and the choice of poems just right. (We are particularly

glad that 'Last Words' is included, for that is one of the best poems written in England in recent years.) If the book can be ordered from ordinary bookshops we should like to order our copies – we shall buy at least four, and probably more – from a brave bookshop fairly recently opened in Chippenham. I'm sure the 1,000 copies will sell easily. This is a great occasion, dear Jim: a time of rich fulfilment. How I wish your mother and your sister were here to relish it!

I'm extremely glad you are going to talk and read in Gloucester Prison. I used to inspect Art in prisons, and visited Gloucester only once. The class was embroidering 'lazy daisies' with thick knitting cotton on huckaback towelling – of all unlikely activities for tough men! I noticed that one man – a young, handsome fellow – sat apart, doing nothing. So I talked to him. I felt him staring with interest at my shoes. 'That's a bloody good bit of bloody doeskin,' he said. 'And I shouldn't be surprised if I made him,' he added. 'Give me one.' So I took off a shoe, and to his delight he read inside it the makers' name, and beside it his number, which he had told me before. He put on both my shoes and I put on his. And while I coped with the lazy daisies he caressed his own handiwork. When I returned to him he chided me for not treating the doeskin properly; he had brushed it with his handkerchief. 'Now if they'd give me a bit of bloody leather I could do some bloody good work instead of that bloody sewing stuff,' he said. When we parted I said I would do what I could, and I did contrive to get a supply of leather for him. Next time I went to my pet shoeshop I told the manager my story. 'Oh, he was our very best craftsman,' he said. 'We would take him back tomorrow!' I've never heard what happened to him.

'The Exile' and 'First to Last' seem perfect to us now; and 'North Cotswold Day' is a most beautiful evocation of that seam of country I know so well. It is taut and spare and searching, and it is quite uncannily true and vivid. You ARE a poet, Jim, and that is a rare human condition. Many people who think they are poets just aren't: to transmute the experience and language of everyday into the language and form of art is a rare, rare gift, given only to the few. . . .

We send you both our love and happy thoughts.

Heather, Dieti and Robin.

To Dust

My clean-burned dust may drift to rest
Silted below a Cotswold stream,
Or caught in tufted cocksfoot crest;
Freed from reality and dream.

The ghosting owl will ride the dark
And wake the wood with hollow call:
The fox's harsh staccato bark
Will echo where no footsteps fall.

If miniscule my dust may lie
Within the happy ways I went,
My memory, whene'er I die,
Will seek no sweeter monument.

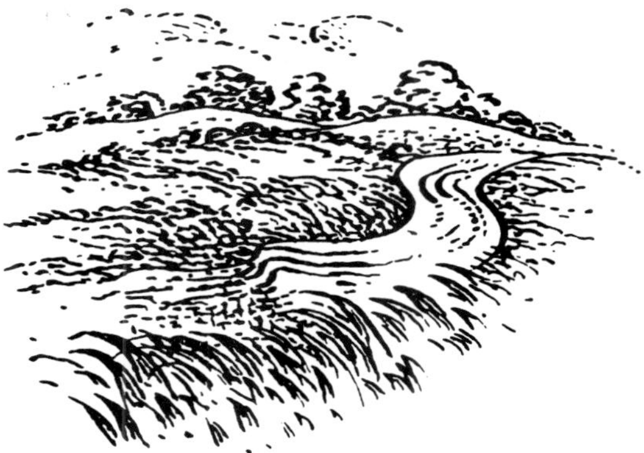

From Jim Turner, *All My Days.*

LETTER 223

[9th December, 1977]

My dear Jim,

Heather and I shared the reading of 'One Small Head' to Baol, and we are all haunted by the terrible story (so vividly told) of your years at that appalling school. It is worse than Charles Lamb's 'Christ's Hospital': it is positively Dickensian. Does it still exist? I had always thought you had had an idyllic Cotswold childhood, uneventful but free and happy. How is it that your shocking experience left you so balanced and optimistic, and without the slightest chip on your shoulder? I remember the very first time we met, Jim, and telling Heather when I reached home that day that I had met a really happy man who celebrated life, and who communicated his sense of well-being to his colleagues and pupils. Your description of that alarming institution is all the more telling because of your restraint. . . .

You have made us very eager to read more! Dieti hasn't yet had a chance to read this chunk. This is the last week of the term, so almost every night there is a party, a dinner, a concert, or some other meeting. But when he has read it we will return the manuscript to you. Also the Collected Poems. We long to see in print quite a bunch that was left behind. The fact is that (like Hardy) your work grows stronger, deeper, more rounded and inevitable as you grow older. 'Pursuit' is an example of what I mean. . . .

I wove a net to meet the need
And catch my sinuous fish of thought.
Too wide the mesh: I netted naught
But foam-flakes on the ribboned weed.

We send you both our love and admiration and warmest thanks and wishes.

Robin.

[4th March, 1979]

My dear Cecil,

. . . Your Shrove Tuesday letter delighted us. We had pancakes for supper – filled with chicken and mushroom – in a school near Bristol! It was a marvellous occasion. The school, which I used to know well, a Grammar School then, and now a Comprehensive one, was burnt down a few years ago, and with it a collection of my work. The new building has a fine library and a quite magnificent theatre, and a new collection of my prints now hangs in the library. The Arts Council sponsored an evening with Yevgeny Yevtushenko and his two translators – reading Yevtushenko's new poems. A packed audience, predominantly young, listened, electrified, for two and a half hours. Yevtushenko is an amazingly persuasive, loving, easy personality and of course an actor. People loved him. He read – or, rather, recited – the Russian of each poem after we had heard the English translation, which proved very successful. Here at last is internationally appealing poetry – uncompromising, brave, deep and most passionate. The man bowled us all over! What an ambassador for the U.S.S.R.! We and six other friends ate a delectable supper with him afterwards, miraculously provided by the school. He was famished, and loved every dish, and drank much wine. We managed to converse easily. We hated parting. We gave him a copy of *Wiltshire Village* when we said goodbye. His (third) wife, who is English, has just had a son, born in Bournemouth – of all places! . . .

Have you the three-volume Kilvert? Or only that hopelessly inadequate and untypical paperback selection? I am copying out every Wiltshire passage from the Diary in a book I made specially for it, which I call 'Kilvert's Wiltshire'. It's a nice job to pick up at odd moments, like knitting! . . .

I've just finished drawing the handsome, rare Violet Helleborine and now I'm drawing the dry seed heads of Spiked Star of Bethlehem ('Bath Asparagus'). It is lovely to go into this pure, unchanging world of plants which are exactly as they were when Chaucer and Shakespeare saw them. It gives me a marvellous feeling. No wonder Blake said 'imagination is the real and eternal world, of which this vegetable kingdom is but a shadow.' . . .

We hope that your fingers are responding well to your piano. Enjoy this release from winter!

Robin.

LETTER 225

[22nd January, 1984]

My dear Cecil,

. . . I've spent today writing out and decorating four new poems by Jim Turner, in a beautiful book he had made specially for this work. So far I've filled 80 pages for him. I may have told you that Jim is disabled, but is content because he is a very good poet, (he was also a very good headmaster of Cirencester Secondary School) and it gives him quite unreasonable pleasure if I read each new poem he writes, twice, by telephone, and then he likes me to record and decorate it in this precious book. Here is his latest, called 'The Spoilers':

When on the windy Cotswold way
The last tall beechen windbreaks fall
And irretrievable decay
Crumbles the last ingenious wall,

When for a mess of pottage, fools
Betray the old unspoken pledge,
To root out with their reeking tools
The charity of sheltering hedge.

When fields once bright with age-old flowers,
Or stoic in the morning frost,
Harbour in shameful latter hours
The Molochs of the holocaust,

Then shadow-eyed we come again
To mourn the ill of no redress,
Forlornly seeking, all in vain,
Old secrets of lost loveliness.

. . . We all three send loving thoughts and hopes and wishes.

Robin.

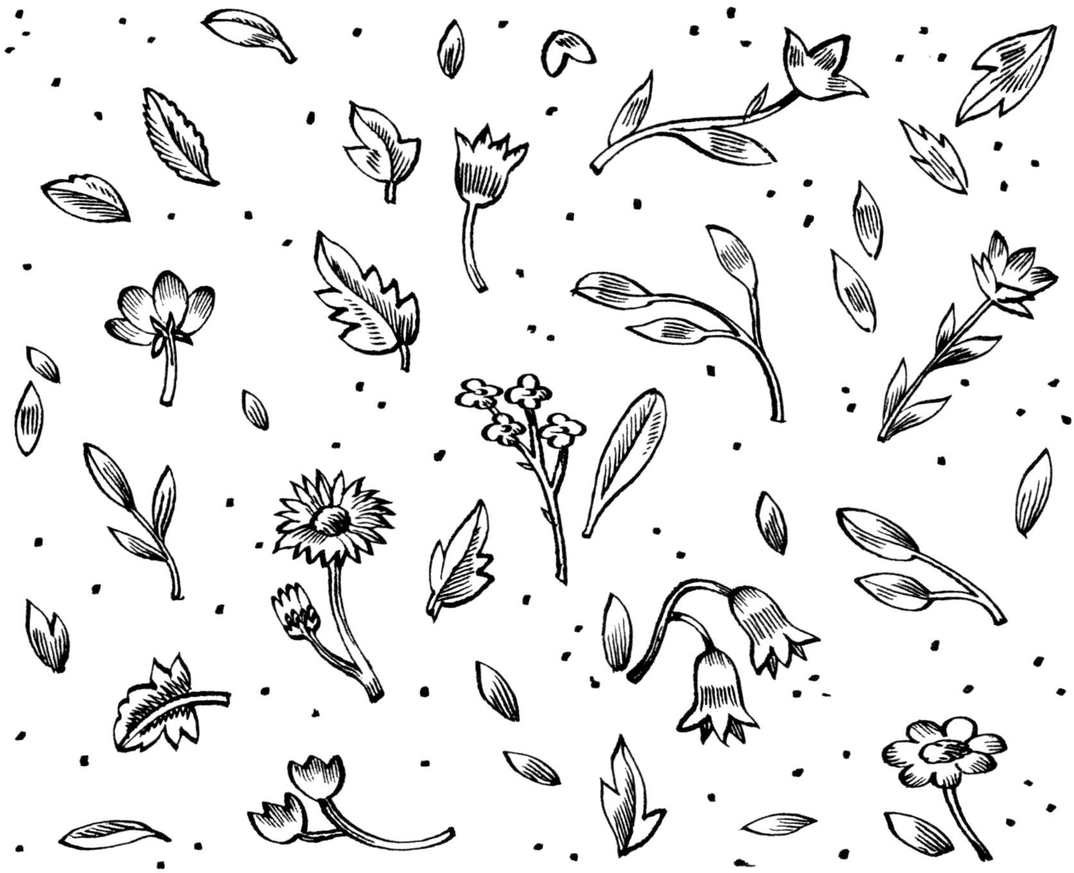

6
Epilogue: 1987–1988

Most of these letters were written after the publication of *Double Harness* in 1987. Robin Tanner died on 19th May, 1988. I am sure he would have approved what Degas said: 'I don't want a funeral oration. Yes . . . you will give one, you will say: "He greatly loved drawing."'

LETTER 226

[19th November, 1986]

My dear Ken [Pritchard],
It was very sweet of you and Pam and Sarah to send me that excellent reproduction of the 'Misty Trees' screen print; I little knew how much the love of friends would sustain me throughout the strange experience I've had.

For some weeks I had had to visit the lavatory too often, so I consulted my doctor, who arranged for me to meet Bath's renowned urologist, Mr Charlton, at The Bath Clinic on Combe Down. He found that a prostate operation was necessary, and he performed it without delay. (In principle, I support the N.H.S., but I couldn't face the inevitable long delay, nor, I'm afraid, the turmoil of a big public ward. At the Clinic I had a peaceful, comfortable room, looking out on great beech trees filled with rooks. And my beloved Heather and Dietrich spent much time with me.)

Now, patiently, I hope, I am coping with the slow return to normality. I feel a deep sense of relief at having put this trouble behind me, and a deep gratitude, too, to the brilliant team who dealt with me. This was the first time ever that my 82½-year-old body had called for help, and my first ever stay in hospital.

I've cancelled all my engagements until 1987. Then I hope to be full of vigour, and we will have some happy times together.

My love to you.
Robin.

[21st March, 1987]

My dear Ken [Pritchard],

It was very good of you to telephone last night. You have been much in my thoughts as May and your departure draw near. I hope you have found a pleasant resting place in or near Chichester. I had in any case intended to write to you today. I've realised that our splendid friendship would be somewhat assailed by your going to Sussex, but now I'm afraid it is even possible that we may never meet again.

Let me explain: because the prostate operation proved ineffective, Mr Charlton proposed a second one, and I spent three days at The Clinic this week. Surprisingly, he found me to be anaemic, so I was given a blood transfusion. Then he performed a cystoscopy, which, alas! revealed a malignant growth in the bladder. He removed what he could, but of course it might grow again. He and Heather and Dietrich and I had a long, frank talk in my room at The Clinic, and he warmly agrees with our determination to face the situation bravely and to continue to live as normally as possible, relishing each day as it comes. I feel so *extremely* well that I find it hard to believe this evil thing is inside me! Unpredictable Nature may even have a surprise for us!

We have cancelled the joint public lectures Heather and I had promised to give; and we are declining all requests from journals for interviews about the superb new edition of *Wiltshire Village*; and I'm hoping soon to print my three new etchings.

I refuse to be downcast. I've been privileged to live a long, full, healthy life – and its end may not be yet.

Thank you for your friendship, dear Ken. I send happy thoughts and my love to you and to Pam and Sarah.

Robin.

To Charlie Naylor.

[7th–8th April, 1987]

. . . Your entire stay was an inspiration and a comfort and joy to us all. We are only sorry that you missed the couple of perfect days since, with the temperature 68°F., and the daffodils marvellous. You weren't a visitor but an essential part of Old Chapel Field. That is why we did nothing special for you but let you share typical days. The harmony of three extended quite naturally to four; and it seemed as though you often stayed here – not that this was a rare and isolated visit. It did us all good, Charlie. Have no doubts about me. I have had NO pain, and except for the water-nuisance I feel extremely well. I've just prepared fine old handmade papers for printing the three new plates on Thursday – *Weeds*, *The Hazel Copse* and '*Still is the Land*' (the A. E. Housman poem). I'm glad you met Molly and Roy, who are quite unlike most of our neighbours. . . .

I think our balanced vegetarian diet can be said to have helped to keep all three of us entirely without colds for three years, by the way. . . .

We have a supper party today for Bruce Kent and the fine vicar of Chippenham before Bruce speaks in the Town Hall. There will be six of us at the long table. We wish you could be with us. How DO you find such marvellous cards? Our collection (i.e. *your* collection!) is most exciting, and we share them with friends.

Our little guest room has been slept in by countless dear friends, and we like to think you are now one of them. My brother designed the sycamore fitment at the head of the bed, and also the low book shelves, and I designed the rest. The tall cupboards and the wash-place are all of wood from the Monkey Puzzle tree, and they were made locally. The Madder bed cover was woven by Rita Beales from her hand-spun wool. The very old and rare Khelim rug I bought more than 50 years ago. The Cat and Bird are Mexican. The black and white teapot etc. are 18th century. The curtains are of undyed Shantung silk. Jim is extremely fond of that room. He likes writing letters at the window table. The wooden calendar was, sadly, never finished. I like to think you've slept there. . . .

LETTER 229

[7th May, 1987]

I've thought of you very often, dear Ken, making your first contacts with your new colleagues and schools. I think you will soon realise that you and Don and your other colleagues achieved what it will call on all your resources to build up. . . . But *you* have those resources; you have all the tact and imagination and skill and quiet power to work that necessary miracle. You will succeed. I have always felt it a privilege to bring light into darkness . . . that was my prime task!

How I wish I could help you in the next few years. What a gentle revolution you and I together could bring about! I will not persecute you with letters, though even through letters I find one can share one's friends' problems and bring reassurance. I cannot express what sustaining comfort the understanding and compassionate letters from countless friends have been to me in my present strange situation. They even make me feel we are all in this together, fighting this sinister cancer. Actually, I'm feeling very well; I've done some mild gardening and quite a lot of etching. . . .

Always know that I am ready to share your triumphs and struggles and even failures; that, surely, is at the very root of true friendship. And I think you must know how much I prize friendship; I could write a book on what I owe to my friends.

We all three send much love to you three.
Robin.

LETTER 230

[25th June, 1987]

My very dear Geraldine, Keith and Peter,
Of all my hundreds of friends it is you who have by far the greatest sense of occasion. And your timing is always so perfect. Today you have humbled and greatly moved me and brought me very great happiness. A friend has sent me this handmade stationery from Italy, so I am using the first sheet to thank you.

First came your vast and exquisite array of roses – all white and cream and gold, and marvellously fragrant. Arranged in two perfect vases – one made by Lucie Rie and the other by Hans Coper – I cannot tell you how they grace this room and give the entire house a feeling of celebration.

Then came your most charmingly presented collection of heartwarming, generous (and as I think, undeserved) messages from these lovely people. What a truly original and typically Taylorian idea!! It must have cost you a lot of time, to say the least, but it is all the loving thought behind it that touches me so. To receive such messages makes me feel it was worth the long travail to give birth to *Double Harness*. What a lot of work it must have given you to collect all these lovely tributes; I don't feel worthy of them. The photograph (is it Peter's?) of Wood Anemone is positively breathtaking: I stare and stare at it!

I am already amassing a large and varied collection of letters about the book, and since many of them speak enthusiastically about the actual production – the material quality – of it I must let Jean-Luc read them. It gives me a nice feeling to know that friends in France, Africa, Australia, New Zealand, America, Holland and elsewhere have received their copies of *Double Harness*. The world seems suddenly very small. . . .

We all three send happy thoughts and our warm love to you; and I cannot thank you enough for making this such a very memorable day.

Robin.

LETTER 231

[14th September, 1987]

Dear Mary [Fooks],
Such a deeply understanding and compassionate letter makes me feel that the long travail to bring *Double Harness* to birth was worth it. Thank you so much.

You see, I only wrote the book because so many artist and educationist friends pressed me to, and I only intended it for private reading. Then a friend to whom I had lent the manuscript asked if she might let one of Harrap's directors – Jean-Luc Barbanneau, who also publishes Impact Books independently – read it, and he straightway begged me to let him publish it. After long discussions and with some misgivings I gave in, and I must say he has been perfect to work with; I explained that all my life I had preached good visual standards; and I got him to agree to pay me no royalties until the book had paid for itself and made a reasonable profit, but that he should spend more than usual on the actual production of the book. His superb designer was responsible for the good paper and nicely disposed Baskerville type, the sections stitched in the traditional way, the real cloth binding, and the high standard of reproduction of the illustrations. Jean-Luc has, fortunately, been rewarded, for about 1,000 copies have already been sold, and The British Council has chosen it for display on their stand at the Frankfurt Book Fair next month.

Yes: tears have been shed by many people reading the story of Dietrich. He has been a more vital part of our lives since 1939 than I can ever say. Why, oh *why* were we so privileged? Heather and I have just finished printing the editions (of 20 impressions in each) of the three etchings I mentioned in the final paragraph of the book, and after each exacting session he regaled us with exquisite vegetarian dishes. He really is a master chef. I shall never forget how he prepared me for my stay at The Bath Clinic last November and March: he was marvellous. I'm glad to say that my cancer appears to be quiescent, and I feel well, but travel is extremely inconvenient. I am reconciled, however, because all that I love and that I want to paint, draw or etch is within a stone's throw of where I sit writing to you.

Two recent surprises have made me very happy – I was afraid I might have lost my cunning as a printer, but the three new editions are quite the best I have ever done! – And this is the second surprise: because some thousands of people know all about me now, and nothing lies hidden, and I've nothing to lose, I find myself repeating that line of John Bunyan's – 'He that is down need fear no fall!' In fact I feel curiously safe and invulnerable! . . .

With our love,
Heather, Dietrich and Robin.

LETTER 232

[21st September, 1987]

My dearest Charlie,
I am picturing you embarking on your fascinating new venture with your sense of humour and humanity uppermost, and a quiet determination to make your mark. This work is going to call on all your tact and tolerance, and you will relish meeting its demands. We wish you well. . . .

We had a splendid day with Jean-Luc and his brilliant designer. . . .

An ecstatic postcard came a few days ago from Jim [Fairbairn] from his beloved Baroque city, Prague. Tony (Heald) seems to have had a quite overwhelmingly moving and impressive holiday in classical Greece. On our holidays in France and Italy and Switzerland, Heather used always to keep meticulous notes, and these – together with Dieti's photographs and my drawings – she worked at on our return home; and these great volumes form a vivid record. I'm enjoying re-reading them and re-living those fabulous times. Similarly I'm re-reading favourite poets, notably Edwin Muir and Louis MacNeice. What a lot they still have to say to us!

One of the most moving and penetrating letters I've had is from someone who once spent a miserable time in the R.A.F. only a few miles from here, and therefore came to hate this area. But *Double Harness* caused him to return to N.W. Wiltshire recently and he came upon Kington Langley! Now I wish he and his wife had called: he said he was afraid! Fools rush in where angels fear to tread! . . .

Robins are singing their wistful little autumn songs already, and the evenings 'draw in' rather early. Fortunately I always enjoy the approach of winter.

Are you working at Woolley at all this term? We all three send you much love.

Robin.

LETTER 233

[25th September, 1987]

Dear Peter [Sowrey],
I read the so-called 'Consultation Document' with dismay and not a little disgust. It is so pitifully ignorant of the nature and needs of young children. It is positively chilling to read these words (page 6):

> 'The majority of curriculum time at Primary level should be devoted to the core subjects (i.e. Maths, Science and English).'

Nothing could be more wide of the mark, more unreal, more wasteful of children's enthusiasms, more certain to produce boredom and a sterile, passive uniformity.

Were I an H.M.I., I should refuse to enforce and inspect and report on the National Curriculum – to civil servants. An H.M.I. is appointed by H.M., and is independent. He views schools as a whole, therefore, and sees 'the core subjects' as only a part of a much wider curriculum. I am quite sure that H.M.I.s will continue to exercise their traditional independence, and that they will attack Baker's ill-considered proposals.

It was good to meet again. All good wishes.
Robin.

LETTER 234

[5th October, 1987]

Dear Janet [Webb].
. . . I have read Baker's so called 'Consultation Document', and have just posted a stinging letter to him. His educational ignorance is abysmal. I've told him that if I were still an H.M.I., I should insist on retaining my independent status and should refuse, therefore, to be answerable to him! . . .

I have done three watercolours, based on etching designs, and I much enjoyed that.

A heavy mail continues to arrive daily. . . . There are still many fine human beings about in this troubled country. Their letters touch me so deeply that I somehow contrive to answer every one. . . .

I'm sure you're enjoying these lovely autumn days. Chiffchaffs are still calling, though soon I suppose they will start on that long, hazardous journey to Africa; they seem too tiny for such a venture. . . .

Everyone has been giving away surplus plums and pears, damsons and apples, courgettes and climbing French beans. Dietrich is making wine with our own damsons. . . .

I'm so glad you have an attractive set of students to teach. . . . Have a good term. Give our love to Christopher. Cherish yourselves! Much love from

Heather, Dietrich and Robin.

LETTER 235

[14th October, 1987]

My dear Win,

Our letters have crossed, but I *must* write again to thank you for your very kind words about my book. I may have told you that I never really wanted to write it, and of course I've never regarded myself as a writer. (I can only write straight from the heart, anyhow!) So it has been a great surprise to me that the book is being so well received, and that people enjoy the writing. Lovely letters – many from strangers – are still arriving. I find it all very strange and unexpected; and it greatly humbles me. I realise how blessed I have been to spend my life in the way I wanted to, and, evidently, to have been able to share my pleasures with so many thousands of people. . . .

It makes me so happy that you are able to identify with all my Langley and Birds' Marsh descriptions. Strangers write to tell me that they have journeyed to Kington Langley and all the places I've etched or described. Some say, 'We were too shy to knock on your door!' Others have boldly called on us!

You were so much a part of my later formative schoolboy years that I was glad to make that clear. I owe a lot to you.

Our warm love and happy thoughts.
From Heather, Dietrich and Robin.

[25th October, 1987]

My dear Sam [Black],
I'm relieved and delighted that Eric Ravilious reached you safely, as our once splendid postal service becomes less and less reliable. I've always felt that Eric R. was your man. You have *so* much in common. I find that the colour plates are faithful enough to allow one to study his technique. What a master he was! And so are *you*! He never admits to having learnt a lot from Cotman, but I'm sure he did. Of course the Wiltshire Downs paintings (e.g. the White Horse seen from inside a 3rd Class railway carriage) specially appeal to me. But I also greatly admire what he did as a War artist; those are stirring, revealing paintings, and nobody else – not even Paul Nash – rivalled him. . . .

The hurricane entirely passed us by. But London, Kew, most of Kent and Sussex have suffered badly. NEVER BEFORE has England known anything like it. It was a major tragedy. What is happening to the world? We rarely have frost in October, yet last night we had five degrees! Now it is a lovely sunny day, and our yellow-berried tall Rowan tree and Fothergilla are ablaze with colour.

Grateful thanks for those charming stamps. They always make me feel ashamed of dull, staid, unenterprising England. We have some fine artists, who could produce spirited and attractive stamps if they were given a chance. We must always have our not very good-looking Queen on every stamp, which cramps every artist's style!

An American friend sent us *Spycatcher*. It is a nasty, boring, ill-written book. Burglary, lying and even murder are callously resorted to. . . .

Much love from us to you all.
Robin.

LETTER 237

[5th December, 1987]

Our dear John and Betty [Parr],
With 300+ friends to send to we are perforce posting our greetings early. You are much in our thoughts. We crave that you are well – as we are. (My cancer never makes itself felt; the only inconvenience is that travelling is out of the question. I rarely go beyond the garden.) But as all I want to draw, paint or etch is close at hand, I don't feel frustrated.

I managed to finish and print a few impressions of those three etchings I mentioned in the final lines of my autobiography and today my ancient back aches! and the entire house smells of the printing ink which I grind with burnt linseed oil.

I am sending you the one called *Weeds*. I greatly enjoyed doing it, and I hope it will give you some pleasure. It won't be officially published until next Spring, when Robin Garton is going to charge £100 for it. That is absurd, and it makes me sad, but that is the fate of my work now, alas! I try to forget it. . . .

LETTER 238

[18th January, 1988]

My dearest Charlie,
At last I've given myself the treat of examining and enjoying the 400+ greeting cards that reached us at Christmas. Some are very beautiful, especially those made by the senders. I particularly love those published by museums of paintings done not later than the 15th century.

Jean-Luc likes to read fan mail; I find there have been more than 100 kind letters about *Double Harness*, and I must share them with him. They all deserve replies, and I make myself answer each one fully, time-taking as that is. Most of those from teachers (who are all strangers to me) reveal dire disheartenment and little hope for the future; but I personally feel sure that . . . no teacher will ever be coerced into a way of teaching which he knows to be wrong: he or she will get round it somehow. It is one thing for a measure to be passed in Parliament and quite another for it to be implemented in the classrooms. . . .

Were you – as we were – able to take some days of complete rest at the end of the old year and the start of the new? We had a delicious few silent and restoring days, with reading and music and Dietrich le Chef's exquisite meals, and 'the first morsels of Spring' from the garden to enjoy, and telephone calls from distant lands, and some rare wines, and pleasant conversations, and log fires of our own wood – hazel and apple. All those joys add up to heaven-on-earth.

A friend sent us the new, enormous biography of Oscar Wilde. The author, Richard Ellmann, died just before it was published. It has left me angry at the cruel British attitudes to such minorities as homosexuals. What Wilde was made to endure in Reading Gaol bore no relation to his actions. Today there is being worked up a revival of persecution. Did not Jesus love *men*, I ask? And what of Shakespeare, Michelangelo and Leonardo da Vinci? Why can't we be utterly simple – and recognise that to be heterosexual, or non-sexual, or homosexual, or *both* hetero- and homosexual (as most really complete human beings are) is neither here nor there. 'Nature' mixes our ingredients without consulting us! Let there be many types and mixtures, I say; and let us accept them unquestioningly.

Our old friend Rita Beales has just died, three days before her 99th birthday. Undoubtedly she has been the world's greatest linen weaver, and every thread she has used has been of her own hand spinning and dyeing. I am one of her two executors, and I'm left her work, which I shall of course give to the Crafts Study Centre. The Centre too will receive her 'estate' and whatever her house fetches. This is their very first substantial windfall. . . .

I'm alarmed to learn of the shocking deterioration of books in the British Library because of the acid in paper. It is quite disastrous. America now bans acid-containing paper, while *we* do nothing. How quickly the evil short cuts of our so-called Technological Age are letting us down! Foam furniture is another dreadful mistake. We think we are so clever, and we fail miserably. . . .

I've been enjoying the remarkably clear moonlight and its dramatic effect in our bedroom. I should like to make moonlight the main subject and focus of an etching; it would be a wonderful subject. . . .

Leap Year Day [1988]

I'm starting a letter today, dear Ken [Pritchard], but may not finish it for some days as I've firmly reserved this week for laying the *July* ground and starting the needling. There were 23 visitors last week – all of them dear, lovely people – but it was very time-taking. We hate isolating ourselves for a few days, but once the ground is safely laid life will be easier: I can then needle as I choose at my big studio window, and I shan't mind receiving friends. Don't be alarmed at my writing to you on this absurd *papier carré*, so beloved of French students! A dear friend of mine who lives in S.W. France sends me consignments from time to time, and it amuses me to obey the discipline of the squares for once. . . .

I can't remember whether I've told you about recent contacts with Ivy Lane? I gave the school a specially rich impression of *Autumn*, in memory of my happy time there from 1929 to 1935, and the Head asked if she could bring some children to interview me. They were wonderfully quick-witted, assured, calm, articulate children. As they sat round our log fire (drinking apple juice and munching Dietrich's biscuits), asking pertinent questions, I wondered what stupid Baker and boorish Thatcher would have made of it.

Another thing I can't remember is whether I've told you about James Roose-Evans' BLEDDFA Centre for Caring and the Arts, at The Old School and Church, Bleddfa, Knighton, Powys. James is one of the most vital and creatively active people we have ever known. He is having a show of my work there in July, which Robin Garton is lending him. I am lending the ten drawings I did to illustrate Gray's *Elegy*. Because I'm hardly likely to be able to travel to Bleddfa I've recorded a 30-minute introductory talk. . . .

Len Marsh intends to establish a National Primary Education Archive at Bishop Grosseteste College. He begged me to contribute. I've sent him a number of National Course programmes and papers, and the texts (with readings) of Heather's Sunday night talks at my Dartington Hall Courses; and I've now combed through my mass of lecture notes (given all over England from 1936 to 1986) and am letting him have 25 of them. As you know, each talk

I give has its notes in book form. Sentimentally, I don't want to part with them, so I'm asking Len to photocopy them.

Robin Garton was here recently. We agreed that three of my etchings that have hitherto only been available in Guichard's book, *British Etchers*, should now be published. They are *Wren and Primroses*, *The Old Road* and *December*.

Jean-Luc has just enabled us to send cheques to The Woodland Trust and Friends of the Earth. He says that *Double Harness* is selling well.

Friends of the Earth is organising a Grand Auction in aid of replacing fallen trees. A number of artists were asked to contribute. I gave a print of *December: Elegy for The English Elm II* which I printed on a precious piece of William Morris' own 'Apple' paper. They hope it will realise £600.

A hospice in Salisbury for terminal cancer cases asked me for a print to sell, and they made £250 on *Flowers of May*. I've been able recently to help that enlightened but neglected body, The Howard League for Penal Reform. . . .

I wonder if you saw Edith Moorhouse's all too brief appearance in the television programme on Primary Education? I thought David Medd and Lady Plowden were good, but best of all was a young Head from Hertfordshire, whose name I failed to catch. . . .

It is extraordinary that I'm still receiving fan mail about *Double Harness* from an incredibly wide range of human beings – teachers everywhere, of course; an H.M.I. who agrees passionately with my condemnation of Thatcher, but who fears that he is in a small minority in the Inspectorate; a postman; a vicar of a poor Leeds parish; a writer of dictionaries who, as a thankyou, would like to make an index for a second edition; a retired don; various booksellers; an old man who lives in a National Trust mansion in Cornwall; and a titled Civil Servant!

No day passes but you are in my thoughts. I picture your tactful handling of delicate situations, or I see you relishing making more and more new contacts and friends. . . .

Continued 1st March.

. . . At odd moments I'm giving myself the pleasure of returning to old loves in my reading – the letters of John Keats; Browning's dramatic monologues and his correspondence with Elizabeth; Matthew Arnold's great sad poems, like

'Dover Beach' and 'Rugby Chapel'; and the poems of the Amherst recluse, Emily Dickinson. All these are a steadying influence, and they bear endless re-reading. . . .

Continued 3rd March.

. . . Three unexpected visitors have arrived, and I'm unable therefore to finish this letter, so forgive its brusque end. It comes with much deep involvement in all you are doing, and with love and warmest thoughts from us three to you three.

Robin.

LETTER 240

[6th March, 1988]

I've just re-read your fine letter – with its masterly JUNIPER drawings – my dear Tony [Heald]; and I realise that in my reply I gave a very feeble account of how I cope with those rare but depressing moments all artists must sometimes experience of sudden blank emptiness and even of failure. That you, Tony, are a member of that strange, small company we call 'artists' is clear to everyone. (Many people who aren't artists think they are!) But to be an artist isn't all honey. I still think Louis MacNeice is right when he asserts that the artist inherits 'a *birthright* and a *burden*' and that he faces 'a *doom* and an *heirloom*'. One doesn't seem possible without the other. So if I wake in the small hours and remember that the cancer in my bladder will certainly shorten my life, and I'm not proud of my latest etching design, I try to concentrate my thoughts on some unsullied lovely object or human being. I let it fill my mind, so that there is no misery. One has to pay pretty dearly for one's sensitivity and joy. But for me the 'panic and emptiness' which occasionally assails me rarely lasts long. I regain my poise by concentrating on one particular friend's special quality, or the perfect form of a certain plant, or an arresting line of poetry, or the air of one of Schubert's or Beethoven's slow movements.

When I tell myself how nice it must be *never* to be assailed by doubt and emptiness I pretty soon realise that I should hate it! Let me accept the dark as well as the light, I say. But let me also find enough strength to do so. I have

Heather to share my struggle and you have Hilary. In this sadly uncertain world we are the greatly privileged ones, Tony. The girl I fell in love with as a schoolboy is still my lover – and that makes *everything* possible.

Bless you, dear Tony! I send you my deepest thoughts and much understanding and love.

Robin.

LETTER 241

[15th March, 1988]

Your magnificent letter, dear Michael [Blaker], was a great inspiration. I read it aloud and we all three rejoiced. We rejoiced because of your good fortune to find a fine house large enough for you both to spread yourselves and all your interests and to let your amazing creative energy produce many Blaker wonders. You really are astonishing, Michael! I am in the throes of my large *July* etching; I needle for about six hours a day, and consider that good. *You* would go on to another job, and then another! and then one more! Oh, what it is to be young! I shall always treasure your letter.

How fortunate for you to make your move in this extraordinary non-winter! We have never known any season like it. Our camellias are earlier and richer than they have ever been, and even magnolias are breaking bud. As I sit working at my large *July* etching (the last of the twelve months) I am entertained by a pair of Greater Spotted Woodpeckers. I tell myself that I am fortunate still to have excellent sight; and my left hand is still steady.

New designs for etchings still come to me, and 'if I'm spared' (as they say in our village) I shall begin one when *July* is as good as I can make it. But the time will come when etching is beyond me. My excellent press and etching apparatus will then need a good home. I shall give it all away. I wonder if you have ideas? An Art School? or a struggling young etcher, or group of etchers?

The portrait photograph you so kindly enclosed is *extremely* beautiful. Yes: what loving care you devoted to the painting of the *flowers*!

Do you hop across to France fairly frequently? And you have Canterbury, of course, nearby, and I seem to remember quiet, open, flat country quite near –

unspoilt and peaceful. I don't imagine that the awful upheaval for the Channel Tunnel will affect you.

It is sad that that great stalwart, Joan Hassall, has died. I've always admired her wood engravings, especially her illustrations to Jane Austen and Mrs Gaskell.

This is no letter. It is only a very warm thankyou for your splendid one.

Our love to you both.
Heather, Dietrich and Robin.

LETTER 242

[20th March, 1988]

Only you, my dearest Charlie, could conceive of an eight postcard letter; it was a joy to receive, and a lovely game to play, going from one surprise to the next. They arrived just as I had finished the exacting but deeply satisfying job of needling my *July* plate and I was feeling very happy: your loving letter made me happier still. It is just a year since I learnt my fate, and I still feel very well, with never a moment's pain. I had wondered whether I might have lost my cunning, but the needle I had as a student in 1924 and I worked happily together, and I now look forward to the long and arduous business of biting. As I've sat at my large studio window, needling, I've been aware of a large missel thrush carrying nesting material and a minute pair of Goldcrests prospecting for a nesting site. And I've looked out on exquisite Camellias and dwarf Rhododendrons. Away in our glade is a drift of wild daffodils, and nearer the house are such fine hybrids as 'February Gold'. The beauty of this astonishing Spring makes me repeat that line by Edward Thomas, 'I cannot bite the day to the core!'

Robin Garton's Retrospective for my 85th birthday will, I hope, contain all twelve months. I expect to have finished *July* by then. . . .

Don't worry about me, dear Charlie. The very thought of you, bearing the Primary torch high, and taking trouble to lighten darkness wherever you find it uplifts me. I am often at your side, so to speak. . . .

All my love.
Robin.

[16th April, 1988]

Dear Kim [Taplin],
You have brought me very great happiness. Your wonderful letter, the excellent reproduction of the Kelmscott bed hanging (which we had never seen before), and most of all your twelve-part poem, 'This Year, Next Year'. It is a marvellous piece of work, Kim: a vivid, personal, arresting calendar. Every detail is deeply and lovingly observed and felt, and the choice of each one is the choice of a true poet – a poet, moreover, with that rare knowledge and understanding that comes from close, daily living with the natural world. How John Clare would love it! I've just put it to the severe test of being read aloud, and it stands up to it manfully. There is nothing derivative or hackneyed here: on the contrary there are lovely shocks of surprise, and each one is absolutely apt. It must have given you deep satisfaction to write. I wish I had all the time in the world to illustrate it, for it asks for that.

'Lapwings', for instance, is a fine poem too, and 'Near Stafford' takes me back to that county I used to know so well. We rejoice that you are writing so much. 'Tongues in Trees' sounds a perfect title for you, and I'm sure you'll find the right publisher. . . .

Many good letters about *Double Harness* are still arriving. In a marvellous one from Jonathan Porritt he said in passing, 'the book should be compulsory reading for all budding political ecologists and teachers.' The best reviews have been in the William Morris Society *Journal* and *The Tablet* and the Hampstead and Highgate newspaper. These last two were by James Roose-Evans (producer of *The Best of Friends*, in which John Gielgud is acting.) This remarkable man spent a day with us recently. He is an unattached Anglican priest, whose chief love is his Centre for Caring and the Arts at The Old School, Bleddfa, Knighton, Powys. He's having a full-dress show of my work there in the summer.

What a fabulous Spring this is! The cuckoo has arrived since I began writing this letter. . . .

We all three send you all many happy thoughts, admiration and much love.

Robin.

[4th May, 1988; unfinished]

My dearest Charlie,
This is the moment when birds 'take over' Old Chapel Field! Jackdaws have built in the studio chimney; great tits occupy a drain pipe, and seven different birds are nesting in our ivied walls. The first young blackbirds of the season are being fed by their parents on the lawn. There is great activity everywhere at this magical moment. Dieti has just given his bees another super – they are working so hard. Every year we think Spring has never been so perfect, but this year it surely excels all others. Cherry and crab blossom, viburnums and species rhododendrons, and drifts of blue, pink and white forget-me-nots among the fading daffodils are all at their best. The cuckoo and a great throng of small birds wake me before 5 a.m., until the air throbs with a mighty chorus. I don't believe they do it just to claim their chosen territory; I believe it is their way of asserting just how good it is to be alive! I wish *Man* would take to copying them! Of course, for far too many people it is by no means good to be alive. And the situation grows worse – not only in the Third World but in that place called *Great* Britain. 'Great' indeed. Thatcher drags it down lower and lower: '"Compassion" is not a word in my vocabulary'!

Did you see that excellent television programme, *Dear Mr Baker*, in which senior pupils from comprehensive schools spoke with clarity and wisdom and passion, firmly showing Baker that he is wrong? I felt proud of them and ashamed of Baker.

Heather and Dieti joined the 30,000 who demonstrated at Aldermaston on Easter Monday. They found it a most moving experience. They met many old friends and renewed many contacts.

My dear old colleague and friend, John Parr, died peacefully in his sleep a few days ago. John was a great human being, large in every way, open-hearted and dedicated. He was a fine photographer, who frequently recorded Christine Smale's and my exhibitions. He married an H.M.I. colleague, and it was a perfect marriage.

Do you receive Robin Garton's catalogues? His latest is magnificent. It is largely devoted to Blake and Palmer, and to us who followed in their footsteps.

Only the excessively high prices disturb me. The reproductions are superb.

. . . We have just proudly planted Camellia Tannerensis – a lusty two-foot bush that I grew from our own seed. I long for it to flower. Why does one so cherish something one has grown from *seed*?

Our sweet bay tree, which is 20 years old, is flowering for the first time, and it is a wonderful and surprising sight. The bosses of little cream flowers look strangely un-English and exotic.

At this moment of high Spring I remember keenly Upper Wharfedale, Wensleydale, and Keld at the end of Swaledale, and I should love to see them again. *Primula farinosa*, cloudberry and mountain pansies will be in bloom, and the peat-brown streams will be rushing down to join the Swale. You are singularly fortunate, Charlie, for here in the south west, for all our beauty, we have nothing comparable to your Dales. Bird cherry will be in flower, and there will be cowslips at Hubberholme. We hear disturbing rumours that those isolated stone barns dotted over the dales are being converted into 'holiday chalets'. Horrible thought! I only hope it isn't true. . . .

LETTER 245

To the Taylor family.

[10th May, 1988]

Our very dear Trio,

We are so glad that the Dusky Cranesbill likes you. Here there are several hundred plants – spreading into the lane and into the open glade! But it shall never be persecuted, but will always be loved. Some plants are growing with that whitest of flowers – the greater stitchwort – and the contrast is quite astonishing. Others are alongside Cornish Garlic, and there is a thick colony under a warm pink-flowered Camellia. How splendid that there are so many cowslips on The Downs! Surely, there has *never* been such an opulent Spring! Heather's favourite Spring flower is Apple blossom. Our vast spreading Bramley is what native Kington Langley people call 'a main vair zoight'! Cherries, viburnums, magnolias, species rhododendrons are all lovely; and single plants of Fothergilla and Rubus 'Tridel' are giving us enormous pleasure. I wish Peter had more time to enjoy this fabulous season.

Yes: we've been able to share some encouraging letters and reviews about *Double Harness* with Jean-Luc. . . .

It is wonderful that you achieve so much. We feel that you three have earned the Freedom of the City of Bristol! You have shown Bristol its hitherto comparatively unknown riches, and you have brought a vital new interest into the lives of many people for whom the natural world had meant very little before. You are doing a most important work. Certainly, the only tremendously encouraging development at this dreadful time is the concern about the fate of the environment; people who once didn't care are now working hard at conservation. No Kington Langley children go birds-nesting now, and the primroses in our hedgerows are left unmolested. We owe a tremendous debt to Friends of the Earth for its great work of enlightenment. Unfortunately Thatcher doesn't care: she would readily sell and sacrifice 'the green belt' for money. Money is God! . . .

We send many happy thoughts and much love.
Heather, Dietrich and Robin.

LETTER 246

[12th May, 1988]

Dearest Tony and Hilary [Heald],
I very rarely want power, but I do now. I wish I could see you installed at . . . The loss is theirs. Not many Heads are artists too. You would have brought something of immense value to the school. However, there must be other vacancies in lovely places from time to time, and it is my hope that you may still find your niche in one of them. How well I understand your sorrow over the rape of Ardsley! This disgusting desecration is happening in many once beautiful places. Everywhere there is a fight against thatcherite developers. Money is God. Beauty and peace count for naught. Even here the Parish Council is constantly fighting proposals for 'an industrial estate with a hotel' or a 'group of choice executive homes', both of which would ruin the village! . . .

This unbelievable Spring is at its zenith, with apple blossom and the later cherries and viburnums. Every day there is fresh and astonishing beauty. How little of it I am able to record with my etching needle!

Your exquisite cards from the Chelsea Physic Garden Company are all new to us, and they will be greatly cherished. What standards those early artists had! I'm grateful to you for this lovely present. My large *July* etching will be bitten as soon as I am able to free a few days for it. I itch to begin.

Alas! my own store of my own prints has almost vanished, and I'm afraid Robin Garton *is* the sole source now. It saddens me to see prints of mine, published originally at £5 (which I considered pretty steep), being sold at £200 or more. Little *Wren and Primroses* was sold recently for £350! It is quite ridiculous, but I am powerless to do anything about it.

A Country Book of Days is to be issued cheaply by Impact Books soon. We have started nothing new. Heather is writing about her family, but not for publication. . . .

Double Harness is still bringing kind and heartening reviews – and many new friends. I wish I had time to be nicer to them, but each day is very full, and it vanishes extremely quickly. Yet friendship is a very precious gift to us human beings, and I am thankful for it.

What I dislike is being forced because of lack of time to be less inviting and generous than I want to be. I only hope that these dear people understand and forgive me. Some have sent me examples of their own work. A nun from . . . Northumberland sent me two of her own exquisite wood engravings, and a teacher from Northamptonshire sent me his own sensitive etching of wild lilies of the valley . . . .

At this season we are 'taken over' by birds. We have three families of robins, three of thrushes, and three of blackbirds; and the following we know are nesting with us: bullfinch, chaffinch, greenfinch; wren, goldcrest, chiffchaff, willow warbler, dunnock; collared dove and wood pigeon; greater spotted woodpecker and nuthatch and tree creeper. The cuckoo starts calling at 4.30 a.m., and calls for most of the day.

Tell me Tony, which etching (or etchings) you would specialy like to have. I don't hold out *great* hopes, I'm afraid, but I'll do my best. In this small house it isn't easy to keep everything in good order. Our many interests – writing, the conservation and peace movements, gardening, overseas correspondence, educational lecturing, and friends worldwide – all call for space! Perhaps we have too many interests.

I long to be able to solve your problem – of finding you a Headship just where you two would like it to be, but alas! I no longer am a voice that counts.

We speak of you all very often,
and we send yearning thoughts and much love.
Heather, Dietrich and Robin.

LETTER 247

This letter was never finished. It was not sent to Ken Pritchard until Dietrich found it, as he explains in his note below.

[9th May, 1988]

My dear Ken,
Reviews of *Double Harness* continue to arrive, and while they are invariably kind they are rarely memorable. But this one, from the current number of the Journal of the William Morris Society, is so vehement and personal that I thought it might interest you. I don't know Nicholas Friend, but I wish I did! There are some remarkable letters, too, that I should like to share with you, but I don't know how.

Today I'm performing the annual ritual of sowing courgette and Hubbard Squash seed in peat pots filled with compost. I shall keep them in the greenhouse until the end of the month. I've also 'started' our French climbing beans. They are lying on wet blotting paper inside a closed box; and as each one begins to shoot I shall carefully plant it in a compost-filled peat pot. When the plants are lusty and there is no risk of frost they will be transferred to the open ground. This method always seems to work perfectly. The white-flowered French bean, 'Désirée', is one of our favourite vegetables.

It is fascinating to see how one particular colour predominates for a week or two at this season, and then gives way to another. At the moment it is a warm, creamy pink. There is much Apple blossom (Heather's favourite spring flower); there are five different pink species of rhododendron, and there is our ten-foot-high specimen of the rare pink form of *Viburnum rhytidophyllum*. Then, of course, there are the lovely and various pink camellias, and there are self-sown pink forget-me-nots among the fading narcissi.

When this pink flush is over, pure white will take its place for some weeks. I always look forward to the tiered 'wedding cake' viburnum (*tomentosum Mariesii*) and a beautiful Rubus called 'Tridel', that I believe may have been a natural hybrid in a Sussex garden. Its great arching branches are thickly set with white flowers like single roses. I can't think why it isn't more popular. When Dietrich was last in America he was impressed by salads containing leaves of Chinese mustard, Roquette, and various small-leaved salad plants. Now seed is available here, so we are growing a few varieties.

Heather and Dietrich are invited to a lunch party at Bleddfa on Saturday, 28 May, to be followed at 2 p.m. by a formal opening of the exhibition, when I 'address' the assembly through my cassette. The Welsh Arts Council wants to give me a fee of £200, but I shall pass it on to the Bleddfa Trust. I don't suppose you will happen to be in Powys then? I still hope to visit Bleddfa before the end of July. . . .

Suddenly we are aware that spotted flycatchers are back – in their favourite haunt on our south-east wall. How do they contrive to find their way back? They are very active, in spite of their long and hazardous journey. . . . The ordered mystery of all this amazes me anew with the coming of Spring each year. . . .

I don't think you've ever had time to wander through this untamed garden of ours. There is one open glade of the ancient untouched pasture – untouched for centuries, I imagine – which we specially cherish. I can walk as far, with the aid of a stick; and I love to note what I call the hay flowers. There are many different grasses; and at the moment there are the following flowers: daisy, hedge parsley, cowslip, selfheal, bugle, ground ivy, cuckoo flowers, greater stitchwort, Cornish garlic, woodruff, forget-me-not and fumitory. There is a wonderful natural world deep down in the lush grass.

The village Common is a blazing sheet of dandelions, which will give place to buttercups later, before the grass is cut for hay. If these two spurned plants were rare and costly they would be highly valued. I think I love the insignificant, humble hay flowers as much as more spectacular plants such as Meadow Cranesbill or poppy.

A host of ideas for a small new etching are starting to wake me in the small hours. It will be hard to choose. I want a design highly charged with feeling yet simple in conception; and I want to convey something fresh. There is always the danger of appearing to repeat oneself, and as this may well be my last etching I want to be doubly careful. Many friends entreat me to etch more plants, while others beg me to leave plants and choose an architectural subject. In the end I expect it will choose itself!

I realise that I ought not to cause you to waste precious time reading about all these very minor matters. They are important to me, but probably seem trivial and insignificant to anyone else. Who is this obscure Robin Tanner who expects you to consider his ruminations seriously? Yet what is friendship for if not for sharing one's deepest thoughts? There is nothing I would hold back from you: I can tell you all.

I have just found this unfinished letter. Could you let us have a photocopy of it? Thank you most warmly for both your beautiful letters to Heather and me. Your last splendid letter to Robin we read round his bedside and enjoyed tremendously. He was completely clear-headed then. Much love to all.

Dietrich.

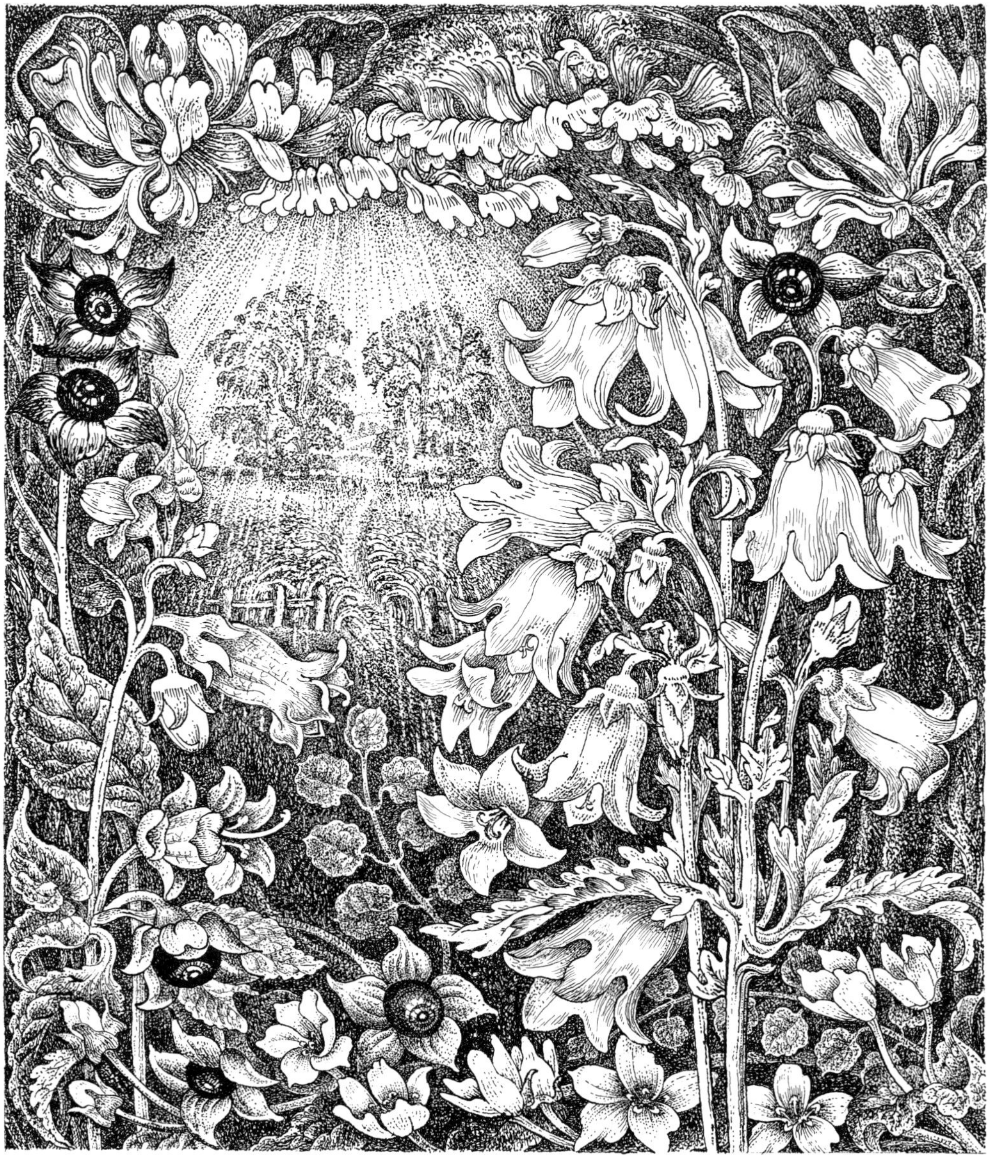

July from a drawing, 1986.

Appendix 1

Publications about Robin Tanner's life and work

MICHAEL BLAKER, 'Letters from Robin Tanner: a selection' (*Printmakers Journal* No.11, 1990)

WILLIAM VAN DER EYKEN AND BARRY TURNER, *Adventures in Education* (Section on Art and Craft)

JAMES FAIRBAIRN, *Robin Tanner as a Teacher*, 1989 Robin Tanner Memorial Lecture (Wiltshire Museum and Library Service)

CHRISTOPHER FRAYLIN *ET AL.*, *Tributes to Robin Tanner (1904–88)* (Holburne Museum and Crafts Study Centre, Bath)

ERNEST HIRD, 'Robin Tanner: Educator and Artist' (*Journal of Art and Design Education* vol.7, no.1, 1988)

JOHN RUSSELL TAYLOR, *Robin Tanner: an Appreciation.* (Merrivale Editions, in association with Garton & Co, 1989)

Appendix 2

Books written and/or illustrated by
Robin Tanner

*Wiltshire Village** (Collins, 1939; Robin Garton, 1978; Impact Books, 1987)

Flowers of the Meadow (text by Geoffrey Grigson) (King Penguin, 1950)

Lettering for Children (Dryad Press, 6th edn, 1962)

Children's Work in Block-Printing (Dryad Press, 6th edn, 1970)

The Etcher's Craft (Friends of Bristol Art Gallery, 1980)

A Corsham Boyhood (edited by Faith Sharp and Heather Tanner) (privately printed, 1981)

Gray's Elegy (Robin Garton, 1981)

*Woodland Plants** (Robin Garton, 1981; Impact Books, 1987)

*A Country Alphabet** (The Old Stile Press, 1984; Impact Books, 1987)

*A Country Book of Days** (The Old Stile Press, 1986; Impact Books, 1988)

Double Harness (Impact Books, 1987)

The More Angels Shall I Paint (pencil drawings) (The Old Stile Press, 1991)

---

* Text by Heather Tanner

Appendix 3

Complete collections of the etchings

These can be seen at:

City of Bristol Museum and Art Gallery

The Ashmolean Museum, Oxford (the copper plates are also there)

In due course the Fitzwilliam Museum, Cambridge will also have a collection.

Devizes Museum, Wiltshire

In the USA, Boston (Mass.) Public Library (incomplete)

Appendix 4

Educational papers by Robin Tanner

Collections can be seen at:

The Wiltshire Museum and Library Service, Bythesea Road, Trowbridge, Wiltshire

Bishop Grosseteste College, Lincoln

Index

(Figures refer to letter numbers)